GOOD TEACHING FOR CHILDREN WITH SEND

Sara Miller McCune founded Sage Publishing in 1965 to support the dissemination of usable knowledge and educate a global community. Sage publishes more than 1000 journals and over 800 new books each year, spanning a wide range of subject areas. Our growing selection of library products includes archives, data, case studies and video. Sage remains majority owned by our founder and after her lifetime will become owned by a charitable trust that secures the company's continued independence.

Los Angeles | London | New Delhi | Singapore | Washington DC | Melbourne

GOOD TEACHING FOR CHILDREN WITH SEND

A GUIDE FOR PRIMARY TEACHER TRAINEES AND EARLY CAREER TEACHERS

ALISON SILBY
ANN CALLANDER

1 Oliver's Yard
55 City Road
London EC1Y 1SP

2455 Teller Road
Thousand Oaks
California 91320

Unit No 323-333, Third Floor, F-Block
International Trade Tower Nehru Place
New Delhi – 110019
India

8 Marina View Suite 43-053
Asia Square Tower 1
Singapore 018960

© 2025 Alison Silby and Ann Callander

Apart from any fair dealing for the purposes of research, private study, or criticism or review, as permitted under the Copyright, Designs and Patents Act, 1988, this publication may not be reproduced, stored or transmitted in any form, or by any means, without the prior permission in writing of the publisher, or in the case of reprographic reproduction, in accordance with the terms of licences issued by the Copyright Licensing Agency. Enquiries concerning reproduction outside those terms should be sent to the publisher.

Library of Congress Control Number: 2025932161

British Library Cataloguing in Publication Data

A catalogue record for this book is available from the British Library.

Editor: Amy Thornton
Senior project editor: Chris Marke
Project management: TNQ Tech Pvt. Ltd.
Cover design: Sheila Tong
Typeset by: TNQ Tech Pvt. Ltd.
Printed and bound by CPI Group (UK) Ltd, Croydon, CR0 4YY

ISBN: 978-1-0362-0647-5
ISBN: 978-1-0362-0646-8 (pbk)

Contents

About the Authors

Alison Silby is a Lecturer in Education at the University of Reading. Her work focuses on Initial Teacher Education at both undergraduate and postgraduate level with a focus on the design and delivery of challenging degree programmes. Her current research focuses on supporting the professional development and practice of trainee teachers with additional needs. Previously, Alison designed and led the specialism pathway for SEND at Brunel University, enhancing trainees' knowledge and understanding of inclusive practice. Her earlier teaching career ranged across the primary and secondary phases where she assumed responsibility for English.

Ann Callander is an educational writer who has worked as a SENCo, Speech and Language Resource Base teacher, County Support and Advisory teacher (SEND), as well as Lead teacher for Gifted and Talented and dual exceptionality. She has been involved in working with children, families, class teachers, teaching assistants and other professionals for over 25 years. Ann has written a range of articles relating to SEND and has co-authored a number of reading books for children as well as resources for teachers.

About This Book

The Education Endowment Foundation's guidance report on special educational needs in mainstream schools (2021) found that, 'To a great extent, good teaching for pupils with SEND is good teaching for all' (p. 9). In this book, we explore ways in which this can be achieved by using the Initial Teacher Training and Early Career Framework [ITTECF] (DfE, 2024) as a guide. The book supports the emphasis placed in the ITTECF (DfE, 2024) on the importance of high-quality teaching; '...high quality teaching is the most important way to improve outcomes for pupils – particularly those with SEND' (p. 5). Nevertheless, the framework recognises that trainees and Early Career Teachers (ECTs) need guidance on how best to support pupils with SEND. This book offers a range of strategies to help pupils overcome or minimise their barriers to learning. These strategies, underpinned by evidence-based research and teacher experience, are accompanied by suggested activities which can be adapted to support all pupils, including those with SEND. Chapters relate to the Teachers' Standards (DfE, 2012) and offer practical activities and school-based case studies to support reflective practice. Additional sections offer specific guidance on supporting pupils with SEND. Although written for the primary phase, many of the suggestions can be used across key stages and are applicable to mainstream classrooms, resource bases and special school settings.

Information Links to the ITTECF

	Int	S1	S2	S3	S4	S5	S6	S7	S8
Adaptive Teaching	-	-	-	-	-	✓	-	-	-
Alternative Methods of Recording	-	-	-	-	-	✓	-	-	-
Assessment	-	-	-	-	-	-	✓	-	-
Attachment Theory	-	✓	-	-	-	-	-	-	-
Augmentative and Alternative Communication (AAC)	-	-	-	-	-	✓	-	-	-
Barriers to learning and Participation	✓	-	-	-	-	-	-	-	-
Behaviour Management	-	-	-	-	-	-	-	✓	-
Cognitive Load	-	-	✓	-	-	-	-	-	-
Cognitive and Metacognitive Strategies	-	-	-	-	✓	-	-	-	-
Communicate Shared Values	-	✓	-	-	-	-	-	-	-
Concepts and Misconceptions	-	-	-	✓	-	-	-	-	-
Collaborative and Cooperative Learning	-	✓	-	-	-	-	-	-	-
Develop Effective Relationships	-	✓	-	-	-	-	-	✓	-
Dual Coding	-	-	✓	-	-	-	-	-	-
Dual Exceptionality	-	✓	-	-	-	-	-	-	-
Educational Settings	✓	-	-	-	-	-	-	-	-
EHCP (Educational Health and Care Plan)	✓	-	-	-	-	-	-	-	-
Engagement Model	-	-	-	-	-	-	✓	-	-
Explicit Instruction	-	-	-	-	✓	-	-	-	-
Feedback	-	-	-	-	✓	-	✓	-	-
Flexible Grouping	-	-	-	-	✓	✓	-	-	-
Graduated Approach	✓	-	-	-	✓	-	✓	-	-
High Expectations	-	✓	-	-	-	-	-	-	-
High Quality Teaching	-	✓	-	-	-	-	-	-	-
Home and Community Environment	-	✓	-	-	-	-	-	-	-
Homework	-	-	-	-	✓	-	-	-	-
Inclusive Education	✓	-	-	-	-	-	-	-	-
Intersectionality	-	✓	-	-	-	-	-	-	-

(Continued)

(Continued)

	Int	S1	S2	S3	S4	S5	S6	S7	S8
Interventions and Tailored Support	-	-	-	-	-	✓	-	-	-
Key Skills for Learning	-	-	-	✓	-	-	-	-	-
Knowledge and Skills	-	-	-	✓	-	-	-	-	-
Liaison with Parents and Carers	-	-	-	-	-	-	-	-	✓
Liaison with SEND Professionals	-	-	-	-	-	-	-	-	✓
Literacy (developing knowledge and skills)	-	-	-	✓	-	-	-	-	-
Maths (developing knowledge and skills)	-	-	-	✓	-	-	-	-	-
Memory	-	-	✓	-	-	-	-	-	-
Modelling	-	-	-	-	✓	-	-	-	-
Motivation	-	-	-	-	-	-	-	✓	-
Multisensory Approach	-	-	-	-	-	✓	-	-	-
Neurodiversity	✓	✓	-	-	-	-	-	-	-
PLP (Personal Learning Plan)	✓	-	-	-	-	-	-	-	-
Planning and Organisation	-	-	-	-	✓	-	-	-	-
Practice	-	-	✓	-	✓	-	-	-	-
Prior Knowledge	-	-	✓	-	-	-	-	-	-
Promote Positive Behaviour	-	✓	-	-	-	-	-	-	-
Role Models	-	✓	-	-	-	-	-	-	-
Questioning and Talking	-	-	-	-	✓	-	-	-	-
Rosenshine's Principles of Instruction	-	-	-	-	✓	-	-	-	-
Routines	-	-	-	-	-	-	-	✓	-
Scaffolding	-	-	-	-	✓	✓	-	-	-
Schema Theory	-	-	-	✓	-	-	-	-	-
Self-awareness	-	✓	-	-	-	-	-	-	-
SEND and Alternative Provision Improvement Plan	✓	-	-	-	-	-	-	-	-
SEND Census Categories	✓	-	-	-	-	-	-	-	-
SENCo (Special Educational Needs and Disabilities Coordinator)	-	-	-	-	-	-	-	-	✓
Teaching Assistants	-	-	-	-	-	-	-	-	✓
Universal Design for Learning	✓	-	-	-	-	-	-	-	-
Using Technology	-	-	-	-	-	✓	-	-	-
Visible Teaching and Learning	-	-	✓	-	-	-	✓	-	-

Part 1

Introduction

Chapter Objectives

This chapter introduces teachers to key information relating to the provision for, and teaching of, pupils with special educational needs and disabilities (SEND). It includes an introduction to the following:

- Inclusive education;
- Barriers to learning and participation;
- Universal Design for Learning;
- Neurodiversity;
- SEND areas of need;
- Educational settings;
- SEND census categories;
- SEND across the UK;
- The Graduated Approach;
- Education, Health and Care plans (EHCPs);
- Personal Learning Plans (PLPs);
- The SEND and Alternative Provision Improvement Plan: Right support, right place, right time (DfE, 2023a).

Inclusive Education

The Warnock Report (1978) recommended that pupils with special educational needs should be educated in their local mainstream school wherever possible. Until then, many pupils with SEND were educated in special schools having very little interaction with their peer group in mainstream schools. Following the Warnock recommendations, the 1981 Education Act required local authorities to integrate pupils with SEND as long as three conditions were met:

1. The school could meet the pupil's needs.
2. The pupil's attendance at the school was not detrimental to the education of other pupils.
3. It was an effective use of local authority resources.

However, it soon became apparent that a pupil's attendance at a mainstream school did not always mean they were an active member of the school community. For many pupils, integration was part of their social experience, but they followed separate learning programmes instead of being able to access the curriculum alongside their peer group in an inclusive setting. The educational philosophy of inclusion is still a work in progress with schools and teachers requiring a range of practical support when working with the needs of a wide variety of pupils in mainstream classes. Nevertheless, many teachers would agree that inclusive pedagogy '...challenges deterministic approaches that exclude certain learners from a positive classroom experience because of adverse labelling by ability, or by diagnosis' (NASEN, 2022, p. 34).

Inclusive education is based on the belief that all children and young people have the potential to make progress, and pupils should not be excluded from opportunities to learn within supportive mainstream classrooms if possible. By creating a flexible and varied learning environment for all pupils, teachers can focus on developing and adapting teaching strategies that benefit everyone in the classroom rather than providing different learning experiences for a small group of individuals.

Losberg and Zwozdiak-Myers (2024) explored inclusive pedagogy with teachers and teaching assistants working with pupils in key stage 2. They highlighted that, although teachers were committed to embedding inclusive practice, they recognised the need for providing individual pupil support when necessary. Losberg and Zwozdiak-Myers concluded:

> *Inclusive education continues to be a topic of great concern and while teachers and TAs exemplify multiple facets of inclusive pedagogy, it can be complex to facilitate in all aspects of classroom life given the complex, diverse needs prescient within our schools. (2024, p. 419)*

Barriers to Learning and Participation

In the *Index for Inclusion* (Booth & Ainscow, 2002), the term 'special educational needs' was replaced by the term 'barriers to learning and participation' indicating that these barriers could be overcome, or at least minimised, if schools could develop effective cultures, policies and practices. It was argued that the approach associated with the term 'special educational needs' had limitations and could act as a barrier to developing inclusive practices. Consequently, the term special needs had been associated with lower expectations for pupils with SEND.

The main barriers to learning experienced by pupils may be cognitive, sensory, physical, emotional or related to social communication difficulties and community environments:

- **Cognitive barriers** may affect a range of skills required for effective learning including prior knowledge, conceptual understanding, working memory, word processing difficulties and other key skills needed for learning.
- **Sensory and physical barriers** may include access problems, cramped classroom space, unsuitable furniture, poor lighting and lack of suitable technology and other resources needed for sensory or physical needs.
- **Emotional barriers** may have their origins in personal, family or community difficulties. They can affect pupil motivation, concentration, behaviour and interactions with their peer group.
- **Social communication barriers** are often related to communication and interaction difficulties. Some social communication barriers may arise from speech and language difficulties or ethnic, cultural and language differences which sit outside of SEND.
- **Community environment barriers** may relate to poor housing and physical environment, poverty and limited access to early years education.

Social and Medical Models of Disability

The social and medical models of disability are just two of the ways in which disability has been viewed. The social model was endorsed by the Government Equalities Office (2014) to be used by all government departments when interacting with disabled people. The social model looks carefully at ways in which barriers to inclusion may be removed, or at least minimised, in all aspects of daily life. For example, a pupil who is blind should not be prevented from learning to read but should be given opportunities to use more suitable formats. Although the social model recognises the medical aspects of disability and the need for individual medical interventions and therapies, it also highlights how negative attitudes in communities can be just as much a barrier to learning as the actual physical or sensory impairment.

The medical model focuses on the individual and their disability as the reason for them being unable to access specific areas of learning. It looks at what they cannot do rather than what they can achieve with the right support. For example, in the past, a pupil with physical needs may not have been able to engage with certain co-curricular activities or trips due to access difficulties. However, most buildings, forms of transport and public attractions now have specific access facilities and assistive technology enabling everyone to take part.

Ensuring a Whole School Approach

Providing an inclusive education for all pupils is a complex process. It requires a whole school approach to teaching strategies and the provision of resources, both people and equipment. Schools need to:

- develop a culture of inclusivity within the educational community where all staff feel supported by the leadership, school systems and environment in which they work (Ainscow & Sandill, 2010);
- develop effective communication systems, considering the culturally diverse needs of all pupils, families and staff. It is important that good communication and relationships are encouraged for the educational success and wellbeing of all pupils;
- train teachers effectively to have a positive attitude to inclusion if they are to be able to make a difference in the classroom (Leatherman & Niemeyer, 2005);
- ensure teachers use flexible teaching strategies and tasks adapted to suit the diverse needs of pupils in the class (Molbaek, 2018);
- use the graduated approach (assess, plan, do, review) as a tool to aid inclusion. It can be used as a '. . .micro-teaching tool to inform and adapt teaching in response to individual learners' (NASEN, 2024, p. 36);
- have an accessibility strategy to increase the extent to which pupils with SEND can participate in the schools' curriculum and physical environment (Equality Act 2010, Schedule 10). Schools should make reasonable adjustments for accessibility which may include applying for funding to provide ramps, carpeting and acoustic tiling, specific lighting, paint décor and sensory areas;
- train and deploy teaching assistants effectively to compliment the role of the teachers, not replace them (Sharples et al., 2018);
- provide suitable resources to support the implementation of inclusive education as well as culturally inclusive teaching materials. This may include some changes in school and classroom infrastructure as well as providing assistive technology, practical equipment and specific support staff.

In addition to the above advice, the National Association for Special Educational Needs (NASEN) states, 'the inclusive teacher challenges that mindset that seeks to predetermine the capacity of each learner, replacing it instead with a curiosity about what the learner can achieve' (2022, p. 35).

Universal Design for Learning

Universal Design for Learning (Gorden et al., 2016) is based on the premise that it is more effective to design an approach that is inclusive from the beginning, rather than having to modify or adapt a learning environment later. However, this approach has been criticised as being expensive and time consuming to implement, though a number of schools and communities have found ways of making reasonable adjustments.

Universal Design for Learning establishes a framework based on three principles:

- **Engagement** – encourages teachers to find a variety of ways to motivate pupils by giving them activities that allow for choice, stimulate their interests and are relevant to their lives.
- **Representation** – advocates introducing pupils to information in more than one format and to allow for multisensory learning.
- **Action and Expression** – suggests that pupils should be encouraged to show what they have learnt using graphic organisers and assistive technology.

As society has become more aware of the diversity of needs within communities, it has provided a range of universal designs which support a variety of people. We can see these designs in both the workplace and classroom. For example:

- Controls for accessible lever door handles, flat panel light switches, touch button blinds and curtains, ergonomic furniture including adjustable chairs and workstations.
- Health and Safety provision including multi-sensory alarm signals, conspicuous emergency equipment clearly labelled, ensuring no obstacles are in an escape route, as well as enough space for manoeuvring a wheelchair.
- Lowered curbs, ramps and walkways which can be used by everyone according to their need.
- Automatic doors and accessible entrances in a range of public buildings and workplaces.
- Communication including the use of subtitles and the use of assistive technology in both the workplace and classroom (adapted I-pads, keyboards, mouse controls, switches, touch pads, touch screens, speech output devices and sensory technology).

Neurodiversity

Neurodiversity is a term that is used increasingly within the context of inclusive education. It was first used by the Australian sociologist Judy Singer in the late 1990s when she began exploring the different facets of autism. Renewed interest in her work has resulted in her ideas being republished (Singer, 2017). Harvey Blume popularised the word in a 1998 issue of *The Atlantic* where he wrote, 'Neurodiversity may be every bit as crucial for the human race as biodiversity is for life in general. Who can say what form of wiring will prove best at any given moment?'

Neurodiversity describes the individual variations in brain functioning within a population and is often used as an umbrella term for pupils with barriers to learning such as Dyslexia, Autistic Spectrum Condition (ASC), Attention Deficit Hyperactivity Disorder (ADHD), among others. Singer (2017) argues that these conditions should be recognised as aspects of the diverse workings of the human brain and should be accepted as such within the context of the community.

Despite political policies and pedagogical research showing evidence of the benefits of inclusive education, there are still many hurdles to overcome in merging policy into practice. Studies show that teachers are faced with daily challenges when trying to implement inclusive practices successfully (Losberg and Zwozdiak-Myers, 2021). Teachers experience multiple pressures when managing neurodiverse classrooms while, at the same time, having to ensure all children make the expected progress (Woodcock and Woolfson, 2019).

Warnes et al. (2022) concluded that, for teachers, '...the highest level of concern was around resources and, more specifically, the availability of support, including specialist and support staff, funding and inappropriate infrastructure' (p. 40). Teachers also cited stress related to the extra workload required when planning and organising for neurodiversity within an inclusive classroom.

SEND Areas of Need

The SEND Code of Practice (DfE, 2015) offers guidance on the special educational needs and disability (SEND) system for children and young people aged 0 to 25.

> *Support for learning difficulties may be required when children and young people learn at a slower pace than their peers, even with appropriate differentiation. Learning difficulties cover a wide range of needs, including moderate learning difficulties (MLD), severe learning difficulties (SLD), where children are likely to need support in all areas of the curriculum and associated difficulties with mobility and communication, through to profound and multiple learning difficulties (PMLD), where children are likely to have severe and complex learning difficulties as well as a physical disability or sensory impairment.*
>
> (DfE, 2015, p. 97)

The Code of Practice positions SEND within four broad areas of need and support:

- cognition and learning;
- communication and interaction;
- sensory or physical needs;
- social, emotional and mental health.

The areas of need are designed to show how particular difficulties impact on a pupil's learning. Further information, including weblinks, covering a range of special educational needs and disabilities can be found in **SEND Areas of Need and Support**. Many children and young people with severe learning difficulties (SLD) and profound and multiple learning difficulties (PMLD) have complex profiles across several categories (see **Pupil Support Profiles in Chapter 9, Tables 9.1–9.4**).

Educational Settings (SEND)

Pupils with SEND in England may be educated within a number of different educational settings.

Mainstream Schools With Resource Bases

The majority of pupils are educated within a mainstream setting including many pupils with SEND.

Some mainstream schools have resource bases which specialise in a particular area of SEND such as speech, language and communication needs and autism. Pupils attending a resource base can receive specialist teaching and therapies but also have access to mainstream classroom resources and activities.

Special Schools

Special schools may be local authority or community schools, non-maintained schools managed by charitable organisations or independent schools run privately. Almost half of all children with an Education, Health and Care Plan (EHCP) are being educated in settings other than mainstream schools (DfE, 2024b). These are pupils whose needs cannot be met through provision in mainstream mixed ability classrooms. Many of these children and young people have severe learning difficulties (SLD) or profound and multiple learning difficulties (PMLD) and require a greater level of individual support. The age range admitted to special schools varies in different parts of the country. While some admit a limited age range, others may cater for pupils aged 3–19 years. Some special schools cater for a wide range of needs, while a few focus on specific areas of need such as autism. For pupils who have PMLD, special schools provide an environment where a range of specialist interventions and tailored support can be made available to meet individual needs. Special schools have staffing ratios that are higher, and more specialised, allowing adults to respond immediately to a pupil's needs. A range of therapies can be offered and integrated into the school day more easily than in a mainstream school. Self-help skills can be taught within a supportive environment allowing each individual to grow in confidence and independence.

Special Units

Special units may be set up for pupils who have been excluded from school because of severe behavioural, social, emotional or mental health problems.

All schools that are controlled by the local authority must follow the national curriculum, including special schools, though some pupils may not be engaged in subject-specific study. While mainstream schools are required to set national curriculum age related targets, special schools have more freedom to consider the specific needs of the individual and deliver the curriculum accordingly.

For some pupils, the right educational setting may need to be flexible with the wishes of the child and their family being taken into consideration.

Case Study: The Right Educational Setting

Emily was considered a miracle child by her parents. She was born with Edward's syndrome and not expected to live beyond her first birthday. She was a fragile baby with a number of conditions including some visual impairment, respiratory difficulties, heart disorder, feeding difficulties and digestive problems. She was also prone to numerous infections. Emily had a significant language delay and used signing to communicate. As she was unable to walk unaided, she used a specially adapted electric mobility scooter.

By the time Emily reached school age, her parents decided they would like her to attend the same mainstream primary school as her siblings. Practical provision for Emily was considered suitable, with the additional support of a teaching assistant for both personal and educational needs via funding from the local authority.

The class teacher introduced symbol cards and signing to the whole class with the TA helping Emily to expand her signing vocabulary alongside her peers. However, Emily found the busy reception class daunting and covered her face when pupils tried to befriend her. A quiet area was organised in the classroom where Emily could interact with one or two other pupils at a time. Although Emily took part in classroom activities with adaptations, she rarely smiled and became stressed during busy sessions such as music, PE, messy play, art and design and playtimes. It was clear that Emily needed regular times where her sensory needs could be addressed. After discussion with her parents, it was decided that Emily should be given the opportunity to visit a sensory room and garden at a nearby special school. These visits proved to be successful, and Emily began to smile more frequently. At the end of the year, Emily's parents commented that both school communities were giving Emily the quality of life they wanted for her.

SEND: PMLD, Edward's syndrome.

Reflective Task 0.1

Why do you think Emily's parents chose for her to attend a mainstream school?

In what ways do you think greater consideration could have been given to Emily's wishes?

SEND Census Categories

In England, although the Government would like to move away from assumptions about pupils' needs based upon their difficulty or disability, they still need information about specific categories of need to allow them to predict levels of future resources and the availability of suitable educational settings. Information is collected through the statutory School Census. The Government first started collecting information on individual pupils in 2002 through the Pupil Level Annual Schools Census (PLASC). In 2006 (for secondary schools) and 2007 (for other educational settings), PLASC was replaced by The School Census. Census categories of SEND include the following:

- specific learning difficulties (SpLD);
- moderate learning difficulty (MLD);
- severe learning difficulty (SLD);
- profound and multiple learning difficulty (PMLD);
- speech, language and communication needs (SLCN);
- social, emotional and mental health (SEMH);
- autistic spectrum condition (ASC);
- visual impairment (VI);
- hearing impairment (HI);
- multisensory impairment (MSI);
- physical disability (PD);
- SEND support but no specialist assessment of type of need (NSA).

SEND Across the UK

Special education is a devolved issue across the nations of the UK with:

- Special Educational Needs and Disabilities (SEND) in England and Northern Ireland.
- Additional Support Needs (ASN) in Scotland.
- Additional Learning Needs (ALN) in Wales.

However, in each nation, the number of pupils being recognised as having SEND, ASN or ALN has risen during the past few years requiring teachers to support a wide range of pupils within inclusive mainstream classrooms.

The Graduated Approach

The graduated approach, **(assess, plan, do, review)**, is a response tool which helps identify and support pupils with SEND.

> *SEN support should take the form of a four-part cycle through which earlier decisions and actions are revisited, refined and revised with a growing understanding of the pupil's needs and of what supports the pupil in making good progress and securing good outcomes.*
>
> (DfE & DoH, 2015, p. 100)

1. **Assess** – Assess pupil's areas of success as well as their barriers to learning using formative and diagnostic assessments. For those pupils who have an EHCP, who are working below the standard of national curriculum assessments and are not engaged in subject-specific study, the government has introduced the engagement model, an observational assessment tool (see **chapter 6 – Assessment**). Professional agencies may be involved in a pupil's regular assessment with the families, teachers and teaching assistants involved in discussing outcomes and the way forward.
2. **Plan** – Organise learning into manageable steps using a multisensory approach. Source support materials and assistive technology that give individuals the opportunity to overcome or minimise barriers to learning where possible. This should be outlined in the pupil's personal learning plan (PLP). The learning targets and success criteria should be linked to prior learning and show next step development. The tailored support and/or interventions provided should meet the targeted outcomes identified in the pupil's EHCP.
3. **Do** – The class teacher and teaching assistant, with the support and advice of the SENCo, work with the pupil daily using support materials, assistive technology and multisensory activities as an integral part of lessons. Flexible grouping can be used to support the pupil's cognitive capability, interests and motivation.

4. **Review** – Progress should be reviewed through a pupil's PLP and EHCP and shared with all concerned. Professionals involved may need to revise their support depending on pupil progress. All pupils with SEND should be part of the graduated approach whether they have an EHCP or not. Details of the graduated approach can be found in the SEN Code of Practice (2015).

Education, Health and Care Plans

Many pupils with SEND attend a mainstream school where teachers are expected to make reasonable adjustments to cater for their areas of need. When a pupil needs specialised support, beyond what can be provided by a maintained school, from their own budgets, then an application can be made for an EHCP. After discussion with everyone, including the pupils, their family, teachers and other professionals involved in the assessment of SEND, a detailed document is drawn up. This outlines all the educational, health and social care needs of the individual including their own concerns, thoughts and aspirations, and names the school or setting chosen. The provision offered must be detailed, specified and quantified. An EHCP is a legally binding document and must be reviewed yearly involving all concerned in its implementation.

Personal Learning Plan

When pupils have been assessed and identified as being in need of specific support, they will be placed on the school SEND register and a PLP will be written by the school. This details the barriers placed on the pupil's learning and outlines ways in which the school aims to support the pupil and minimise their barriers to learning. A PLP is a statutory document and needs to be maintained and reviewed regularly as the pupil makes progress. An effective PLP should be SMART (Specific, Measurable, Achievable, Relevant and Time limited).

- **Specific** – targets should outline a pupil's barriers to learning and specify the strategies and resources available to support the pupil in making progress. The targets should motivate and give pupils confidence to make progress.
- **Measurable** – targets should allow teachers, teaching assistants and other professionals to assess progress through observations or formative, diagnostic and summative tests. The PLP should state what criteria will be used to evaluate outcomes.
- **Achievable** – targets should be appropriate to a pupil's ability range and give them the opportunity to recognise their own progress.
- **Relevant** – targets should reflect the pupil's needs.

- **Time limited** – targets should be reviewed regularly allowing progress to be monitored by all those involved with the pupil. The PLP should state review dates allowing for some flexibility according to pupil progress.

SEND and Alternative Provision Improvement Plan

The SEND and Alternative Provision Improvement Plan (DfE, 2023a) looked at ways to ensure the SEND system offered consistency, high quality and integrated provision across education, health and care. It considered the following:

- Setting new national standards across education, health and care detailing what support should be made available in mainstream settings and when an EHCP is needed.
- Developing simplified digital EHCPs to help reduce bureaucracy and support families in making informed choices on placements for their child/children. These standardised ECHPs would help to reduce variations between councils and would be used to review and update standards.
- Setting a new legal requirement for councils to introduce local inclusion plans showing joined up responsibility across education, health and care services. Families would be provided with a list of settings based on local inclusion plans which would include mainstream and special schools.
- Publishing new local inclusion dashboards to make roles and responsibilities of all partners within the system clearer for families and young people. The dashboards would help the DfE collect data on outcomes and experiences.
- Providing a new national framework for councils for banding and tariffs relating to high level needs funding. This should match national standards and give clarity on the level of support being offered, providing greater consistency.
- Changing the culture and practice in mainstream education to be more inclusive and better at identifying and supporting needs, including through earlier intervention and improved targeted support.
- Improving staff training by introducing a new leadership SENCo national professional qualification and increasing the number of staff with an accredited NVQ level 3 qualification in early years settings.
- Introducing a new delivery model in every local area for alternative provision focusing on early intervention and improvements to educational settings.
- Updating performance measures to recognise schools and colleges that are doing well for children identified with SEND.

NASEN responded positively to the new proposals and many professionals welcomed the suggested improvements. At the present time, the new Labour government has not indicated whether it will carry the SEND proposals forward. It appears to be adhering to its manifesto where it indicated it would take a community-wide approach to SEND. It aims to improve inclusivity and expertise in mainstream schools while ensuring those pupils with complex needs have a placement in a special school. There seems to be an interest in improving specialist resourced provision (SRP) in mainstream schools where pupils can attend mainstream school, while accessing SRPs. Whatever decisions are made, it's certain that Ofsted will rate inclusivity as part of their new report card system.

Useful Resources and Information: You Don't Need to be an Expert

Teachers don't need to be experts in relation to the range of needs in schools. School colleagues, SENCos and other professionals can provide support and suggest ways in which all learners can be encouraged to make progress. *The Teacher Handbook: SEND*, developed by NASEN (2024), is an excellent resource to use as a reference. It contains guidance on a wide range of teaching approaches to support children and young people with SEND within an inclusive environment.

1

High Expectations

Chapter Objectives

This chapter recognises the importance of high-quality teaching for all pupils including those with SEND. It also explores:

- promoting positive behaviour;
- collaborative and cooperative learning;
- role models;
- high expectations;
- neurodiversity and dual exceptionality;
- communicating shared values;
- supporting the development of effective relationships;
- intersectionality;
- self-awareness;
- attachment theory;
- home and community factors.

High Quality Teaching

Links to the ITTECF 1.1

- **1.6 Learn that** high quality teaching has a long-term positive effect on pupils' life chances, particularly for children from disadvantaged backgrounds.
- **1.7 Learn that** high quality teaching is underpinned by positive interactions between pupils, their teachers and their peers (DfE, 2024a, p. 11).

The Education Endowment Foundation's report on *Special Educational Needs in Mainstream Schools* (2021a) found that, 'to a great extent, good teaching for pupils with SEND is good teaching for all' (p. 9). Mould (2020) highlights teaching strategies that enhance high quality teaching for pupils with SEND. These strategies are:

- **Flexible grouping**
  This is a way of grouping pupils, according to need, for specific activities. Grouping can change according to the nature of the task, the cognitive capability and interests of the pupils.
- **Explicit instruction**
  Explicit instruction should follow a sequence which helps all learners. Teachers explain learning objectives and success criteria clearly, organise information into manageable chunks, model tasks while verbalising the thinking process, allow pupils time for practice and give clear feedback.
- **Using technology**
  Technology may be used to support and enhance learning for pupils in mainstream schools, but for some pupils with SEND, it may be their only form of communication. Advances in eye tracking technology has given many pupils with PMLD a practical way to express their thoughts and feelings.
- **Scaffolding**
  Instructional scaffolding has been described as, 'I do, we do, you do'. The teacher demonstrates how something is done, then gives pupils time to practise and work together on the task. Finally, the teacher gives pupils the opportunity to work individually on a similar task without support. For some pupils with SEND, this may be a small step process.
- **Cognitive and metacognitive strategies**
  Cognitive strategies refer to the mental techniques we use to process information and achieve certain goals. Metacognitive strategies help pupils become aware of and understand their own thought processes.

High quality teaching does not mean that teachers can be all things to all pupils. It does mean that the inclusive ethos created in both school and classroom encompasses all learners whatever their cognitive capability and that activities can be adapted to support the development of key learning skills. For high quality teaching to take place for all pupils, teachers need to:

- use formative assessment effectively when planning a lesson sequence, taking into consideration the level of knowledge and skills development within the class;
- use the graduated approach (assess, plan, do, review) to ensure a continuum of support for pupils with SEND;

- recognise a pupil's barriers to learning within an area of the curriculum and help them to overcome these barriers where possible;
- activate pupils' prior knowledge and identify misconceptions;
- use modelling and scaffolding strategies;
- adapt activities to ensure that all pupils can take part and make good personal progress;
- provide a range of multi-sensory activities where pupils can choose options;
- use technology and specific resources to support learning;
- encourage positive behaviour and cooperative learning;
- ask open-ended questions where all answers are valued;
- give specific and encouraging feedback in real time;
- show pupils how to review their own learning regularly.

Packer (2019) encapsulates the essence of high-quality teaching stating:

> *High-quality teaching is about the day-to-day interactions that take place in your classroom and the different pedagogical approaches you use to engage, motivate and challenge learners. It is about the way you use assessment and feedback to identify gaps and help children move on in their learning. It is about providing both support and challenge in order to enable children to achieve more. (p. 1)*

Promoting Positive Behaviour

Links to the ITTECF 1.2

- **1.1 Learn that** teachers have the ability to affect and improve the well-being, motivation and behaviour of their pupils.
- **1.2 Learn that** teachers are key role models, who can influence the attitudes, values and behaviours of their pupils (DfE, 2024a, p. 11).

Promoting positive behaviour in schools is fundamental to a teacher's role. Allowing negative behaviour to flourish affects the learning environment for everyone. The EEF's (2019) guidance report entitled *Improving Behaviour in Schools* emphasises that 'consistency and coherence at a whole-school level are paramount' (p. 2). It's important to have a school behaviour policy which gives clear guidelines to all staff and is used as part of a consistent approach to behaviour. Strategies for promoting positive behaviour in schools may include:

- modelling positive learning behaviours;
- encouraging mutual respect;
- giving positive, constructive feedback;
- establishing structure and routines;
- planning motivating activities;
- praising and rewarding positive social interactions;
- setting clear behaviour expectations;
- providing opportunities for guided cooperative learning;
- encouraging pupils to be self-reflective on their own behaviours.

Suggested strategies for understanding behaviour for learning and managing specific pupil behaviours are explored further in **7 – Managing Behaviour**.

Activities to Promote Positive Behaviour

Activities to promote positive behaviour and the development of social communication skills are particularly helpful for pupils with Social, Emotional and Mental Health difficulties (SEMH). Suggested activities may include:

- **Circle Time** which helps to develop positive relationships through listening and speaking activities. It can be used to address specific issues identified in the class.
- **Role Play** which helps pupils develop their communication and social skills as they act out and make sense of real life and imaginary situations. Pupils can express their thoughts and feelings more freely as a character. Role play activities can be linked to several subject areas.
- **Creating Rules** – Ask pupils to brainstorm some helpful classroom rules, giving reasons for their choices. Let the class vote for the three or four they consider to be the most important to implement.
- **Responsibilities** – Give pupils classroom and community responsibilities. This not only raises their self-esteem but also encourages a shared appreciation for the community environment.

- **Time to Talk Book and Game (LDA)** is a programme of activities to develop oral language and social interaction skills. It includes the skills of turn-taking, giving and following instructions, eye contact, listening and attention.
- **Rainbow Parachute** activities help to improve spatial awareness, interaction and social skills through a wide range of games. They can be used with all primary age ranges.
- **Catch them being kind** – Praise pupils for acts of kindness to each other. Encourage the use of kind words such as please, thank you, we can share, I'll be your friend.
- **Playground Buddies** – Pupils can volunteer to act as buddies to those children who may be left alone on the playground. This helps to encourage the development of friendly, sociable play times.
- **Social Stories** are short descriptions of situations, events or activities written by a supportive adult for an individual with ASC. Each story includes specific information about what to expect in a certain situation and how to respond appropriately. *The New Social Story Book* by Carol Gray offers a wealth of social stories which can be used with different age ranges and shared with families.
- **Team Sports** such as football, netball and hockey involve social and communication skills. Some pupils with ASC avoid contact sports because of oversensitivity to certain stimuli. Team activities, where you can compete as an individual but also as part of a team, can be beneficial. Sports such as swimming, gymnastics, athletics, horse riding and sailing are some of the team sports more suitable for pupils with social communication and sensory difficulties.
- **Comic Strip Conversations** are a technique developed by Carol Gray to assist individuals with autism to develop greater social understanding. Comic Strip Conversations provide visual representations of the different levels of communication that take place in a conversation, using symbols, stick figure drawings and colour.
- **Puppets** can be used to address specific emotional and behavioural issues using adult/pupil interaction through puppets. Puppet play with other pupils allows children to express their thoughts and feelings, learn conversational skills and act out difficult social scenarios without stress.

Collaborative and Cooperative Learning

Collaborative learning can help provide an environment where positive behaviour is promoted, where all thoughts and ideas are valued, and pupils can develop a shared understanding of each other's needs. Collaborative learning theory is founded on social constructivism and, in particular, the work of Vygotsky who suggested that learning happens through interactions between pupils, teachers and other adults. Vygotsky (1978) argued that language helps us develop reasoning skills and supports the development of cultural activities such as reading and writing. He suggested we learn by following the rules, values, skills and knowledge of our culture through group collaboration and discussion as we work together.

All pupils benefit from taking part in group activities but putting them in a group does not mean they will cooperate effectively (Johnson & Johnson, 1994; 2014). Cooperative learning is where groupwork is carefully prepared, planned and monitored. Initially, some pupils with SEND may need to work with a trusted partner instead of a group. Key elements of cooperative learning include the following:

1. **Positive interdependence** – pupils are expected to work together for the good of all and not in competition with each other.
2. **Individual accountability** – pupils take responsibility for their own part of the learning task and, in helping the group, complete the activity as a cooperative effort.
3. **Face-to-face promotive interaction** – pupils are given opportunities to take part in balanced discussion and interaction. They are encouraged to discuss their learning and support each other's strengths and difficulties.
4. **Social skills** – pupils are given opportunities to develop social skills such as active listening, taking turns, sharing ideas, showing respect for the feelings of others, compromising and conflict resolution.
5. **Group processing** – pupils are encouraged to reflect on their task performance, to listen to feedback and think about ways to make improvements if necessary.

Cooperative learning can help promote positive behaviour if pupils are shown how to work together and recognise each other's strengths. Teachers and other adults can model positive behaviour within a cooperative learning situation. Feedback during these learning activities should praise positive interactions. In this way, all pupils can begin to develop interpersonal skills within a safe, inclusive environment. Some pupils with SEND may need the support of assistive technology, multisensory resources, physical adaptations and adult guidance.

Cooperative Learning Strategies

- Think, Pair, Share activities can be linked to a topic or subject. The adult asks an open-ended question, giving pupils time to pause and think. Pupils discuss with a partner, then share their ideas with the group. The adult may expand discussion with a larger group or with the class.
- Jigsaw Tasks are linked to a topic or subject. Each pupil within a group has part of the topic to learn about. They then take turns to share their learning with the group. When all the learning has been shared, the jigsaw is completed.

- Design and Technology challenges are where pupils work together in pairs, or within a group to support each other with making decisions, overcoming any barriers to learning, coping with difficulties and solving problems.
- Peer review can help pupils develop critical thinking skills regarding both their own work and that of others. The adult needs to model peer review to ensure that only constructive criticism is given alongside ideas for possible improvement.
- Round robin involves each pupil in the group taking turns to share their thoughts and ideas related to a specific topic. Round robins help to structure brainstorming sessions at the beginning and end of topics. They also ensure that all pupils are encouraged to participate. Group thoughts can be collated by an adult and shared with the class.
- See, Think, Wonder is a strategy that involves pupils in making careful observations (see), thinking about what they have observed (think) and asking questions about their observations (wonder). This strategy can be used across a range of subjects. Adults may need to model each part of this strategy at first.

Role Models

Teachers can influence pupils in a positive way, but can they be considered role models? A role model is generally recognised as a person whose behaviour, qualities, success or social position is one to which others may aspire. Children and young people often idolise and try to emulate professional athletes, music artists or influencers.

Research by the National Literacy Trust (2022) found that role models are an important influence in children and young people's lives. The Trust was looking specifically at the influence of role models on children and young people's attitude to reading, but it is important to note that the influence of role models can spread much wider.

1.1 Did You Know?

- 93.4% of children and young people aged 7 to 18 had at least one role model.
- 52.6% said that they looked up to a YouTuber (38.3%, a sibling and 36.5%, a teacher).
- 52.9% of children and young people who had a role model agreed that seeing their role model read would make them think it is okay to read.
- 27.2% agreed that seeing their role model read would make them think that reading would help them to pursue a career they are interested in.
- The most popular role models were mums (67.4%) and dads (60.2%).

National Literacy Trust (2022)

Teachers may not be considered role models by pupils, but they do have a tremendous influence on their lives. The decisions they make, and the teaching strategies used to encourage pupils to develop lifelong learning skills, are important. School values, as exemplified by all staff, can help raise self-esteem and confidence when all pupils are encouraged to be proud of their personal achievements as well as the achievements of others.

Case Study: I Can

Roshan was an anxious member of a year 4 class who often refused to take part in literacy activities, muttering 'I can't do it'. His teacher recognised that Roshan had been in and out of hospital over the past two years for cancer treatment and, for much of the time, he had been too ill to attend school.

It was during circle time, when Roshan's teacher introduced a story trail activity, that she noticed Roshan's mature use of vocabulary during oral storytelling. She decided to use Roshan's oral strengths to support his reading development by organising read, think, share groups where pupils read a text together, thought about the content, then discussed open-ended questions about it. Although shy at first, Roshan began to interact enthusiastically with his reading group often sharing some thought-provoking ideas. Alongside this strategy, the teacher organised small group targeted support with systematic synthetic phonics to help Roshan develop his phonemic and phonological skills. To minimise the stress associated with writing activities, Roshan and others were given the choice of using alternative methods of recording. Gradually Roshan began to develop an 'I can' attitude though he continued to need some targeted support.

SEND: Anxiety, Cancer treatment.

Reflective Task 1.1

Which literacy activities may have made Roshan the most anxious?

How do you think Roshan's illness had impacted on his literacy development?

Positive attitudes to learning and the sharing of a school's ethos and values can have an impact on the character development of pupils with SEND. Character education can encompass both curricular and co-curricular activities. The Character Education Framework Guidance (2019a) states, 'Schools have a statutory duty, as part of a broad and balanced curriculum, to promote the spiritual, moral, social, and cultural (SMSC) development of pupils and prepare them for the opportunities, responsibilities and experiences of later life' (p. 4).

In the fast-paced world of ever changing social and political views, it's important that schools and classrooms provide safe havens where pupils can grow in their personal awareness of the world around them without being pressurised into following imposed ideologies or influences from social media. Teachers can share joy and enthusiasm for learning and, in doing so, give pupils a purpose in their lives.

High Expectations

Links to the ITTECF 1.3

- **1.3 Learn that** teacher expectations can affect pupil outcomes; setting goals that challenge and stretch pupils is essential (DfE, 2024a, p. 11).

The results of classroom-based research undertaken by Rosenthal and Jacobsen (1968) highlighted the power of positive expectations. The research findings demonstrated that what one person expected of another could serve as a self-fulfilling prophecy. Rosenthal and Jacobsen (1968) termed this the Pygmalion Effect. Conversely, when a teacher had low expectations of a pupil, the pupil's performance became lower; termed the Golem Effect. Rosenthal and Babad (1985) emphasised, 'Teachers tend to treat less favourably and obtain inferior performance from students for whom they have less favourable expectations' (p. 38).

Rubie-Davies (2014) explored the expectations of teachers in New Zealand. Her research showed that teachers' different levels of expectation were conveyed in their teaching practices. Those teachers who had low expectations of pupils often offered learning experiences which were less cognitively demanding. They were prepared to accept a lower standard of work from certain pupils and provided little challenge in the tasks given. Rubie-Davies also noted that, in general, the most effective teaching practices were employed when a teacher had high expectations of their pupils. This, in turn, gave pupils more opportunities to make progress.

Rubie-Davies et al. (2015) set up a teacher expectation intervention where teachers were asked to model the practices of high expectation teachers. Key elements of the intervention were to:

1. provide a positive and inclusive learning environment;
2. organise tasks using flexible grouping;
3. provide pupils with choice during activities;
4. ask open-ended questions;
5. praise pupils for effort as well as accuracy;
6. give constructive feedback.

The findings of this teacher expectation intervention revealed positive results for pupil attainment when these practices were implemented.

High expectations act as a foundation for building an inclusive learning environment. Within that environment, pupils with SEND can be given opportunities to make progress if teaching strategies are adopted that help pupils overcome, or at least minimise, some of their barriers to learning.

Strategies that recognise and support high expectations for pupils with SEND may include the following:

- Communicating belief in a pupil's potential, using language that promotes challenge and aspiration but also offers support.
- Encouraging pupils to develop self-belief, using pupils' strengths to support their difficulties.
- Making learning outcomes explicit and encouraging pupils to contribute to task success criteria.
- Setting tasks which are achievable by breaking larger activities into smaller more manageable tasks.
- Asking open-ended questions to encourage the sharing of ideas and the understanding that all points of view are relevant.
- Making effective use of assistive technology to support learning.
- Giving clearly defined task expectations and making expectations clear for learning task behaviour.
- Giving pupils thinking time before starting a task and setting realistic time management challenges.
- Giving effective feedback to pupils in real time which recognises motivation and progress made.
- Suggesting realistic ideas for continued improvement using clear, constructive language.

Both teachers and pupils can experience pressure in relation to expectations in education (Murdock-Perriera et al., 2018). If some pupils with SEND do not reach age-related expectations, it's important to use the graduated approach (assess, plan, do, review) to explore and identify each stage of a pupil's learning development. Rather than putting pressure on pupils with SEND to achieve age-related expectations, teachers should encourage them to achieve personal success. Recognition of progress, however small, is important to a pupil's well-being and self-efficacy. In this way, expectations can be set that are realistic and achievable.

Malmberg and Martin (2019) studied the effect of applying 'pressure expectations' on children's learning experiences. They found that pupils reported they felt less confident in subjects where high-pressure expectations were applied and had less enjoyment in these lessons. The study suggested that teachers should place greater emphasis on sharing the joy of learning with their pupils, providing appropriate learning goals and feedback, according to pupil needs, while at the same time taking into consideration pupils' interests, motivation and enjoyment of a topic or subject.

Case Study: Providing Feedback

Olivia, aged seven, was secure in all the end of year assessments. However, her teacher felt she could achieve greater depth in her writing. After completing a piece of descriptive writing, the teacher suggested Olivia made some improvements in her use of descriptive language. When the teacher returned, she found Olivia sobbing quietly with her writing covered in tears. At the time Olivia was yet to receive a SEND diagnosis and appeared socially and emotionally immature. She had interpreted the teacher's feedback as a criticism of her efforts.

SEND: Dyslexia, Semantic Pragmatic difficulties.

Reflective Task 1.2

How could the teacher have adapted her feedback to meet Olivia's needs?

In what ways do you think feedback can affect pupil motivation?

Neurodiversity

Within the context of inclusive education, neurodiversity is an area of research which emphasises the importance of having high expectations. Many pupils who, in the past were diagnosed with dyslexia, dyscalculia, Attention Deficit Hyperactivity Disorder (ADHD), autism and Tourette syndrome, were offered learning experiences which were less cognitively demanding, and their abilities often went unrecognised. As many pupils are neurotypical, and their brains process information in a similar way, certain teaching strategies have been developed that work for most pupils. Yet many of the strategies used to support pupils who are neurodivergent are effective for all pupils.

It's estimated that 15%–20% of pupils in England are neurodivergent (DfE, 2024b). Therefore, for pupils who have neurodivergent traits, it's important that teachers and families recognise their achievements while, at the same time, helping them find ways to minimise their barriers to learning.

> *Some people with dyslexia, for example, have been noted for their visual thinking ability and entrepreneurial strengths. Some people with ADHD can thrive where they can use their skills in developing novel solutions to complex problems. People with ADHD may also be more inclined to take calculated risks and be more entrepreneurial. Some individuals with autism spectrum traits have good analytical skills relating to computer programming or mathematical computation.*
>
> (Ellis et al., 2023, p. 15)

In any mixed ability mainstream classroom, pupils have a range of learning needs requiring flexible arrangements in both teaching style and classroom organisation. These may include the following:

- A multisensory approach with step-by-step activities.
- Flexible grouping considering pupil strengths, interests and needs.
- Quiet areas or spaces with limited distractions.
- Visual timetables and clear instructions.
- Use of assistive technology to support a range of needs.
- Personalised provision such as room layout, portable desk screens, specific lighting and furniture.

Dual Exceptionality

Dual exceptionality is a term used for pupils who are high attainers while, at the same time, have a learning difficulty or disability. These pupils may feel doubly isolated. Some may feel under challenged and this may generate feelings of low self-esteem as well as a negative attitude to learning. For pupils with dual exceptionality, it's important to organise suitable learning activities that both challenge and support. Montgomery (2015) provides practical guidance on how to support pupils' learning, extend their thinking skills and provide appropriate degrees of challenge in *Teaching Gifted Children with Special Educational Needs*.

Case Study: Dual Exceptionality

Sam did not attend pre-school. His mother was concerned he'd be ostracised by parents and pupils because of his aggressive behaviour towards other children. She felt his behaviour had been aggravated by the break-up of her marriage. When Sam started

(Continued)

(Continued)

school, he was withdrawn but aggressive when asked to take part in group activities. If challenged he would run out of the classroom, hide in the toilets and shout at any child who entered. He refused to learn to read but sat in the book corner, muttering loudly. At break times, he walked around the perimeter of the playground, threatening children who got in his way. One violent outburst resulted in his exclusion from school and an appointment was made for Sam to see an educational psychologist. At this point, his mother decided to educate him at home.

After some weeks, the Educational Psychologist diagnosed Sam with autism but, to receive support, a multi-professional diagnosis needed to be made. While waiting for a decision, Sam's mother continued to educate him at home, where he learnt to read and play the piano.

When Sam was eight years old, his mother moved to an area where he could attend a small primary school. It was agreed that funding would be provided for one-to-one support in a mainstream classroom. Sam was given a visual timetable and prepared in advance for any changes in routine. He was given an area in the classroom for personal space and often worked on his own individual projects linked to class themes. He continued to have outbursts of anger and made very few friends. Both at home and at school, Sam became obsessively interested in reading dictionaries and encyclopaedias.

When Sam was aged 10, his mother needed to move again for work reasons. Sam was given a place in a mainstream class at a large primary school with a speech and language resource base. He was monitored by the SENCo and resource base teacher and then assessed by the Speech and Language Therapist (SALT) using the British Picture Vocabulary Scales (BPVS). He scored highly and was encouraged to use his interest in words by devising word challenges, quizzes and crosswords for small groups of interested pupils. He also became a library monitor.

Although Sam continued to need sensory integration therapy as well as support in the speech and language resource base to develop his grammatical, semantic and pragmatic understanding of language, he spent much of his time in the mainstream classroom. Sam's class teacher often used music as a calming strategy and during practices for the school concert Sam showed he was a talented singer. Although he could not be persuaded to sing on stage, he agreed to sing a solo backstage.

With both school and parental support, Sam achieved above age-related scores in maths and science in his year 6 SATs. He moved on to secondary education, with a learning support package. His mother was thrilled that he was also part of the school's high attainer group with the reputation for being a formidable chess player.

SEND: Autism, Dual Exceptionality.

Reflective Task 1.3

Why do you think it took so long to discover Sam's dual exceptionality?

How do you think Sam's interest in music could be encouraged?

Communicating Shared Values and Supporting the Development of Effective Relationships

Links to the ITTECF 1.4

- **1.4 Learn that** setting clear expectations can help communicate shared values that improve classroom and school culture.
- **1.5 Learn that** a culture of mutual trust and respect supports effective relationships.
- **1.8 Learn that** pupils' experiences of school and their readiness to learn can be impacted by their home life and circumstances, particularly for EAL pupils, young carers, and those living in poverty (DfE, 2024a, pp. 11-12).

The government report on *Behaviour in schools* emphasises that, 'Schools should be clear about which behaviours are permitted and prohibited; the values, attitudes, and beliefs they promote and the social norms and routines that should be encouraged throughout the school community' (DfE, 2024c, p. 6).

Supporting the development of positive relationships within both the school and classroom is an important part of providing a learning environment where everyone feels valued and high-quality teaching can take place. Establishing trust and clear communication between families, pupils, teachers and supporting adults means that everyone can work more effectively. Children and young people with SEND thrive on structured routines and established expectations where they can experience explicit instruction, feedback, task adaptation and opportunities to become part of a friendly learning community.

To begin developing positive relationships, pupils and adults need to learn each other's names to strengthen associations and develop stronger relationships. Many of the activities below can be organised using speaking, signing or assistive technology, depending on individual pupil communication needs.

Interactive games and activities are a good way of encouraging both adults and children to learn each other's names. For example:

- **Good morning** – The adult says good morning to each child by name as they arrive at the classroom door or as part of taking the register, ensuring eye contact is used appropriately.
- **Name badges** can be worn for the first few weeks of term as prompts for both adults and other children. Allow pupils ownership of the design and production so they feel comfortable with the look and feel of them.
- **Birthday calendar** – Have a calendar on display with each child's name printed next to their birth date. For those who need visual cues, small photos of children can be attached (with parent/carer's permission). Most pupils enjoy some recognition on their birthdays.
- **Alphabetical name poster** – Print out a poster with class names arranged alphabetically by first name and display prominently. For those who need visual cues, photos of children can be attached (with parent/carer's permission).
- **Bean bag name game** – Pupils take turns to say the name of someone in the group and throw the bean bag to them. That pupil then calls out the name of another pupil and throws the bean bag to them. If someone drops the bean bag, it must be returned to the child who started the activity.
- **Wordsearch** – Compile printed word searches using pupil names (use a lower-case font with initial letters capitalised, e.g. Liam). These can be based on groups or randomly picked names.
- **Name/pair/share** – Adult can model this activity by introducing themselves and their favourite activity. In pairs, pupils tell each other their name and favourite activity, 'I'm Sophie and my favourite game is football'. Introduce your partner to another pair, 'This is Sophie, and her favourite game is football'. Repeat with a different pair around the group table.
- **Name rhythms** – Pupils take turns to clap or tap the syllables in their name. When pupils are used to clapping the rhythms of their own names, they can be encouraged to clap the name of another pupil who then must respond by clapping the name of a different pupil to encourage relating a name to a person.
- **I came to school, and I saw**... – Adult models the activity with a group of children. Then pupils try the activity in groups. First pupil says, 'I came to school, and I saw (name of any child in the class)'. Second pupil says, 'I came to school, and I saw (repeats first name and adds another)'. The aim is to see how many names can be remembered at any one time.
- **Stand Up, Sit Down** is an action activity and can be adapted for physically disabilities (wave your hand, nod/shake your head, press a light). You can use a range of instructions

that involve pupils in listening and responding to different descriptive commands (stand if you walk to school/sit down if you have brown eyes). Be aware of any pupil who is self-conscious of a physical feature and do not wish attention to be drawn to this.

The statutory guidance on relationships states that pupils should know:

- the importance of respecting others, even when they are very different from themselves (for example, physically, in character, personality or backgrounds), or make different choices or have different preferences or beliefs
- practical steps they can take in a range of different contexts to improve or support respectful relationships
- the conventions of courtesy and manners
- the importance of self-respect and how this links to their own happiness
- that in school and in wider society they can expect to be treated with respect by others, and that in turn they should show due respect to others, including those in positions of authority
- about different types of bullying (including cyberbullying), the impact of bullying, responsibilities of bystanders (primarily reporting bullying to an adult) and how to get help
- what a stereotype is, and how stereotypes can be unfair, negative or destructive
- the importance of permission-seeking and giving in relationships with friends, peers and adults.

(DfE, 2021, p. 21)

For primary school pupils, and especially those with SEND, the conventions of building positive relationships may need to be taught explicitly. In the early years, role play and planned practical activities are an appropriate way of learning about relationships. Later, games and activities, which help pupils learn more about each other, can also support the building of positive relationships. Some suggestions for games:

- **I'm happy when I**... – This is an action or signing game. Pupils mime or sign things that make them happy for their group to guess. Some pupils may need the support of assistive technology to take part.
- **My favourite things** – Pupils create a collage or digitally generated pictorial representation of favourite things.
- **Pass the hat** – A group game to be played as pass the parcel with adult support for some pupils. Pupil takes a question card out of the hat. Questions should aim to discover more about each pupil in the group (What is your favourite food/game/book?).

- **Just a minute** – Allow each pupil a set time to talk about themselves to their group. Use a visual timer such as a physical sand timer or one generated on the Interactive White Board. Communication can be verbal, signing or using assistive technology.
- **Yes or no?** In pairs, pupils ask questions to get to know each other but can only answer yes or no. This activity is not suitable for pupils with communication and interaction difficulties unless using assistive technology or signing with adult support.
- **Picnic** – On a paper plate, pupils to draw food they'd like to take on a picnic. This activity is suitable for small classes in special schools or resource bases, where pupils can express preferences and be given targeted support with coping with their own sensory reactions to foods they dislike.
- **All about me booklet** – Pupils can compile booklets with signposted headings about themselves and their family using words and/or pictures. Headings will depend on age and cognitive ability of pupils.

Intersectionality

Learning is a multi-faceted lifetime process with each pupil facing a different journey depending on their individual needs and lived experiences. For some children and young people, home life is positive and supportive. For others, there may be hidden difficulties which leave them vulnerable and isolated.

Intersectionality was a term used by Kimberle Crenshaw (1994) when exploring the barriers to participation experienced by Black women. Crenshaw used the term to refer to the double discrimination of racism and sexism faced by Black women. The term was extended further by Patricia Collins (2019) who highlighted how some people with different characteristics and identities (gender, ethnicity, social status, poverty, sexuality and disability) may experience barriers to participation in everyday life as well as in the school community. 'Intersectionality is the complex, dynamic way in which the effects of multiple vulnerabilities combine, overlap or intersect. This deeply impacts an individual's lived experience, including the specific barriers to access that they face' (NASEN, 2024, p. 12).

Assumptions that are based on a pupil's outward identity and behaviour can sometimes influence the decisions made by teachers. Often there is a need to investigate beyond the outward persona of a pupil and enlist the help of the SENCo, the family and other educational professionals.

Case Study: Understanding Pupils' Backgrounds

Dylan was a noisy, seemingly hyperactive year 3 pupil who caused regular disruption in the classroom despite a variety of strategies being used. His teacher referred him to the SENCo querying a possible diagnosis of ADHD. After talking to Dylan, the SENCo found

(Continued)

that he lived in a high rise flat where he was rarely allowed to play outside. His mother was concerned he would be persuaded to join the gangs operating in the area. He was also forbidden to play any noisy, physical games in the flat because the family were afraid of complaints from the neighbours. School was the only place where Dylan could let off steam.

The class teacher encouraged Dylan's mother to allow him to join some after school sports clubs and he was given the responsibility of organising equipment for PE lessons. After a while, Dylan became a regular member of the school football team.

Although Dylan continued to struggle with listening and attention skills at times, his teacher found that he benefitted from learning through a multisensory approach. Playing literacy and maths games to support the development of listening and attention skills also helped Dylan focus in the classroom.

No SEND identified, supported by a multisensory approach to learning.

Reflective Task 1.4

In what ways do you think community factors affected Dylan's learning in school?

Consider a maths lesson you have planned and taught. In what ways could you adapt it using a more multisensory approach?

Self-Awareness

Developing self-awareness is a skill which helps all pupils, including those with SEND, to cope with the challenges they encounter in life. Teachers have a responsibility to support pupils in developing an awareness of self, allowing them to:

- recognise their areas of strength and barriers to learning;
- identify ways in which barriers may be overcome or minimised;
- recognise their own feelings and those of others;
- talk about their thoughts and feelings;
- recognise how their attitude and behaviour may affect others.

The EEF report, *Improving Social and Emotional Learning*, notes that, 'Self-awareness is concerned with the ability to recognise our emotions and thoughts, and to understand how they influence our behaviour. It also means being aware of our strengths and having a belief in oneself ("self-efficacy")' (EEF, 2021b, p. 10).

For some pupils with SEND, gaining self-efficacy is a slow process and needs small step encouragement. Zimmerman (1995) recognised motivation as a factor in developing self-efficacy, for when pupils experience success it can motivate them to continue learning.

Attachment Theory

A pupil's self-awareness does not begin at school but within the home and community to which they belong. Good experiences in the early years affect the development of language and social skills and provide a firm foundation for future learning. Attachment theory, developed by John Bowlby (1969), captures the importance of bonds established in the early years.

> *This theory tells us that a strong emotional and physical bond to a primary caregiver (parent, carer, sibling, grandparent) is critical to childhood development. If children have 'good enough' care (sensitive, attuned care which meets their physical and emotional needs), they feel safe to explore the world in the knowledge that they have a secure base to return to. With this secure attachment, children receive and develop a positive 'internal working model' of themselves, others and the world around them.*
>
> (NASEN, 2024, p. 17)

Home and Community Factors

There are many pupils whose learning experiences are impacted negatively by their home life and circumstances. These may include the following:

- perinatal factors;
- community disadvantage (poor housing and physical environment);
- poverty and limited access to early years education;
- Special Educational Needs and Disabilities (SEND);
- language and cultural barriers (ethnicity);
- family stress and dysfunction.

1.2 Did You Know?

Disadvantaged children start school behind their more advantaged peers, and the gap in performance widens as they progress through the education system. Our analysis shows that, on average, disadvantaged pupils are 4.3 months behind in the early years phase, 9.4 months

(Continued)

behind in primary school, and 18.4 months behind at Key Stage 4, with persistently disadvantaged pupils 23.4 months behind at KS4. For this analysis, we used the DfE definition of disadvantage i.e. pupils who are eligible for the Pupil Premium; persistently disadvantaged pupils are those who have been eligible for Free School Meals for at least 80 per cent of their school lives.

(Crenna-Jennings, 2018, p. 4)

Young carers are children and young people under 18 who provide care and support for a family member who is disabled or ill. This may be on a temporary or permanent basis. Young carers take on a level of responsibility that is sometimes inappropriate for their age and level of development, where they often have to offer both personal and emotional support. Surveys have shown that as many as 1 in 10 young people may be acting as carers.

Case Study: Hidden Care

Kira was a quiet child who rarely talked about home activities or interests. At the beginning of year 4, Kira began to arrive at school independently and was often a few minutes late. She showed signs of fatigue during afternoon sessions and her academic progress suffered. Contact was made with her mother, via a phone call as she was unable to visit the school. Kira's mother organised a visit to the GP and reported back that the doctor could find nothing wrong. Kira continued to look pale and withdrawn and one afternoon burst into tears.

The class teacher organised a one-to-one session with the SENCo, and Kira began to unburden herself. It appeared that her mother had been ill for some time and needed help with self-care which Kira was providing. This involved helping her get washed and dressed, both in the morning and evening, as well as doing most of the cooking and cleaning. Kira's father worked away from home frequently but, when he was at home, he refused to let his wife visit a doctor, shouting at her and calling her a hypochondriac. That morning, he had announced he was leaving. The weight of worry fell upon Kira.

A home visit from the health visitor was organised immediately and an appointment made with the GP. After tests, it was discovered that Kira's mother was suffering with multiple sclerosis. Home help was arranged, and the father contacted. Although he refused to return home, he was willing to make some financial provision for Kira and her mother. At school, Kira was assigned a mentor who helped her find her way through the separation of her parents and a move to more suitable accommodation. Gradually Kira began to develop a sense of well-being and confidence that she had almost lost.

No SEND identified: Young Carer.

Reflective Task 1.5

In what ways can schools build and strengthen relationships between teachers, pupils, their families and the wider community?

In primary schools, teachers not only have responsibility for teaching a broad and balanced curriculum but also need to take into consideration the individual, family and community barriers to learning faced by pupils with SEND. Some individuals and families may have complex needs, which are already recognised and supported, while others may have hidden challenges. Identifying vulnerable learners is a starting point, but the advice and help of other staff and professionals is needed when setting up support packages. Once in place, the support provided will impact a pupil's belief that they are a valued part of the school community.

2
How Pupils Learn

Chapter Objectives

This chapter examines the educational theories of cognitivism, behaviourism and constructivism and introduces Bloom's taxonomy. It also emphasises the importance of achieving a balance in the way we educate our children and young people by considering the two meanings of the word education. It explores:

- how pupils learn;
- visible teaching and learning;
- prior knowledge;
- memory in learning;
- cognitive load;
- purposeful practice.

How Pupils Learn

Links to the ITTECF 2.1

- **2.1 Learn that** learning involves a lasting change in pupils' capabilities or understanding (DfE, 2024a, p. 13).

If learning is to involve making a lasting change to pupils' capabilities or understanding, it's important for teachers to explore ways in which children develop and learn how to learn. Ideas developed by educational theorists on how children learn have been debated for many years. Several theories have been explored, but probably the most well-known are summarised below.

Cognitive learning theory explores the idea that both internal and external forces affect how well pupils learn. Internal forces such as the ability to think about how you think (metacognition) and external forces such as the environment, both at home and school, have an impact on how children learn. How well pupils respond to stimulus, and learn new concepts, depends on both internal and external influences. Cognitivism has produced a few evidence-based theories such as social cognitive theory, cognitive load theory and schema theory. Key theorists in the area of cognitivism include Albert Bandura, Lawrence Kohlberg, George Miller, Jean Piaget and John Sweller.

Behavioural learning theory explores the idea that the learner is a 'tabula rasa' (a blank slate) and needs to be provided with environmental stimuli. The theory is based on the premise that all behaviours are acquired through conditioning. Learners need to experience repeated actions, verbal reinforcement and rewards to achieve a goal. Some theorists argue that an individual can be trained to perform any task, within the limits of their physical capability, if the right conditioning is provided. Key theorists in the area of behaviourism include Ivan Pavlov, Burrhus Frederic Skinner and John Watson.

Constructivist learning theory explores the idea that pupils construct their learning of new ideas based on prior knowledge and experiences. For this to be effective, pupils need to have established clear prior knowledge bases with resolved misconceptions. Bruner (1960) advocated developing a curriculum which presented ideas repeatedly but with increasing complexity and depth of difficulty. This was termed the 'spiral curriculum' and was aimed at reinforcing previous learning. Key theorists in the area of constructivism include Jerome Bruner, John Dewey, Jean Piaget and Lev Vygotsky.

Taxonomies for Learning

In education, a taxonomy is a hierarchical model used to classify educational learning objectives by levels of specificity and complexity. A number have been developed, but perhaps the best known is Bloom's Taxonomy (1956) which originally described the cognitive learning processes and the development of subject mastery. This initial framework has been expanded to three learning domains – cognitive, affective and psychomotor.

The **cognitive** domain (Bloom, 1956) involves the hierarchical development of intellectual knowledge and skills.

The **affective** domain (Krathwohl et al., 1964) describes emotional growth and includes the way in which individuals deal with things such as feelings, attitudes and values.

The **psychomotor** domain (Simpson, 1972) includes physical movement, coordination and the development of motor skills from simple to complex.

The original taxonomy was revised by Krathwohl and Anderson (2001). However, it has been argued that the hierarchical nature of the design of Bloom's taxonomy is too rigid and does not take into account the complexities involved in the learning process, particularly for pupils with SEND. It has also been suggested that it's important to recognise, when using the taxonomy, how the different domains as well as the hierarchical levels are interrelated. For example, designing and making a model may require the use of a range of interconnected knowledge and skills across domains and levels.

Although some useful theories on how children learn have been developed, the cognitive, affective and psychomotor processes of the brain are hugely complex and theories do not necessarily reflect the many individual variations, especially in pupils with SEND. For example, Piaget saw learning development as taking place in stages from birth to adulthood, while some theorists see stages of development as continuous with children moving between them at different times and for different reasons.

Educare versus Educere

It's interesting to note that the word education is derived from two Latin words: 'educare' meaning to train or mould, and 'educere' meaning to draw out. These two meanings are often seen as opposing arguments in the way education is delivered. Some view education as preserving and passing down knowledge from generation to generation, emphasising the need for rote learning, memorisation and working to a one size fits all. Others view education as 'drawing out' the best in each individual by developing enquiry, creative and critical thinking skills. In practice, as Bass and Good (2004) suggest, both meanings are important.

> *In the overall scheme of things, educare and educere are of equal importance. Education that ignores educare dooms its students to starting over each generation. Omitting educere produces citizens who are incapable of solving new problems. Thus, any system of education that supplies its students with only one of these has failed miserably.*
>
> (2004, p. 164)

Mathematics is a subject where there needs to be a balance between educare and educere for pupils with SEND. Pupils need to be familiar with facts as well as being able to use these facts when solving problems. Traditionally, rote learning has been used when teaching multiplication tables. Rote learning can help some pupils recall facts quickly and build a foundation of basic knowledge. However, rote learning alone does not encourage pupils to make connections between facts or explore a fuller understanding of a concept.

Some pupils with SEND, particularly those with dyscalculia, have difficulty with a variety of skills which puts them at a disadvantage when involved in mathematical problem-solving activities.

Difficulties children may experience with problem solving in mathematics:

- using working memory when loaded with information;
- recalling number facts quickly from long-term memory;
- recalling both auditory and visual sequences of numerical information;
- making connections between number facts and abstract concepts such as time or money.

Case Study: Multiple Maths

A class of year 2 pupils were encouraged to learn the 2, 5 and 10 multiplication tables by rote. Keisha and Tom found this particularly difficult, so their teacher introduced chants, rhymes and songs as a support. When asking pupils to solve problems involving multiplication, the teacher adapted the activities to include the use of a range of manipulatives. Some pupils were able to recall multiplication facts when problem solving, others had difficulty in making connections between their practical experiences, rote learning and the nature of the problem.

The teacher decided to provide regular experiences each day to make the concept of multiplication visible. Pupils counted in 2s when lining up in pairs or being praised as helping hands or good listeners (I have six good listeners, how many ears are listening?). They counted in 5s and 10s when checking resources (pencils in a pot, balls in a box, hoops on a hook). The teacher regularly posed 'real life' problems for the pupils to discuss as well as introducing the link between multiplication and division (sharing out resources).

Gradually, most of the pupils began to use their knowledge base to help solve mathematical problems using the 2, 5 and 10 multiplication tables. The teacher noted that Keisha, Tom and a few others continued to need the support of worked examples, multisensory resources, games and IT activities when involved in other areas of mathematical problem solving.

SEND: Dyslexia, Dyscalculia.

Reflective Task 2.1

How do you think multisensory resources can help pupils with understanding mathematical concepts?

What characteristics might you observe in a pupil with dyscalculia?

Social and Emotional Learning

Recently, developmental learning theories have been criticised for not reflecting the impact and influences of 21st century social, emotional and cultural life on pupils, in particular the affective learning issues they face both inside and outside the classroom. McNess et al. (2003) reviewed the findings from two projects which showed that teachers felt:

> *perceived demand for a delivery of 'performance', for both themselves and their pupils, had created a policy focus that emphasised the managerially 'effective', in the interests of accountability, while ignoring teachers' deeply rooted commitment to the affective aspects of teaching and learning. (p. 1)*

Although some aspects of the teachers' concerns have been addressed, schools continue to struggle with the tensions between effective and affective learning. In addition, the Covid-19 pandemic has highlighted the challenges many pupils with SEND face when families and communities are put under stress.

Case Study: Affective Learning Issues

Reena joined a year 6 class after being isolated with her family during the Covid-19 lockdown. Her parents, both NHS workers, had suffered with covid, with her mother being hospitalised for several weeks. During this time, Reena developed stomach pains, sickness and headaches, but her very real symptoms were dismissed as psychological or possibly a food allergy. Reena began limiting her food intake to small amounts of bland food which didn't give her stomach pains.

After lockdown, Reena had a blood test which revealed she had *Helicobacter pylori*. The doctor explained to her that it was an infection caused by bacteria and could be cured by antibiotics. Soon after this, Reena began to scrub her mouth both before and after eating. She continued with her very restrictive diet and had an intense fear of touching anything which might harbour bacteria. Reena was referred to CAMHS (Child and Adolescent Mental Health Services) where, after several months waiting, she was offered a combination of cognitive behavioural therapy and medication.

At school, staff were made aware of Reena's difficulties and the class teacher liaised regularly with Reena's parents regarding her progress. With her parents' permission, Reena was given the responsibility of helping lunchtime staff clean the tables with anti-bacterial spray before washing her hands and eating her packed lunch. Reena was also encouraged to share her eating anxieties with a few close friends. By the end of the year, Reena was eating a more varied diet and no longer scrubbing her mouth. She continued to need support with overcoming her fear of bacteria, but with the encouragement of family, friends and teachers, she was able to become more self-aware and ask for help when necessary.

SEND: Obsessive Compulsive Disorder (OCD).

Reflective Task 2.2

What other characteristics might you observe in a pupil with OCD?

Why is it important for the pupil and family to actively seek professional help for OCD?

The Education Endowment Foundation (EEF) reported that evidence suggests pupils from disadvantaged backgrounds have weaker social and emotional learning (SEL) skills than their more advantaged peers. The EEF guidance report on SEL suggests a range of strategies to support pupils in developing SEL skills. They are as follows:

- 'Self-awareness: expand children's emotional vocabulary and support them to express emotions.
- Self-regulation: teach children to use self-calming strategies and positive self-talk to help deal with intense emotions.
- Social awareness: use stories to discuss others' emotions and perspectives.
- Relationship skills: role play good communication and listening skills.
- Responsible decision-making: teach and practise problem solving strategies.
- Model the social and emotional behaviours you want children to adopt.
- Give specific and focused praise when children display SEL skills.
- Do not rely on 'crisis moments' for teaching skills.
- Embed SEL teaching across a range of subject areas: literacy, history, drama and PE all provide good opportunities to link to SEL.
- Use simple ground-rules in groupwork and classroom discussion to reinforce SEL skills'.

(EEF, 2021b, p. 8)

Visible Teaching and Learning

A great deal of research exists emphasising different ways in which teachers can be effective in the classroom. Hattie (2012) explored not only the evidence-based teaching practices that worked but also the underlying principles as to why some practices were more successful than others. Hattie identified the approaches that had the most and least effect on pupil achievement. He suggested that the most effective learning takes place when there is clarity of intent on the part of both the pupil and the teacher and where there is visible pupil/teacher interaction and feedback. When the learning is visible, the pupils show whether they understand how to complete a task, and the teacher can see whether learning has occurred. This approach is particularly important for pupils with SEND.

The data analysed by Hattie (2012) characterised effective teachers as those who are:

- passionate about teaching and learning with high levels of personal competence;
- able to develop a shared language of learning with pupils and encourage them to reflect on their learning explicitly;

- able to provide challenging learning experiences that are made explicit to pupils through learning intentions and success criteria;
- able to monitor and evaluate teaching interventions;
- able to develop a learning climate where all pupil efforts and abilities are valued;
- able to adapt their teaching as a result of observations and feedback from learners;
- able to provide a balance of both surface and deep learning;
- able to assess the difference between what is learnt and what is taught.

Hattie's (2012) concept of visible teaching and learning suggests that a teacher's focus should be on:

> *seeing learning through the eyes of the students, appreciating their fits and starts in learning and their often, non-linear progression to the goals, supporting their deliberate practice, providing feedback about their errors and misdirections, and caring that the students get to the goals and that the students share the teacher's passion for the material being learnt. (p. 23)*

Case Study: Visible Rivers

A year 6 class were learning about rivers and their effect on the landscape. The pupils, including Kai in an all-terrain wheelchair, had followed part of the path of a nearby river and, with adult prompting, had noted some of the key features. Visual material such as maps, photographs, diagrams, labelled pictures and key vocabulary were on display in the classroom. Yet, despite the environmental visit and visual displays, several pupils had difficulty in understanding and using key concept vocabulary with Gregor commenting 'river words are difficult'.

The teacher took the class outside where they gathered materials to represent natural river features. In groups, pupils were given wet sand to represent soil and a container of water to represent the source of the river. The groups were asked to arrange their materials as riverbank features on the sloping part of the playground. Each member of the group was given a role, and the teacher noted that Kai proved to have excellent observational skills.

Back in the classroom, Gregor and Albin described their practical experiences using some key concept vocabulary. Gregor noted that their sand eroded quicker because they made the water source go faster. Albin noticed that it made a floodplain at the bottom of their river. Other groups talked about flow rate influencing the river features. The teacher noted that, as the children talked about their experiences, they made use of key concept vocabulary and explained some concepts to each other as part of their natural conversation.

SEND: Muscular Dystrophy, SLCN.

Reflective Task 2.3

Kai needed no support with understanding concept vocabulary. In what other ways do you think he was supported?

Why was it important for each member of the group to be given a role?

Prior Knowledge

Links to the ITTECF 2.2

- **2.2 Learn that** prior knowledge plays an important role in how pupils learn; committing some key facts to their long-term memory is likely to help pupils learn more complex ideas.
- **2.7 Learn that** where prior knowledge is weak, pupils are more likely to develop misconceptions, particularly if new ideas are introduced too quickly (DfE, 2024a, p. 13).

Prior knowledge is an important part of the constructivist learning theory which explores the idea that pupils construct new learning based on prior knowledge and experiences. Sousa (2015) suggests that pupils can make more sense of new information if they are able to make connections with their own past knowledge and experiences. To integrate new ideas with existing knowledge, pupils need to be able to store prior knowledge in their long-term memory. Although pupils may have appropriate knowledge stored in their long-term memory, they may need prompting to recall it before being presented with new knowledge (Howard-Jones et al., 2018).

Pupils with SEND benefit from having new concepts and skills introduced gradually with teachers anticipating common misconceptions. Misconceptions can become part of a learner's long-term memory if allowed to continue (see **3 – Subject and Curriculum**).

Activities for Activating Prior Knowledge

Assistive technology can be used to adapt these activities to suit specific needs.

- **Mind maps** – pupils write or draw a topic in the centre of a page, then make connections and add key ideas around it to show what is already known. New ideas can be added as pupils acquire new knowledge.

- **Word walls** support the understanding of vocabulary across key learning areas but particularly with specific topic or subject words. Word walls can be useful when making connections with other topics.
- **Visualisation** – pupils build a picture in their minds about a given word, sentence or topic, then draw what they see in their 'mind's eye' using their prior knowledge.
- **Picture books** relating to a subject or topic can stimulate prior knowledge. These can be presented on the interactive whiteboard as a class or group activity.
- **Multimedia** – use audio-visual resources to review specific areas of a topic or subject, making connections between previous knowledge and new learning. Subtitles or assistive technology may support those with hearing impairments.
- **Brainstorm** prior knowledge of a topic with visual or concrete prompts. Ideas can be recorded using labelled drawings or Widget symbols.
- **Colorcards: Everyday Objects (Winslow)** – These cards can be used to assess pupils' prior vocabulary knowledge and understanding of the function of everyday items. Used for individual or small group speech and language intervention activities.
- **Flow charts** – pictorial/symbol flow charts can remind pupils of the order of a maths or science process, the timeline of an historical event and help to stimulate prior knowledge of the order of personal or everyday events.
- **Questions** – simple questionnaires using assistive technology can assess basic prior knowledge of a subject.
- **Think/pair/share** – pupils think about prior knowledge of a given topic, share knowledge with a partner and then with the group or class.

Activating Prior Knowledge for Pupils With SLD and PMLD

Pupils with SLD (Severe Learning Difficulties) and PMLD (Profound and Multiple Learning Difficulties) should be given opportunities to engage in games, activities and targeted support, using signing and assistive technology, to activate prior knowledge. Activities may include the following:

- Choosing preferred objects or toys from a container to use for an activity.
- Responding to concrete and visual cues to complete a simple activity.
- Recognising photos, pictures and symbols relating to an activity.
- Anticipating the next activity through visual timetables.

- Having opportunities to make both positive and negative responses to sensory stimuli and to anticipate remembered reactions.
- Recognising and matching shapes to complete simple puzzles or when posting shapes into a container.
- Recalling and taking part in action songs and rhymes using preferred communication skills.
- Anticipating results by operating toys and games that are controlled by one or more switches.
- Using prior knowledge to build and create with simple constructional toys.
- Selecting appropriate resources for a familiar activity.
- Building on previous learning to develop self-help skills.
- Selecting appropriate resources for familiar routines.

Memory in Learning

Links to the ITTECF 2.3

- **2.3 Learn that** an important factor in learning is memory, which can be thought of as comprising two elements: working memory and long-term memory.
- **2.5 Learn that** long-term memory can be considered as a store of knowledge that changes as pupils learn by integrating new ideas with existing knowledge (DfE, 2024a, p. 13).

Use of the terms working memory, short-term memory and long-term memory have been debated for several years. Cowan (2005) described short-term memory as the area where information is held temporarily and working memory as the area where information is both held and in active use. Some researchers feel that the two terms are interchangeable. It's thought that short-term memory can hold limited amounts of information. Cowan (2008) suggested four items of information could be the limit. Beyond this amount pupils may suffer cognitive overload.

If working memory is the area where information is both held and in active use, then it's important to explore ways to support pupils who have poorer working memory capacity. Gathercole and Alloway (2007) introduce the role working memory plays in everyday life and educational learning. They highlight the difficulties faced by pupils who have poorer working memory skills such as not being able to retain instructions, recall sequences or follow a task through to completion which can be characteristic of a wider need such as dyslexia or ADHD. Below are Gathercole and Alloway's (2007) recommendations for supporting pupils with poorer working memories:

Strategies for supporting working memory:

- Evaluate the working demands of learning activities.
- Reduce working memory loads.
- Be aware that processing demands increase working memory loads.
- Develop pupils' use of memory-relieving strategies.
- Encourage the use of memory aids.
- Frequently repeat important information.

Long-term memory differs from short-term memory and working memory in that it has two fundamental aspects, duration and capacity. It's thought that long-term memory may have a duration of months and years, or even an unlimited capacity. Sousa (2015) suggested that long-term memory can weaken over time due to lack of recall. Therefore, new information needs to be introduced in small chunks and rehearsed regularly.

Long-term memory has been divided into two types, explicit and implicit. Explicit memory, also referred to as declarative memory, is divided further into two types:

- Episodic memory which stores information details about individual life events.
- Semantic memory which stores information such as word meanings and general knowledge.

Implicit memory involves the implicit actions of the mind and body when learning new skills such as riding a bicycle, reading, writing or driving a car. Implicit memory includes the following:

- Procedural memory which is responsible for the memory of motor skills.
- Associative memory which refers to the ability to recall relationships between concepts and the ability to store and retrieve information through association.
- Non-associative memory which refers to the learning of new behaviours through repeated experience of a specific stimuli.

For new information to be encoded into a pupil's long-term memory, Hattie and Yates (2014) suggest information needs to be relevant and make sense to the learner. This is especially important for pupils with SEND. They emphasise that pupils need to be able to relate new information to their existing knowledge for it to be remembered. Some pupils with SEND need to be shown how to organise and structure meaning as they learn.

2.1 Did You Know?

The forgetting curve is a mathematical formula by Hermann Ebbinghaus (1885), a German psychologist, who found that within an hour of learning new information, people tend to forget up to 50% of it. Within 24 hours, this can increase to 70%. By the end of the week, people tend to retain only about 25% of what they've learnt. (Ebbinghaus, 2013).

Dual Coding

The Education Endowment Foundation state that:

> *Dual coding theory is based on the theory that working memory has two distinct components, one that deals with visual and spatial information and another that deals with auditory information. By presenting content in multiple formats, it is possible that teachers can appeal to both subsystems of the working memory, which subsequently strengthens learning. (2021c, p. 37)*

Chandler and Sweller (1992) suggest that a pupil's working memory has different points of entry when accepting information and that the burden on working memory, when encoding, is far less when the strategies used to give information are clearly integrated such as verbal/concrete, verbal/pictorial. The strategy of providing pupils with verbal and visual materials at the same time is termed 'dual coding' and can support the development of working memory, especially for those pupils with limited working memory capacity. This combination has been identified as being effective in improving long-term memory (Clark & Pavio, 1991).

Cognitive Load

Links to the ITTECF 2.4

- **2.4 Learn that** working memory is where information that is being actively processed is held, but its capacity is limited and can be overloaded.
- **2.6 Learn that** pupils have different working memory capacities; some pupils with SEND may have more limited working memory capacity than their peers without SEND (DfE, 2024a, p. 13).

Cognitive load theory originated from the work of cognitive educational psychologist John Sweller (1988) and highlighted the effect that instructional design and learning materials have on a learner's ability to process information. Cognitive load theory emphasises that a pupil's working memory has a limited capacity for learning new information. The load imposed on their cognitive system may be intrinsic, extraneous or germane.

Intrinsic load is imposed by the level of difficulty of the material presented and the level of pupil expertise in the subject/topic.

Extraneous load is imposed by the provision of activities and resources that are extraneous to the specific learning objective and can form a distraction.

Germane load refers to the load imposed on the working memory as the learner begins to understand the information and transfer it into their long-term memory.

When working memory is overloaded, learning can be unsuccessful for some pupils with SEND. Sweller (2010) notes that this is often the result of extra extraneous and intrinsic load being imposed on the learner. Teachers need to reduce extraneous load and ensure that lessons are designed to provide a balance between intrinsic load and germane load to best support those pupils with poorer working memories (Van Merrienboer & Sweller, 2005).

Case Study: Classroom Practice

Using the Jigsaw cooperative learning strategy, a year 6 teacher provided four mixed ability groups with replica WW2 artefacts, information sheets, books and illustrations showing the artefacts in use. Learning objectives and success criteria for the lesson were displayed on the interactive whiteboard. Each member of the group was asked to choose an artefact from the jigsaw activity to explore (Table 2.1).

Table 2.1 Reducing cognitive load for pupils

During the lesson	Adult response
Theo was excited by the number of interesting objects. He visited each group frequently, handling the artefacts and distracting other pupils. **SEND: ADHD**	Teacher guided Theo to choose one artefact, then encouraged him to work with a partner away from the distractions of the group. He presented his information as a 'Did You Know' poster.
Freya took the WW2 coins, sat down behind her portable desk screen and began to draw them. **SEND: Autism**	Teacher directed the TA to support Freya with reading information about the coins, then encouraged her to relay the information to her group visually/orally.
Omari was excited by the activity initially but became lethargic and needed to be taken for an afternoon rest halfway through the lesson. **SEND: Sickle Cell Disorder**	Teacher noted that such a visually busy activity might be better organised in the morning. A class presentation of findings was organised for the next morning.
Mia became fascinated by the gas mask but struggled with reading information and recording her findings. **SEND: Dyslexia**	Teacher suggested Mia and her friend read information together, relating to both their jigsaw tasks. Mia chose to record her information as a labelled picture.

Reflective Task 2.4

Did the teacher provide a balance between intrinsic load and germane load?

What adaptive strategies did the teacher employ?

In any mainstream classroom, there may be several pupils who have a more limited working memory capacity than their peers. Some may experience difficulties with developing **auditory memory skills**. Pupils who have difficulties in this area may:

- be unable to retain more than one or two items of information from a lesson presented orally;
- have difficulty recalling information in the correct sequence;
- have difficulty recalling information after a period of time;
- need regular spaced practice of knowledge, concepts and skills.

Some pupils may experience difficulties with developing **visual memory skills**. Those who have difficulties in this area may:

- be unable to recall patterns, shapes and designs;
- have problems with reading and spelling high frequency non-phonetic or common exception words;
- have immature drawing skills (drawings lack detail);
- have difficulty with letter and number orientation.

Information retained for a short while in the working memory needs to be rehearsed to help pupils retain it in their long-term memory. Games, activities and interventions, linked to a topic or subject, can encourage pupils to develop both auditory and visual memory skills. Suggested activities to develop these skills can be found in **10 – Key Learning Skills.**

Purposeful Practice

Links to the ITTECF 2.5

- **2.8 Learn that** regular purposeful practice of what has previously been taught can help consolidate material and help pupils remember what they have learnt.

(Continued)

- **2.9 Learn that** requiring pupils to retrieve information from memory, and spacing practice so that pupils revisit ideas after a gap are also likely to strengthen recall.
- **2.10 Learn that** worked examples that take pupils through each step of a new process are also likely to support pupils to learn (DfE, 2024a, p. 14).

Mastering a skill requires practise, but practice needs to be purposeful. Medical research has established that repetition creates and strengthens neural connections in the brain. When babies move their limbs and grasp objects, they are developing neural connections. Similarly, young children learn self-help skills such as getting dressed and undressed by daily repetition. New skills, such as learning to ride a bike or playing an instrument, are only developed through regular, purposeful practice. Depending on their barriers to learning, pupils with SEND benefit from revisiting new concepts and skills in different ways. Practice through a multisensory approach can make learning enjoyable and encourage pupils to embed information into their long-term memory. It's interesting to note that many musicians and top-level sports people rely on the basic practice of learnt skills as well as incorporating new ones into their routines. In the same way, pupils need to be provided with opportunities to revisit concepts and skills across the curriculum while being supported to make relevant connections to new learning.

Spaced learning and retrieval practice are strategies that have been reviewed for their effectiveness by the EEF (2021c). They have produced definitions for both strategies.

- **Spaced learning** – distributing learning and retrieval opportunities over a longer period rather than concentrating them in 'massed' practice.
- Retrieval **practice** – using a variety of strategies to recall information from memory, for example flash cards, practice tests or quizzing, or mind-mapping.

(EEF, 2021c, p. 5)

For many pupils with SEND, being asked to listen, process and absorb knowledge and skills in large amounts can be intimidating. Although every child is different, their attention span is generally considered to be 2–3 minutes per year of their age (Brain Balance, n.d.). For children with listening and attention difficulties, the time would be much shorter. However,

> *While spaced practice is thought to make learning more challenging for pupils as it prohibits information being held in the working memory, it may be able to increase the likelihood of knowledge being embedded in pupils' long-term memory. In having pupils revisit key concepts, ideas, or skills over longer periods of time in which content is almost forgotten, teachers may be able to improve learning retention.*
>
> (EEF, 2021c, p. 15)

Agarwal et al. (2017) noted that retrieval practice with feedback benefitted pupils with lower working memory. Revisiting and reviewing concepts and skills by employing spaced practice can strengthen recall for pupils with SEND. Similarly, the importance of giving effective feedback, and adapting it to the needs of the pupils, as part of the ongoing progress towards the next step of learning, is highlighted by Hattie and Yates (2014).

All pupils, but particularly those with SEND, benefit from having worked examples to support their learning. Worked examples provide clear explanations of the process for completing a task and the expected criteria for success. By having the support of worked examples, pupils have less stress on their working memory. Clark et al. (2006) suggest that 'a worked example is a step-by-step demonstration of how to perform a task or how to solve a problem' (p. 190). Practical examples of spaced practice can be found in **4 – Classroom Practice**.

Vygotsky reminds us, 'What a child can do with assistance today, she will be able to do by herself tomorrow' (Vygotsky, 1978, p. 87).

3

Subject and Curriculum

Chapter Objectives

This chapter focuses on ways in which pupils develop knowledge and skills across the primary curriculum and specifically in the areas of English and maths. The chapter identifies key skills for learning and highlights how some pupils with SEND may experience difficulties in these areas. The chapter also explores:

- pedagogical knowledge;
- concepts and misconceptions;
- knowledge and skills (a partnership);
- building schemata;
- transferring knowledge and skills between contexts;
- developing knowledge and skills for English;
- developing knowledge and skills for maths.

Pedagogical Knowledge

Links to the ITTECF 3.1

- **3.1 Learn that** a school's curriculum enables it to set out its vision for the knowledge, skills and values that its pupils will learn, encompassing the national curriculum within a coherent wider vision for successful learning.
- **3.2 Learn that** secure subject knowledge helps teachers to motivate pupils and teach effectively (DfE, 2024a, p. 15).

A school is not just an environment where pupils learn knowledge and skills for later life, it's also a place where they can develop values and attitudes that help them become thoughtful members of a community. Primary schools that have a clear curriculum vision:

1. encourage understanding of the range of spiritual, moral, social and cultural life experiences within the community;
2. support the development of the pupils' self-awareness and self-efficacy;
3. support the development of cross-curricula skills (English, maths and information technology) as well as the knowledge and key skills needed for learning (see **10 – Key Learning Skills)**;
4. encourage positive attitudes to collaborative and cooperative learning, where all pupils' ideas are valued;
5. incorporate appropriate assessment and adaptive teaching for all pupils by responding to their needs within an inclusive environment.

Primary school teachers are expected to have varied cross-curricular knowledge though they may be a specialist in a particular subject. Guerriero (2017) highlighted the need for teachers to ensure they are up to date not only with subject knowledge but also with research on teaching practices. Some studies of teachers' pedagogical knowledge distinguish between declarative knowledge (knowing that) and procedural knowledge (knowing how) (Guerriero, 2017). This is emphasised in the Initial Teacher Training Early Career Framework (2024a) which highlights the importance of having not only a firm subject knowledge base but also an understanding of effective teaching methods.

Research for the education inspection framework identifies three types of essential knowledge:

> *These three types of essential knowledge are known as content knowledge, pedagogical knowledge and pedagogical content knowledge. Content knowledge can be defined as teachers' knowledge of the subject they are teaching, pedagogical knowledge as teachers' knowledge of effective teaching methods, and pedagogical content knowledge as teachers' knowledge of how to teach the particular subject or topic.*
>
> (Ofsted, 2019, p. 10)

Primary teachers need to deliver a carefully sequenced coherent and multi-subject curriculum. No primary teacher can be an expert in all areas of the national curriculum and therefore, it's important to work in collaboration with colleagues to plan for the learning development of all pupils.

Concepts and Misconceptions

Links to the ITTECF 3.2

- **3.3 Learn that** ensuring pupils master foundational concepts and knowledge before moving on is likely to build pupils' confidence and help them succeed.
- **3.4 Learn that** anticipating common misconceptions within particular subjects is also an important aspect of curricular knowledge; working closely with colleagues to develop an understanding of likely misconceptions is valuable (DfE, 2024a, p. 15).

Concept vocabulary refers to those words that encapsulate a thought or idea. Some concept vocabulary expresses abstract ideas which are difficult for pupils with SEND to understand without practical examples. The vocabulary of position (above, below, behind, around, between), of time (before, after, first, last) and of quantity (more, less, few, many) represent just a small part of the concept vocabulary used in primary classrooms. The ability to understand the meanings of words in different contexts as well as the knowledge of relationships between words (categories, opposites, synonyms, word associations) supports the learning of new ideas. Many activities, such as scientific and mathematical investigations, historical and geographical enquiries and creative and critical thinking across the curriculum, require an understanding of complex concept vocabulary. It's useful to work with colleagues to identify ways in which misconceptions may be minimised in specific subject areas for pupils with SEND.

Support strategies for learning new concept vocabulary may include the following:

1. Ensuring pupils learn new words in real life situations where possible.
2. Teaching the meaning of concept vocabulary explicitly, using clear explanations and visual cues.
3. Modelling the use of key concept vocabulary across a variety of learning experiences.
4. Providing opportunities for pupils to use new vocabulary within practical contexts.
5. Using multisensory resources to support understanding.
6. Encouraging the natural use of key concept vocabulary in cooperative learning situations.

The following Case Study illustrates how misconceptions may be based on conceptual learning processes that were not fully experienced or understood.

Case Study: A Chocolate Experience

A year 5 class were studying reversible and irreversible changes of state in materials. The class had experienced dissolving and freezing and discussed their findings. The teacher organised a cooking activity where groups of pupils experienced melting chocolate to make chocolate crispy cakes. Some of the melted chocolate was put in the fridge, where it hardened. When discussing whether this was a reversible or irreversible change, both Hanan and Jack were adamant that the change was irreversible.

Hanan: It was in squares at the beginning. Now it's just a lump so it's not the same.

Jack: You could share it out before but now you can't.

SEND: Global Developmental Delay, SLCN.

Reflective Task 3.1

Discuss with your colleagues and peers possible reasons why Hanan and Jack developed this misconception.

How could the teacher support Hanan and Jack with understanding the concept of reversible and irreversible changes of state?

Table 3.1 lists activities to support pupils' understanding of concept vocabulary. Activities for developing an understanding of concept vocabulary can be adapted using signing, multi-sensory resources and assistive technology.

Table 3.1 Activities for developing an understanding of concept vocabulary

Subject areas	Activities
Vocabulary Games	
Maths and PE	Simon Says for body awareness and motor development using vocabulary of position and direction.
English	I Spy - teach concept vocabulary such as opposites (narrow/wide, long/short, old/new).
History	What am I? Ask pupils to identify an item from a given group when given form, function and feature clues.
Geography	Treasure Hunt - give directional clues using a map of the school grounds.
Audio-Visual Resources	
Cross-Curricular	IT programmes and videos can provide visual prompts to support conceptual understanding.

Concept Cartoons (Millgate House Education)	
Science and maths	Cartoons show a visual representation of a scientific or mathematical concept with characters discussing alternative views. They are designed to develop conceptual vocabulary and stimulate thinking.
Sorting and grouping	
Maths	Sort into groups using given criteria or own chosen criteria. Discuss reasons for choices. Sorting and grouping for size, shape, length, height, colour.
English	Sorting words into groups using given classification (verbs, adjectives, nouns, synonyms)
Science	Grouping living things, materials.
History	Grouping types of toys and games past and present, grouping household objects past and present.
PE	Sorting and grouping PE equipment according to use.
Art	Sorting and grouping different types of media when preparing for an activity.
Cue Cards	
Cross-Curricular	Can be created using Widget Symbols. They can be used to support individual pupils with relating specific concept vocabulary to a topic or subject.
Concept Charts and Posters	
Cross-Curricular	Can be created using Widget Symbols. They can be used as a visual reminder of specific concept vocabulary relating to a topic or subject.
Multisensory Activities	
Cross-Curricular	Can be used to support pupils with learning concept vocabulary related to size, shape, texture, sound, taste and smell. Be aware of pupils who may have an adverse reaction to a particular texture, sound, taste or smell.
Mind Maps	
Cross-Curricular	Help pupils to organise information visually to understand how new concepts can be linked with those already known.

Knowledge and Skills

Links to the ITTECF 3.3

- **3.5 Learn that** explicitly teaching pupils the knowledge and skills they need to succeed within particular subject areas is beneficial.
- **3.6 Learn that** in order for pupils to think critically, they must have a secure understanding of knowledge within the subject area they are being asked to think critically about (DfE, 2024a, p. 15).

In 2014, the education secretary Michael Gove emphasised that the new national curriculum would be influenced by E.D. Hirsch, an American educator who advocated a knowledge-rich approach. Consequently, the content of the national curriculum has a strong emphasis on knowledge. In 2021, Nick Gibb MP also emphasised that the gap between pupils with greater prior knowledge and those with less continued to widen. Gibb advocated strongly that all pupils, whatever their barriers to learning, should be given opportunities to access what Hirsh termed 'communal knowledge'. This communal knowledge is often developed in the home where some children are exposed to a wide range of language rich experiences such as shared reading and interaction through discourse. For pupils who are less advantaged than their peers, it's the responsibility of teachers to facilitate such opportunities.

Perkins (1993) used the term 'fragile knowledge' to describe when pupils do not remember, understand or actively use the information they learn in school. Perkins theorised that, pupils with a deep understanding focus not only on having prior knowledge embedded in their long-term memory but also on being able to think critically, explain and apply that knowledge across the curriculum.

Although first introduced in 1968, by Benjamin Bloom, mastery learning is still considered an effective teaching method. The EEF (2021d) provides theoretical and practical advice on the theory.

Mastery learning works through designing units of work so that each task has a clear learning outcome which pupils must master prior to moving on to the next task. Core components of the mastery approach that schools should be careful to implement include:

- Effective diagnostic assessment to identify areas of strength and weakness.
- Carefully sequencing topics so that they gradually build on foundational knowledge.
- Flexibility for teachers on how long they need to spend on any particular topic.
- Monitoring of pupil learning and regular feedback so that pupils can master topics prior to moving to the next
- Additional support for pupils that struggle to master topic areas.

(EEF, 2021d)

The graduated approach (assess, plan, do, review) is an essential part of ensuring that all pupils with SEND are given opportunities to follow a carefully planned sequence of lessons linked to mastery learning. However, some pupils may need specific interventions and/or tailored support to reach a personal level of mastery.

Young children construct knowledge through play and learn new skills as they experience practical tasks. Some self-help skills can be developed through everyday activities such as learning how to get dressed in the morning. Other skills, such as reading or learning to ride a bicycle, may be more complex and need to be learnt within particular contexts. Pupils need both knowledge and skills to make progress. For example, to access information through reading, pupils need to develop a range of key skills to become effective readers and to think critically about what they read. Some pupils with SEND need to be given opportunities to develop a range of skills alongside adapted academic experiences. Planning for developing these skills will be part of a pupil's EHCP and PLP and may require advice on suitable interventions and support strategies from key professionals such as educational psychologists, occupational therapists, physiotherapists, speech and language therapists and visual and hearing impairment services. These professionals may identify specific key skills where a pupil needs support. This may include:

Key Learning Skills

- auditory discrimination;
- auditory memory;
- creative thinking;
- critical thinking;
- enquiry skills;
- fine motor skills;
- grammar, syntax and morphology;
- gross motor skills;
- listening and attention;
- organisational skills;
- phonemic and phonological awareness;
- semantic knowledge;
- social communication (pragmatics);
- spatial awareness;
- verbal reasoning;
- visual discrimination;
- visual memory;
- word finding.

Practical activities to support the development of these skills can be found in **10 – Key Learning Skills.**

Building Schemata

Links to the ITTECF 3.4

- **3.7 Learn that** in all subject areas, pupils learn new ideas by linking those ideas to existing knowledge, organising this knowledge into increasingly complex mental models (or 'schemata'); carefully sequencing teaching to facilitate this process is important (DfE, 2024a, p. 16).

Schema theory explores how the brain structures and connects knowledge throughout the learning process. The grouping of linked experiences, knowledge, concepts and vocabulary, stored in the long-term memory, supports new learning and helps pupils build a mental model of the world around them. Piaget and Cook (1952) suggested that a child's knowledge was composed of schemata (organised units of knowledge) which served as a foundation for understanding new concepts and experiences. Piaget and Cook (1952) defined a schema as, 'a cohesive, repeatable action sequence possessing component actions that are tightly interconnected and governed by a core meaning' (p. 7).

Inclusive teaching strategies should aim to encourage and support pupils with SEND to build their own schemata. Strategies may include the following:

1. Making explicit links between previous topics and a new topic.
2. Providing scaffolded activities and graphic organisers to help pupils structure and organise information.
3. Introducing and discussing new topic vocabulary, a few words at a time – ask pupils to map new vocabulary using mind maps, checking for any misconceptions.
4. Using multisensory resources to help consolidate understanding of concept vocabulary and new knowledge.
5. Introducing audio/visual experiences related to the new topic (picture book, animation, video, visit or visitor).
6. Providing a range of information as visual, concrete and written resources for pupils to explore the topic.
7. Giving pupils time to discuss and question any thoughts and ideas related to the topic.
8. Providing opportunities for spaced practise to support the building of new schema into the long-term memory.

Transferring Knowledge and Skills Between Contexts

Links to the ITTECF 3.5

- **3.8 Learn that** pupils are likely to struggle to transfer what has been learnt in one discipline to a new or unfamiliar context (DfE, 2024a, p. 16).

Willingham (2002) suggests, 'cognitive science has shown us that when new material is first learned, the mind is biased to remember things in concrete forms that are difficult to apply to new situations' (p. 31). He terms this 'inflexible knowledge' characterised by the fact that it's surface knowledge which pupils can recognise in specific contexts. Willingham emphasises that inflexible knowledge differs from rote knowledge because it's meaningful. When new knowledge is acquired at first, it's surface knowledge and, for some, may remain inflexible if the knowledge is not used in other contexts. Pupils with SEND need to have access to surface knowledge as it provides a foundation upon which they can build a deeper understanding of a topic. In contrast, 'knowledge is flexible when it can be accessed out of the context in which it was learned and applied in new contexts' (Willingham, 2002, p. 32). Barnett and Ceci (2002) highlight some reasons why transfer may be difficult.

1. The social context is different.
2. The learning environment is different.
3. The mode of learning is different.
4. The knowledge domain is different.

For many pupils with SEND, the transfer of knowledge and skills between contexts needs to be taught explicitly.

1. **Different social contexts**
   Organise activities using flexible grouping to ensure all pupils experience a variety of social learning contexts during which knowledge and skills transfer can be practised.
2. **Different learning environments**
   Organise a range of learning activities both inside and outside the classroom including exploration of the school environment, visits to places of interest with links to topics.
3. **Different modes of learning**
   Ensure pupils have opportunities to develop knowledge and skills via different modes of learning - practical, visual, auditory, tactile, kinaesthetic.

4. **Different knowledge domains**
   Organise cross-curricula topics with knowledge and skills transfer being an integral part of the study. For example, knowledge and understanding of the use of shapes in mathematics, art, design and technology.

Developing Knowledge and Skills for Literacy

Links to the ITTECF 3.6

- **3.9 Learn that** to access the curriculum, early literacy provides fundamental knowledge; reading comprises two elements: word reading and language comprehension; systematic synthetic phonics is the most effective approach for teaching pupils to decode.
- **3.10 Learn that** every teacher can improve pupils' communication and literacy, including by explicitly teaching reading, writing and oral language skills specific to individual disciplines.
- **3.12 Learn that** pupils' oral language skills can be supported by teaching new words and how to use and understand words within sentences or longer texts. This can help to address speech and language difficulties, especially for children in their early school years (DfE, 2024a, pp. 16–17).

The National Literacy Trust (2017) defines literacy as, 'the ability to read, write, speak and listen in a way that lets us communicate effectively and make sense of the world' (para. 1). It's not surprising that, in primary education, a strong assessment focus is placed on English for without functional literacy skills pupils struggle to find their place in the modern community. Breadmore et al. (2019) explain that:

> *Literacy includes the word-level skills of word reading and spelling and the text-level skills of reading comprehension and writing composition. These skills are involved in virtually all everyday activities. As a result, poor literacy impacts on every aspect of life. (p. 4)*

Certain pupils with SEND, such as those with hearing, visual, speech or motor-related needs, may find it more challenging to develop literacy skills.

To become literate in the 21st century requires the development of a complex range of knowledge and skills. Literacy abilities, within a global environment, need to encompass a variety of cultures and contexts as well as understanding how to interact with others through oral, aural, visual, digital and printed material. Literacy is fundamental to all areas of the curriculum. Though each subject may have its own specific knowledge and vocabulary, if pupils have not developed the key learning skills needed to access that knowledge, they will have difficulty in making progress.

Perkins et al. (2009) emphasise the importance of all teachers being aware of how learners develop literacy skills, arguing that the early years right up to adolescence is a crucial period in which attitudes and skills are embedded. Literacy development does not stop at the school gate, it's part of a partnership between home and school and requires cooperation between families, pupils and staff. Functional literacy plays an essential role in everyday life whether shopping in a supermarket, interacting on social media or following a recipe. Pupils with SEND are surrounded by communication in all its different forms and need to be encouraged to develop critical thinking skills in order to make reasoned judgements on what they hear, see and read.

3.1 Did You Know?

'Despite the Government's covid recovery programmes, the number of children estimated to have speech and language challenges has increased from 1.5 million in 2021 to 1.7 million in 2022' (Speech and Language UK, 2023, p. 2). Speech and Language UK report teachers estimate the number to be closer to 1.9 million in 2024.

Oracy

The majority of children learn to talk before they learn to read or write so the development of both oral (speaking) and aural (listening) language skills is an important part of learning. Oracy (the capacity to express oneself using spoken language and to understand speech) involves the use of both expressive and receptive language skills. Oral language is composed of the following:

- **Vocabulary** – including semantics (the study of meaning in language). A pupil may have a large vocabulary but not necessarily a depth of semantic knowledge such as relationships between words, shades of meaning in different contexts and figurative language.
- **Phonology** – the organisation of phonemes (speech sounds) within language. Pupils begin to develop phonological awareness as they learn to talk. Sharing stories, rhymes, alliterative sentences and syllable games with children supports the development of phonemic and phonological awareness.
- **Grammar** – the organisation of words into sentences using correct grammatical structure. Syntax – the way in which words are sequenced to convey meaning. Morphology – the way words are formed. A morpheme represents the smallest unit of meaning in a word. Inflectional endings such as 's' or 'es' can change a noun from singular to plural, while endings such as 'ing' and 'ed' can alter the tense of a verb.
- **Pragmatics** – the ability to understand how to communicate in social situations. This includes the understanding of how to behave in social groupings such as taking turns during games and activities.

- **Discourse** – the ability to use written or spoken communication for a purpose. It involves pupils being able to share their thoughts and ideas via meaningful discussion and debate.

Pupils who have difficulties with oracy may be identified as needing support with developing specific key learning skills. Suggested activities to support the development of these skills can be found in **10 – Key Learning Skills.**

Case Study: Finding a Voice

Katie joined a primary school in year 1 to benefit from having regular speech therapy provided through the attached Language Resource Base. She presented with an expressive language impairment and had difficulties with phonology (speech sound development) and articulation (the production of meaningful speech sounds by the coordinated movements of the lips, tongue, jaw, teeth and palate). Katie had weekly individual therapy sessions with the speech and language therapist and daily sessions with a trained teaching assistant. The resource base teacher organised small group literacy and numeracy lessons in the resource base, but Katie joined her class for other lessons.

When in year 2 Katie's group were preparing to give a talk on their project, Katie asked the TA for help. She wanted to take part but was afraid some pupils would laugh at her speech. The resource base teacher met with Katie's group, and they discussed the importance of using everyone's strengths. Katie's artistic skills were put to good use, and she practised introducing both parts of the presentation with a simple sentence and an illustration. Gradually, as Katie became more confident, she began to take an active part in cooperative learning activities.

SEND: Speech, Language and Communication Needs (SLCN).

Reflective Task 3.2

In what ways do you think the class teacher and the resource base teacher worked together to help Katie gain confidence in taking an active part in cooperative learning activities?

Reading

> *Children who are good at reading do more of it: they learn more, about all sorts of things, and their expanded vocabulary, gained from their reading, increases their ease of access to more reading. Conversely, those for whom reading is difficult fall behind, not just in their reading but in all subjects and a vicious circle develops.*
>
> (DfE, 2023b, p. 14)

Reading is an essential skill needed in all areas of daily life. Pupils with SEND should not only be encouraged to become confident, fluent and independent readers but also to gain pleasure from reading. Some pupils may take small steps in their reading journey, but it is important to ensure that each step brings pleasure.

Case Study: A Shared Experience

Discussion between a year 5 teacher and a colleague teaching year 3 revealed that many of their pupils did not read for pleasure. They decided to organise a literacy link involving the two classes meeting twice a week to share reading sessions. Reading material included playscripts, poetry, stories in different formats and genres and information books. The SENCo and teaching assistants were part of the literacy link and helped with choosing reading material. Pupils were assigned to a given classroom, to ensure a mix of age ranges, but within the classroom were given freedom to choose a reading partner and reading material. Some notable observations were as follows:

- **Graeme (year 5)** displayed an amazing ability to role play different characters when reading playscripts. Previously, when reading aloud, his delivery was hesitant.
- **Elina (year 3)** was anxious about reading aloud with another pupil. Frequent absences from school had left her with difficulty in making friends. **Alex (Year 5)** chose Elina as a partner and, despite their age difference, they were often seen chatting together on the playground.
- **Mali (year 5)** read with accuracy and speed but needed guidance when answering questions requiring inference or deduction. Paired with **Eva (Year 3)** she began to read more slowly and helped Eva with developing her phonemic and phonological skills. Both pupils enjoyed reading some mystery stories where they had to make deductions about characters and events.
- **Liam (year 3)** and **Riley (Year 5)** discovered a shared interest in dinosaurs. With Riley's help, Liam began to decode the multisyllabic names of dinosaurs. This gave him confidence to develop his phonological skills. Previously he had refused to read unknown words. Riley, who was self-conscious when reading aloud, grew in confidence and self-esteem in his role as teacher to Liam.

SEND: Hearing Impaired, Dyslexia, Stammer, Cystic Fibrosis.

Reflective Task 3.3

Which pupils do you think were identified with SEND? How do you think the shared experience helped them?

3.2 Did You Know?

Just 2 in 5 (43%) of children and young people aged 8 to 18 said they enjoyed reading in their free time in 2023, the lowest level since 2005.

Fewer than 3 in 10 (28%) of children and young people aged 8 to 18 said that they read daily in 2023, matching levels seen in 2022.

(Clark et al., 2023a)

Research into the teaching of reading has often become polarised with some theorists advocating a whole language approach and others a phonics approach. The ITTECF (DfE, 2024a) states that, 'reading comprises two elements: word reading and language comprehension; systematic synthetic phonics is the most effective approach for teaching pupils to decode' (p. 16). In primary classrooms, it's now a statutory requirement to teach systematic synthetic phonics using a DfE validated teaching programme. It's also statutory to administer the phonics screening check to pupils in key stage 1.

Glazzard and Stones (2020) explore the focus that has been placed on the discrete teaching of synthetic phonics as a basis for teaching reading. They express concern that this approach is mandatory in the teachers' standards and the inspection framework for initial teacher education in England. Glazzard and Stones also query the research evidence which gives prominence to just one area of the teaching of reading. They state, 'this attempt to regulate the way new teachers are prepared to support children's reading development is extremely concerning, given the body of research which demonstrates that no single approach is necessarily more effective than another' (2020, p. 1).

The prominence given to the discrete teaching of synthetic phonics rather than providing a balanced approach which includes teaching systematic synthetic phonics alongside other strategies continues to be questioned. Glazzard and Stones conclude:

> *the approach does not work for all children. If it did, there would not be a tail of underachievement in reading in England. It is worrying that by limiting trainees' knowledge of a repertoire of strategies to promote reading development, their capacity to support reading development in all children will be severely restricted. (2020, p. 5)*

For many pupils with SEND, particularly those with speech, language and communication difficulties, the pressure of trying to keep pace with age-related, synthetic phonics lessons can cause anxiety. NASEN (2024) recognised that pupils with specific reading difficulties may need small group focused teaching.

The move towards a more phonics-based approach to the teaching of reading does not mean excluding other aspects of learning to read. Developing reading for pupils with SEND involves making effective use of a range of knowledge and skills and relies on the ability to:

- recognise and read common exception words;
- decode by using phonemic awareness skills (the ability to hear and organise sounds in words) and phonological awareness skills (the use of rhyme, alliteration, syllables and morphemes);
- build vocabulary knowledge and understanding of how words relate to each other in different contexts;
- understand how sentences are structured and how punctuation aids meaning;
- understand how sentences can be related to each other;
- read a text and be able to process and understand its meaning;
- use working memory to process, interpret and recall information being read;
- make use of prior knowledge when reading a text;
- develop fluency when reading both aloud and silently (fluency is the ability to read with pace, accuracy and intonation);
- read a text and be able to use critical thinking skills.

Reading requires the development of a complex set of skills with phonemic and phonological awareness being an important part of that development. Pupils who have difficulties with reading may be identified as needing support with developing a range of key learning skills such as:

- auditory discrimination;
- auditory memory;
- critical thinking;
- grammar (syntax and morphology);
- listening and attention;
- phonemic and phonological awareness;
- semantic knowledge;
- pragmatics;
- verbal reasoning;
- visual discrimination;
- visual memory;
- word finding.

Suggested activities to support the development of these skills can be found in **10 – Key Learning Skills.**

Writing

The national curriculum programmes of study for writing at key stages 1 and 2 are organised in two areas:

- **Composition**, which includes generating ideas, considering the audience, understanding genre structure, planning and reviewing work, using suitable vocabulary and sentence construction.
- **Transcription**, which involves the skills of spelling, grammar, punctuation and handwriting.

Writing, in the primary classroom, is a process which requires the formation of ideas and the shaping and ordering of those ideas into a genre structure. It's a complex process involving the simultaneous interaction between composition and transcription. Silby (2013) noted that, for many pupils, a gap between their composition and transcription skills can be observed as they move from the age-related expectations at key stage 1 to those of key stage 2. Some pupils with SEND may be able to generate ideas, with the help of graphic organisers, but need support with developing transcription skills as age-related expectations become more complex.

3.3 Did You Know?

Research findings from Clark et al. (2023b) state the following:

- While 3 in 4 children enjoyed writing when they started school, this drops to 1 in 4 by the age of 16.
- Only 1 in 3 children said they enjoyed writing in their free time.
- This is alongside a rise in children leaving primary school without reaching the expected levels in writing.

Pupils need to be given opportunities to develop the knowledge and understanding of how composition and transcription support one another in the writing process. Supportive strategies for pupils with SEND include the following:

- Providing opportunities to explore genres by shared and guided reading of a range of texts.
- Identifying an audience for the completed writing (this may be for classroom display or a wider audience).

- Allowing pupils to express their ideas visually, using graphic organisers before beginning to write.
- Using assistive technology to aid the process of planning and composition.
- Modelling the process of sentence construction required for the task by providing examples from expert writers.
- Scaffolding the process of writing in the chosen genre by chunking (breaking down the task into smaller parts).
- Providing scaffolds such as writing frames for pupils who have difficulty in structuring their writing. These can be reduced gradually as pupils become more confident.
- Teaching the skills of drafting, revising and editing explicitly, remembering that editing is not just about spelling (some pupils may need support with specific transcription skills).
- Providing opportunities for pupils to share the processes of revising and editing with peer/ adult feedback.
- Ensuring that the presentation of written work is about personal progress.

Some pupils may have very specific difficulties with presenting their written work and need to use speech-to-text software which can allow a pupil to dictate their writing, alleviating both memory and spelling barriers. Others may have difficulties with particular areas of the writing process (Tables 3.2 and 3.3).

Some pupils with SEND may be identified as needing support with developing specific key learning skills for writing. Suggested activities to support the development of these skills can be found in **10 – Key Learning Skills.**

A number of pupils with SEND have very specific barriers to learning which impact on their ability to develop literacy skills. These difficulties can be overcome or minimised, with support, which may require additional resources and reasonable adjustments in mainstream classrooms. The following sections explore specific needs with suggested strategies for developing pupils' literacy skills.

Literacy and Pupils With Hearing Impairment

Children who are deaf or hard of hearing may experience difficulties associated with language development including building a broad vocabulary and phonological skills. Consequently, forming links between spoken and written language and reading and writing for purpose and meaning may be more challenging (Breadmore et al., 2019). Most pupils with hearing impairments in mainstream classrooms have moderate to severe hearing loss. The term 'deaf' usually refers to a hearing loss so severe that there is little or no functional hearing. Pupils with hearing impairment need to use alternative ways of developing literacy skills particularly in areas like reading and spelling which rely on identifying sounds.

Table 3.2 Difficulties with composition – Support activities

Difficulties with composition	**Support activities**
• Generating ideas for a writing activity	• Class, group or paired idea generation • Visual prompts such as photographs or pictures • Oral story chains - small group generating sentence sequences for a story • Audio/visual stimulus (fiction and non-fiction) • Story starters - visual/verbal (open choice) • Drama and role play related to writing activity
• Identifying vocabulary suitable for the writing activity	• Pre-teach key vocabulary using word webs • Use Clicker 8 to give pupils instant access to more adventurous or topic-specific vocabulary • Word mats for common exception words • Word banks in Clicker 8 for topic or subject-specific vocabulary
• Sequencing events, personal experiences or a familiar story	• Draw a story map showing the sequence of events • Rewrite a well-known story in the correct sequence using comic strip format • What's the Story? Sequencing Cards (LDA) • Role-play to retell events in correct sequence
• Planning and organising a story	• Concertina plan - fold paper into three sections for beginning, middle and ending • Character, context, problem, solution (writing frame) • Story boards and story maps
• Writing for different purposes and audiences using simple sentences	• Write clues for a treasure hunt • Write simple forfeits for a board game • Write comic strip stories using templates
• Writing in the style of a specific genre	• Provide opportunities for shared reading and writing of texts in the genre being studied • Scaffold genre through guided writing • Use writing frames linked to genre
• Information processing difficulties when planning and creating non-fiction texts	• Guided/paired reading and planning (adult and peer group) • Speech to text software (for planning ideas) • Visual cue cards related to topic
• Difficulties with organising and presenting information	• Did you know? (topic posters or cards) • Use suitable graphic organisers to convey information (charts, tables, diagrams)

Table 3.3 Difficulties with transcription – support activities

Difficulties with transcription	Support activities
• Inconsistent letter formation (irregular size and shape of letters, mixture of upper and lower case)	• Sandpaper letters (LDA) • Letter formation (Top Marks) • Skywriter (Top marks) • Write from the Start (LDA)
• Poor spatial planning of written work, inconsistent spacing between words and letters	• Finger or lolly stick space reminders • Lined paper or line guides for presentation • Regular practise using space bar when using a keyboard
• Mirror writing (reversal of letters and numbers)	• Individual alphabet strips in lower and upper case on table as visual reminder • Learn to write letters in formation groups using air writing (c, o, a, d, g, q) • Play noughts and crosses (using letters commonly confused - d/b, p/q, m/n) with each player using a different colour for their letter
• Poor posture, weak pencil grip and possible writing fatigue	• Suitable chair size and height • Left/right-handed pens and pencils as appropriate • Writing slope and pencil grips as needed
• Phonemic and phonological awareness difficulties	• See a range of phonemic and phonological awareness activities in **Key Learning Skills**
• Recall and spelling of common words	• Cued Spelling as part of targeted support • Word mats, word banks (high frequency words) • Wordshark for tricky words
• Sentence construction	• Sentence sorting (words into sentences) • Sentence completion (open-ended) • Colourful Semantics (grammar guidance) • Clicker 8 (visual/verbal syntax support) • Cloze (open-ended) for nouns, adjectives, verbs

- **BSL (British Sign Language)** is the language mostly used by the deaf community in the UK. It has its own grammar, word order and regional variations. In some schools, Makaton is used to help pupils with additional learning or communication difficulties. It uses signs and symbols with speech.

- **Cued speech** is a system which helps deaf pupils see what someone is saying. It uses a system of eight handshapes in four positions near the mouth which help to clarify the lip patterns of speech turning spoken language into a visual language.
- **Visual Phonics by Hand** is designed to support the most profoundly deaf pupils. It's a system of visual hand cues for teaching and using phonics. Although we associate phonological awareness with the ability to hear sounds, lip reading, visual systems, finger spelling and the written alphabet can be used to build up a visual knowledge of spelling patterns.

Useful Resources and Information: Literacy and Pupils With Hearing Impairment

- British Sign Language: https://www.british-sign.co.uk/
- Cued Speech: https://www.cuedspeech.co.uk/cued-speech-2/
- NDCS (2016) Teaching phonics to deaf children: Guidance for teachers: https://www.ndcs.org.uk/documents-and-resources/teaching-phonics-to-deaf-children-guidance-for-teachers/
- Visual Phonics by Hand: https://www.visualphonicsbyhand.co.uk/

Literacy and Pupils With Visual Impairment

Pupils with visual impairment may have mild, moderate or severe vision, but with a visual acuity worse than 3/60 they would be registered as blind. Whatever level of vision they have, pupils with visual impairment need more time to develop literacy skills. Pupils with both visual and motor difficulties may also experience challenges with the eye and hand movements needed for reading and writing. In addition, 'Broader cognitive skills and processes such as rapid automatized naming, executive function, metacognition, and memory impact on the child's ability to read and write' (Breadmore et al., 2019, p. 63). Depending on their level of vision and cognitive capability, these pupils can develop literacy skills through:

- sensory stories, tactile pictures, sensory objects and games, tactile and textured letter shapes;
- shared reading using the interactive whiteboard ensuring clarity of type face;
- guided reading using braille books;

- specially designed screen reading software;
- listening books;
- speech technology and dictation software;
- portable recorders;
- tactile Lego braille bricks used for developing motor coordination and early phonic skills through play;
- handwriting guides or templates for pupils who have some vision;
- scan recorder pens;
- magnifiers;
- braille keyboard stickers and touch typing.

Useful References and Information: Literacy and Pupils With Visual Impairment

- Literacy through Moon: https://www.sense.org.uk/information-and-advice/communication/moon/
- RNIB (Royal National Institute of Blind People) has a series of guides showing some of the different types of literacy support available for blind and partially sighted people: https://www.rnib.org.uk/living-with-sight-loss/assistive-aids-and-technology/everyday-tech/reading-and-writing/
- Plymouth City Council: Choosing and producing reading materials for visually impaired children: https://www.plymouth.gov.uk/sites/default/files/choosingbooks.pdf
- Tameside MBC: Curriculum Framework for Children and Young People with Vision Impairment (CFVI): https://www.tameside.gov.uk/TamesideMBC/media/Children/CFVI-Framework.pdf

Literacy and Pupils with Speech, Language and Communication Needs (SLCN)

SLCN is the term used to describe learning difficulties which can range from mild to severe difficulties with the understanding and use of language. Many children have speech and language difficulties associated with physical, sensory, neurological and cognitive impairment. Pupils with SLCN may have difficulties with one or more of these areas: phonology, grammar (syntax and morphology), word finding, semantics, listening and attention and pragmatics. For more detailed information on these difficulties, see **9 - SEND Areas of Need and Support.**

Strategies to support pupils with SLCN may include the following:

- Providing visual timetables and visual task plans.
- Using visual resources and manipulatives and other multisensory resources to support conceptual understanding.
- Giving pupils time for processing language.
- Being consistent with rules and routines.
- Giving clear, simple instructions and modifying questions if not understood.
- Using assistive technology and different forms of communication (symbols, pictures).
- Avoiding idioms and phrases with dual meanings or ensure clear explanations.
- Modelling correct grammar without correcting pupils.

Useful References and Information: Literacy and Pupils With Speech, Language and Communication Needs (SLCN)

- Blacksheep Resources: BSP, speech & language resources for schools, therapists & parents (https://www.blacksheeppress.co.uk/)
- ICAN: Developmental Language Disorder: https://speechandlanguage.org.uk/wp-content/uploads/2023/12/ican_dld_guide_final_aug4.pdf
- Colourful Semantics: https://resourcecentre.routledge.com/books/9780367210502
- Walking the Talk: a vocabulary recovery plan for primary schools - a report compiled by Widget Symbols https://www.widgit.com/about-symbols/booklets/vocabulary-recovery-guide.pdf
- Colorcards (Winslow) are activity cards designed to develop a range of speech and language skills.

Literacy and Autistic Spectrum Condition (ASC)

Pupils with autism may experience many of the same difficulties as pupils with SLCN, but, in addition, autism affects a pupil's ability to develop social interaction skills. For more detailed information on these difficulties, see **9 – SEND Areas of Need and Support.**

Strategies to support pupils with autism may be similar to those for pupils with SLCN but in addition may include the following:

- Providing a structured learning environment with verbal and visual signposting of changes in routine.
- Using assistive technology and specific forms of communication suitable for the pupil, for example, PECS (Picture Exchange Communication System).
- Being aware of sensory processing needs, avoiding sensory overload.
- Providing and modelling use of personal workspaces.
- Using social stories for specific social situations.

Useful Resources and Information: Literacy and Autistic Spectrum Condition

- Autism Toolkit for Primary Schools: https://sites.southglos.gov.uk/safeguarding/wp-content/uploads/sites/221/2020/07/autism_toolkit_primary_sg_version_07_03_19.pdf
- Teach Starter: https://www.teachstarter.com/gb/teaching-resource-collection/autism/
- PECS (Picture Exchange Communication System): https://nationalautismresources.com/the-picture-exchange-communication-system-pecs?
- Social Stories: https://www.autism.org.uk/advice-and-guidance/topics/communication/communication-tools/social-stories-and-comic-strip-coversations

Literacy and Pupils With Specific Learning Difficulties

Pupils with specific learning difficulties (SpLD), which may include dyslexia, Attention Deficit Hyperactivity Disorder (ADHD), dyscalculia, dysgraphia and dyspraxia, need support with a variety of literacy skills. They may have difficulties with word interpretation and perception, working memory, sequencing, information processing, phonemic and phonological awareness, orientation of letters and numbers and organisational skills. Most pupils with SpLD are taught in mainstream classes and benefit from adaptive teaching in an inclusive environment. In addition, pupils may need to:

- use multi-sensory resources to support learning;
- make use of assistive technology when necessary;

- use coloured overlays and line trackers where necessary;
- learn keyboard skills and use spell checkers;
- refer to visual timetables and planners;
- create mind maps to help link ideas;
- use graphic organisers and other alternative methods of recording such as writing frames, diagrams, labelled drawings, flow charts, story maps and comic strip stories;
- make use of audio-visual aids.

Useful Resources and Information: Literacy and Pupils With Specific Learning Difficulties

- Helen Arkell Dyslexia Charity: https://helenarkell.org.uk/about-dyslexia/what-is-an-spld/
- A practical guide to teaching children with dyslexia: https://my.optimus-education.com/practical-guide-teaching-children-dyslexia
- Nessy: https://www.nessy.com/en-gb
- Clicker: https://www.cricksoft.com/uk/clicker
- Wordshark: https://www.wordshark.co.uk/

Developing Knowledge and Skills for Mathematics

Links to the ITTECF 3.7

- **3.11 Learn that** pupils' positive dispositions and attitudes towards mathematics are associated with positive outcomes on learning (DfE, 2024a, p. 16).

Ofsted's (2023) mathematics subject report stated that the quality of maths education has improved over the last decade but there is still a gap between the disadvantaged and advantaged pupils. Therefore, it's essential to create a classroom atmosphere that encourages pupils to develop an interest and enthusiasm for maths while, at the same time, understanding their difficulties and potential anxieties. If pupils develop a negative disposition, they lose confidence in their ability to make progress in mathematics. Feelings of anxiety may develop if a pupil feels inadequate when mathematical demands are placed on them. Interestingly, Skyrme and Hunt (2022) note how students training to teach the primary age range are the most anxious about teaching maths. However, they note that, 'Most teachers with maths anxiety are extremely empathetic to their learners and often present as highly effective teachers as a result' (2022, p. 4).

Case Study: A Tale of Two Teachers

Teacher A had achieved a first-class honours degree in mathematics and, in her first teaching post, was eager to share her enthusiasm for the subject with her year 6 class. Although a small group of pupils caught their teacher's enthusiasm and made excellent progress, a number struggled with understanding how to apply the concepts being taught and made little progress.

Teacher B had always struggled with mathematics and had to retake the subject at GCSE level. He lacked enthusiasm for the subject and spent twice as much time preparing mathematics lessons compared with other subjects. Most of his class made reasonable progress, but the more able mathematicians became disruptive when tasks were completed early.

During the headteacher's appraisal, both teachers' concerns were identified with supportive suggestions and objectives set. Teacher A received mentoring from the key stage 1 lead who demonstrated how concepts could be broken down into smaller steps with greater use of visual resources and manipulatives. Teacher B experienced team teaching with the subject leader for mathematics who was able to model how tasks could be increased in both challenge and depth.

Reflective Task 3.4

Consider what actions would help support maths anxiety in a pupil, peer or yourself.

Pedagogical content knowledge (the ability to demonstrate good subject and curriculum knowledge as well as being aware of the most effective strategies for teaching a subject) is an essential element of mathematics teaching. It's important to be aware of the stages of pupils' learning development in mathematics. The EEF (2021e) highlights the need for teachers to be aware of developmental progression and the impact of high-quality targeted support for pupils. The understanding of mathematical concepts and terminology can be difficult to comprehend for some pupils with SEND. The concept of time, for instance, is complex and needs to be linked to pupils' everyday experiences. If mathematical concepts are introduced before pupils are cognitively able to understand them, then misconceptions develop.

Pupils need to develop an understanding of the mathematical concepts and skills required in everyday life. Shopping, cooking, playing games and many other activities need a certain amount of mathematical understanding to support the development of essential life skills. For some pupils, understanding the language associated with mathematical concepts can be a barrier to their learning. It's important to provide activities within a practical context and at a stage suitable to the pupil to ensure links are formed between the manipulatives or representations used and the mathematical concept being taught. Stages may include the following:

- **Concrete stage:** At this stage, pupils will be introduced to mathematical ideas or skills by using manipulatives (counting cubes/counters, sorting by shape/size).
- **Pictorial stage:** At this stage, pupils will begin to visualise and relate their concrete experiences to pictorial representations of real objects. These may include simple pictorial computation, number games and bar charts.
- **Abstract stage:** It is at this stage that pupils will begin to use mathematical notation ($6 + 4 = 10$). They will show that they can use abstract symbols to answer a question or solve a problem.

Some pupils with SEND may have been diagnosed with dyscalculia which is a specific learning difficulty affecting the ability to understand the number system and the relationships and connections in mathematics. For these pupils, it's important they are given time to understand mathematical ideas and develop learning skills at the concrete and pictorial stages before they are asked to attempt learning at the abstract stage.

Pupils with dyscalculia or dyslexia may have difficulty with:

- understanding the properties of numbers;
- making connections between numbers, symbols and words;
- recognising and recalling patterns and sequences (numbers and shapes);
- understanding the concepts of addition, subtraction, multiplication and division;
- understanding place value;
- understanding the practical application of using number for measurement;
- making connections between numbers and money values;
- following directions and understanding positional language;
- understanding and using mathematical language for problem solving;
- processing information and using working memory;

- visual perception and spatial awareness;
- telling the time and time related activities, following directions, sequencing, organisational skills and information processing.

For pupils with SEND, mathematical understanding may be developed through a number of practical and everyday activities which can be used for pre-teaching a specific concept or for whole class and group experiences (Table 3.4).

Table 3.4 Practical support for developing mathematical concepts and skills

Multi-sensory number activities - tactile shape objects and numerals giving strong sensory feedback	Number songs and rhymes that provide repetition and aid retention
Visual timetables to aid an understanding of the passing of time	Timed games using a stopwatch in mathematics and PE
Role play shopping activities and games - simple money exchange	Investigating shapes in the environment both in nature and in buildings
Sorting and categorising objects, shapes and numbers using Venn and Carroll diagrams	Tessellation - design flooring using 2D shapes. Design products using 3D shapes
Food Fractions - use the idea of sharing food such as pizza or chocolate to realise having a part of a whole before moving to fraction tiles	Introduce vocabulary of length, height, weight and capacity through practical paired and group activities
Numicon SEND resources use a multisensory approach to exploring mathematical concepts	Stile maths resources (LDA) cover several areas and provide self-checking activities
Numbershark is a games-based learning programme	Top Maths - provides online maths games
Two-colour counters www.mathsbot.com build counting skills and support visual and tactile exploration of number and operations concepts	Playing games with dominoes and dice support subitising (instantly knowing how many objects there are)
Geoboards (pegboards) - stretch elastic bands to create shapes supporting understanding of the properties of 2D shapes.	Books - share stories that build numeracy skills. Visit: https://www.mathsthroughstories.org/

Positive experiences for pupils with SEND can be fostered through carefully planned encounters with mathematics. By supporting the concrete, pictorial and abstract stages flexibly, all learners can engage and be helped towards mastery of mathematical concepts. The scaffolded activities outlined above will not only support pupils with understanding and retaining mathematical vocabulary but aid those who may struggle with literacy skills, attention, number fluency and confidence levels, enabling them to develop a greater sense of self-efficacy.

4

Classroom Practice

Chapter Objectives

This chapter highlights evidence-based research on approaches, knowledge and skills leading to effective pedagogy. It outlines the ideas of Rosenshine, emphasising that they are a set of principles, not a rigid structure for lesson planning and delivery. The chapter highlights teaching strategies and practical activities that have been effective for all pupils, including those with SEND. Areas covered include the following:

- effective teaching;
- explicit instruction;
- planning and organising for pupils with SEND in different settings;
- modelling and scaffolding;
- cognitive and metacognitive strategies;
- questioning and talking;
- practice;
- flexible grouping;
- homework.

Effective Teaching

Links to the ITTECF 4.1

- **Learn that** effective teaching can transform pupils' knowledge, capabilities and beliefs about learning.
- **Learn that** effective teachers introduce new material in steps, explicitly linking new ideas to what has been previously studied and learned (DfE, 2024a, p. 18).

As highlighted by Coe et al. (2014), defining what constitutes effective teaching can be challenging. In their review of the research, they define effective teaching as 'that which leads to improved student achievement using outcomes that matter to their future success' (p. 2). The review highlights six areas where there is evidence-based research of approaches, knowledge and skills leading to effective pedagogy for all pupils. The areas highlighted are as follows:

1. **Content knowledge** – strong evidence showing that effective teachers have a good understanding not only of the content knowledge of a subject but also of the way pupils develop their own thinking and understanding. Effective teachers can identify common pupil misconceptions and rectify them.
2. **Quality of instruction** – strong evidence to suggest that quality of instruction is fundamental. Specific strategies such as activating prior knowledge, modelling, scaffolding, questioning and discussion are just some of the elements of effective teaching.
3. **Classroom climate** – some evidence that effective teaching and learning takes place when all pupils are valued and motivated to overcome barriers to learning and when teacher/pupil relationships are based on trust and mutual understanding.
4. **Classroom management** – some evidence that the organisation of classroom space and resources, as well as good management of pupil behaviour, is necessary for effective teaching and learning to take place.
5. **Teacher beliefs** – some evidence that an understanding of evidence-based theories about learning and the ability to use these in practice can contribute to effective teaching.
6. **Professional behaviours** – some evidence that teachers who reflect on and develop their own professional practice, support colleagues and communicate regularly with pupils and families, can improve pupil outcomes and progress.

Case Study: It Was Magic!

In a crowded shopping centre, a young man called loudly to a grey-haired woman, 'It's me Miss! It's Ryan'.

'Goodness me, Ryan', smiled the woman. 'I hardly recognised you'.

Ryan smiled and reminded his teacher of one of his fondest memories of being in her class - the trip to a local manor house during his last year at primary school. One of Ryan's distinct memories was of the intricate wooden carvings inside. He remembered how beautiful they were and his sense of awe and wonder. 'It was magic!' he said.

(Continued)

(Continued)

Ryan's teacher recalled how the class were unable to touch or handle any of the wooden interiors or artefacts, so she borrowed several carvings from the local library to display and share with the children in the classroom. She remembered how much Ryan had been inspired by the wooden carvings.

Ryan reminded his teacher how she'd encouraged him to develop his strengths and interests and told her he had a brilliant job. He'd always been good at design and technology and had joined the DT club when he started secondary school. He'd worked hard to develop his skills and was now an apprentice furniture restorer.

Ryan's teacher listened to his enthusiasm for a career that was just beginning. She thought about her own, now coming to an end. With some pupils, it had been hard work, but with others, like Ryan, it was magic.

SEND: Dyslexia.

Reflective Task 4.1

In what ways do you think Ryan's teacher helped him?

Do you think she exemplified any of the qualities of an effective teacher?

Explicit Instruction

Explicit instruction is a method of teaching in a clear, direct, structured way, linking new ideas to what has been previously studied and learnt. It's an important aspect of teaching for all pupils but especially for those with SEND (Aubin, 2023a). It's one of five teaching strategies highlighted in a guidance report by Davies and Henderson (2021) as being an element of high-quality teaching for pupils with SEND. The guidance report states,

Common aspects of explicit instruction include:

- teaching skills and concepts in small steps
- using examples and non-examples
- using clear and unambiguous language
- anticipating and planning for common misconceptions
- highlighting essential content and removing distracting information (p. 24).

Rosenshine's Principles of Instruction (2012) highlight explicit teaching strategies that have been effective for most pupils. They are as follows:

- Daily review of previous learning.
- Small step presentation of new material.
- Asking questions.
- Providing models.
- Giving opportunities for guided practice.
- Checking understanding.
- Obtaining a high success rate – Rosenshine suggests a success rate of 80% shows that pupils are learning and being challenged. He believes that 70% is too low and 95%–100% is too easy.
- Scaffolding.
- Independent practice.
- Weekly and monthly reviews of previous learning.

However, it must be emphasised, Rosenshine's ideas are a set of principles and should not restrict a teachers' ability to plan creatively for the needs of all pupils.

Effective planning provides structure and direction in all educational settings and should be based on the whole school ethos and vision for successful learning for all pupils, whatever their needs. Davies and Henderson (2021) state:

> *Supporting pupils with special educational needs should be part of a proactive approach to supporting all pupils – it is not an 'add on'. It means understanding the specific barriers pupils face to learning and what they need in order to thrive so that they can be included in all that the school has to offer. (p. 7)*

Planning and organising for inclusive learning means:

- Assessing pupils' needs through the graduated approach.
- Ensuring an inclusive ethos within the classroom environment.
- Ensuring physical access and safety throughout the day.
- Employing a variety of adaptive teaching strategies.
- Providing suitable multisensory resources and assistive technology.
- Using teaching assistants effectively.

Case Study: Aadan

Aadan, aged 9, is the eldest of two children (see Pupil Support Profiles in **9 - SEND Areas of Need and Support** and attends the same mainstream school as his sister. Aadan has a cheerful, outgoing personality with a supportive family and friends. He uses a wheelchair to move around the school and a walker in the classroom. He enjoys using IT for topic research, has excellent art and design skills, likes puzzles and gaming.

Aadan needs support with some self-help skills, fine and gross motor skills, auditory memory and phonemic and phonological awareness skills. The teaching assistant is available to support Aadan, but he is given opportunities to be independent in areas where he is confident. He needs rest and recuperation times. Table 4.1 shows Aadan's weekly support timetable.

Table 4.1 Support timetable for Aadan

	Monday	**Tuesday**	**Wednesday**	**Thursday**	**Friday**
Session 1	Adaptive teaching	Literacy - support with keyboard skills (TA)	Literacy - 15 mins phonic intervention group (TA)	Adaptive teaching	Literacy - 15 mins phonic intervention group (TA)
Session 2	Literacy - 15 mins phonic intervention group (TA)	Maths support with problem solving (TA)	Adaptive teaching	Literacy - support with keyboard skills (TA)	Adaptive teaching
BREAK	Playground buddy	Playground buddy	Playground buddy	Playground buddy	Playground buddy
Session 3	OT visit to assess Aadan's chair and seating arrangements.	Adaptive teaching	PE - adapted ball games (peer support)	Adaptive teaching	Adaptive teaching
LUNCH	Art Club	15 mins physio exercises with TA	15 mins physio exercises with TA	15 mins physio exercises with TA	Board Games activity group
Session 4	PE (TA support) adapted ball skill activities.	Adaptive teaching	Adaptive teaching	Topic - TA support with presentation of information.	Hydrotherapy with parents
Session 5	Adaptive teaching	Adaptive teaching	Adaptive teaching	Topic - TA support with presentation of information.	Hydrotherapy with parents

SEND: Duchenne Muscular Dystrophy, respiratory difficulties.

Case Study: Support Timetable for Sam

Sam, aged 10, is an only child in a one parent family (see Pupil Support Profiles in **9 - SEND Areas of Need and Support**). His mother is keen to support her son in all aspects of his development. Sam likes to work in a contained space but will work with a partner. He is hypersensitive to light, bright colours and specific smells.

Sam enjoys listening to music, singing and playing the piano. He has a talent for devising word challenges, quizzes and crosswords. He is also a gifted chess player. He receives no support during music, design and technology, PE and IT lessons.

Sam attends a mainstream school, with support in the Resource Base (RB) for grammatical, semantic and pragmatic understanding of both oral and written language. He has class-based support with verbal reasoning and sensory integration and uses assistive technology, visual resources and graphic organisers Table 4.2 shows Sam's weekly support timetable.

Table 4.2 Support timetable for Sam

	Monday	**Tuesday**	**Wednesday**	**Thursday**	**Friday**
Session 1	Literacy (small group support in RB)	Maths (TA support In class)	Maths (TA support in class)	Literacy (small group support in RB)	Literacy (small group support in RB)
Session 2	Adaptive teaching	Literacy (small group support in RB)	Literacy (small group support in RB)	Science Topic (TA support in class)	Maths (TA support in class)
BREAK	Playground buddy	Playground buddy	Playground buddy	Playground buddy	Playground buddy
Session 3	Maths (TA support in class)	Therapy session with SLT	Adaptive teaching	Maths (TA support in class)	Adaptive teaching
LUNCH	Library monitor	Buddy system	Chess club	Buddy system	Quiz group in library
Session 4	Adaptive teaching	Adaptive teaching	Science Topic (TA support in class)	Art (TA support with sensory integration)	Semantic, pragmatic games in RB
Session 5	Adaptive teaching	PSHE - TA support, link to social stories	Science Topic (TA support in class)	Art (TA support with sensory integration)	Homework pre learning (TA support)

SEND: Autism, Sensory integration difficulties.

Reflective Task 4.2

Do you think supportive and inclusive timetables have been organised for Aadan and Sam?

Ask your school colleagues about ways in which a pupil's specific needs (therapy sessions, targeted support) and their curriculum needs are managed.

Modelling and Scaffolding

Links to the ITTECF 4.2

- **Learn that** modelling helps pupils understand new processes and ideas; good models make abstract ideas concrete and accessible.
- **Learn that** guides, scaffolds and worked examples can help pupils apply new ideas but should be gradually removed as pupils' expertise increases (DfE, 2024a, p. 18).

Traditional modelling is when the adult demonstrates a concept or skill, verbalising their thought processes and pointing out what is happening at each stage. Interactive modelling is when the adult demonstrates and narrates what is happening but also encourages pupils to make observations, ask questions and explain their thinking. Salisu and Ransom (2014) suggest that 'a model makes the process of understanding a domain of knowledge easier because it is a visual expression of the topic' (p. 59). The use of models as learning aides has two primary benefits. First, models provide accurate and useful representations of knowledge that are needed when solving problems in particular domains. Second, a model makes the process of understanding a domain of knowledge easier because it is a visual expression of the topic. Modelling can have a positive impact on pupils with SEND. It helps them:

- make cognitive connections;
- develop listening and attention skills;
- understand new concepts and skills;
- overcome some working memory and processing problems;
- develop communication and interaction skills.

Below are the steps teachers can work through when modelling.

1. Activate prior learning of both concepts and skills required for the task.
2. Break down the task into smaller manageable steps.

3. Link each step to both the previous and the next step in learning.
4. Remodel steps if misconceptions occur.
5. Encourage interactive modelling using multi-sensory strategies.
6. Be aware of possible working memory and processing difficulties.

Davies and Henderson (2021) conceptualise scaffolding as, '...a metaphor for temporary support that is removed when no longer required. It may be visual, verbal or written' (p. 26). Instructional scaffolding has been described as 'I do, we do, you do' and represents the support given by teachers to help pupils with tasks they would find difficult to complete on their own. Many pupils with SEND need to spend more time being supported at the 'we do' stage.

I do (modelled instruction) – adult presents tasks in small steps using clear, direct instruction and multisensory resources to support learning. Pupils are encouraged to request clarification as each step is demonstrated.

We do (shared practice) – adults work alongside pupils encouraging them to predict next steps for the task. Some pupils benefit from following a visual task flow chart showing each step.

You do (guided practice) – pupils gradually take control of the learning process and are given opportunities to work together in pairs or small groups sharing knowledge and practising skills. Adults act as mentors providing prompts and asking questions to help identify any misconceptions.

You do (independent practice) – pupils should be able to complete tasks (similar to those already experienced) with little or no adult support, though some pupils with SEND may continue to need the support of concrete resources, audio/visual aids, assistive technology and graphic organisers.

Some ways in which scaffolding can be used:

- Visual task organisers showing clear stages of a task.
- Audio/visual media resources to enhance understanding.
- Think, pair, share activities where peer group support each other.
- Wall charts with key words or ideas linked to topic/subject.
- Think-aloud activities where thought processes can be modelled by adults.
- Cue cards for specific concept vocabulary related to the task.
- English and mathematics table mats providing reinforcement of key vocabulary and ideas.
- Assistive technology and AAC resources to aid communication both verbally and written.
- Multi-sensory resources to aid the understanding of new concepts and the development of key learning skills.

- Graphic organisers (labelled pictures, writing frames, charts, diagrams, word webs, story maps, timelines) to support pupils with organising information and representing their ideas.

Cognitive and Metacognitive Strategies

Links to the ITTECF 4.3

- **4.5 Learn that** explicitly teaching pupils metacognitive strategies linked to subject knowledge, including how to plan, monitor and evaluate, supports independence and academic success (DfE, 2024a, p. 18).

Cognition refers to the mental processes used to gain knowledge and understanding. Metacognition refers to an individual's knowledge and understanding of their own cognitive processes and being able to plan, monitor and evaluate those processes. Supporting pupils in developing metacognitive strategies helps them become independent learners but, as the EEF state, 'It is important that supporting pupils' metacognition and self-regulation skills isn't seen as something 'extra' for teachers to do, but an effective pedagogy that can be used to support their normal classroom practice' (2018a, p. 26).

Swartz and Perkins (1989) developed a framework to identify levels of awareness in thinking which they considered to be increasingly metacognitive. They suggested:

- **Tacit learners** do not think about the strategies they need to use for specific tasks but just accept that they know, or do not know, what to do.
- **Aware learners** recognise some of the thinking they do, such as generating ideas to begin a task and choosing a strategy to help complete a task. They apply known strategies to suit certain tasks, but they do not plan their thinking.
- **Strategic learners** know and apply strategies that can help them learn. They organise their thinking by being able to use a range of skills.
- **Reflective learners** can reflect on their learning while they are undertaking a task. They know and apply strategies that help them learn and can consider the success, or not, of any strategies they're using and revise them as appropriate.

Without encouragement and support, many pupils with SEND are unaware of the strategies they use to complete a task. To become independent learners, pupils with SEND need to be shown how to plan, monitor and evaluate their own learning:

- **Plan** – understand how to approach a task before starting.
- **Monitor** – be aware of their own progress and understanding of a task.

- **Evaluate** – review their own learning experience and outcomes, deciding on possible improvements.

Case Study: A New Ball Game

Year 5 pupils, organised in groups of six, were asked to devise and demonstrate a new ball game. The groups were of mixed ability, but one group had the addition of a Teaching Assistant who noted responses.

TA: What do you think we need to do first?

H: Get some balls before the other groups take them.

B: What shall we get, big ones or small ones?

S: Let's use the big, coloured ones. Then we can make up a game for teams.

G: How many balls shall we get?

S: Five cos there are five groups.

H: Let's do a kicking game. I'm good at football.

A: That's not fair. What about everyone else?

TA: What do you think D?

D: We could roll the ball into something.

TA: How did you think of that idea?

D: I don't know. It just came into my head.

G: It could be like skittles.

A: We need to try it out and we haven't got any skittles.

TA: What could you use instead?

B: We could use a hoop and roll the ball into the hoop.

(After trying out the game)

A: It was a bit hard.

TA: How could you make it easier?

B: Put the hoop a bit nearer.

H: But not too near or it'll be easy.

(The group practised the game until they were all happy with it.)

SEND: Cerebral Palsy, ADHD.

Reflective Task 4.4

How many different levels of thinking were used in this group interaction?

What can you learn about each pupil from their responses?

How did the TA extend the pupils' thinking?

Questioning and Talking

Links to the ITTECF 4.4

- **4.6 Learn that** questioning is an essential tool for teachers; questions can be used for many purposes, including to check pupils' prior knowledge, assess understanding and break down problems.
- **4.7 Learn that** high-quality classroom talk (sometimes referred to as oracy), can support pupils to articulate key ideas, consolidate understanding and extend their vocabulary (DfE, 2024a, pp. 18-19).

Developing the quality of classroom talk is an effective way of improving pupils' cognitive and metacognitive skills (Alexander, 2020). Jay et al. (2017) suggested that pilot studies of dialogic teaching in the UK show evidence of improvement in language, mathematics and science for pupils who have engaged in challenging classroom talk. Alexander (2020) emphasised the importance of 'dialogic teaching' involving pupils and adults in quality classroom discussion. He acknowledged that talk should be reciprocal for it to be meaningful, 'If students need talk in order to learn about the world, teachers need talk in order to learn about students. The first condition is more generally understood than the second' (Alexander, 2020, p. 1).

It's particularly important for pupils with SEND to take part in classroom discussion that reflects an understanding of their barriers to learning. All pupils should be given opportunities to express their thoughts and ideas in whatever way is appropriate to their needs. Using a variety of questioning strategies can help with the development of language skills for pupils with SEND. Questioning can:

- assess what has been learnt and understood;
- provide opportunities for pupils to express their views;

- foster collaborative thinking and discussion;
- create a shared learning environment;
- help pupils consider different ways of approaching a task;
- challenge the level of thinking and encourage creative thought.

For some pupils with SEND, it's important that lines of communication are open before effective discussion and questioning can take place. This may be through signing, symbols, picture cards, Braille, PECS, multisensory resources or assistive technology. An important element of questioning for all pupils, but particularly for those with SEND, is to allow pupils time to think.

Rosenshine (2012) suggests that teachers need to ask different kinds of questions in order to enhance pupil learning and facilitate the development of thinking skills. Some questions require factual answers while others may ask pupils to explain a process or make a personal response. Table 4.3 shows a range of factual, process and personal response questions.

Table 4.3 Factual, process or personal response questions

Factual	Process	Personal response
Which seeds did you plant?	How can you help your seeds to grow?	What is your favourite flower?
What did you need to make your model?	How did you make your model?	What do you like best about your model?
What two colours can be mixed together to make green?	How do you make different shades of green?	Which shade of green do you like best?

Generally, in primary classrooms, adults use either open or closed questions. Open questions encourage pupils to think and give reasoned explanations for their answers. Closed questions are usually those which require a simple factual answer or yes/no response. Some pupils with SEND, particularly those with communication and interaction difficulties, may find open-ended questions confusing, but they can be modified.

Questions Related to *The Gruffalo* by Julia Donaldson:

- Open question – How did the mouse frighten the animals in the wood?
- Modified question – What did the mouse tell the animals to frighten them?
- Open question – Why do you think the Gruffalo was frightened of the mouse?
- Modified question – What did the mouse tell the Gruffalo to frighten it?

Case Study: Questions and Responses

Year 3 pupils were discussing Van Gogh's painting *The Starry Night*. The following represents just a few noted responses.

Q: What do you think Van Gogh called this painting? Why?

A: Dark night because it's dark and the lights are on in the houses.

Q: What colours has Van Gogh used the most and why?

A: Blue and black. I think they are his favourite colours.

Q: How do you think Van Gogh felt when he created the painting?

A: I think he was tired because it was nighttime.

Q: How do you feel when you look at the painting?

A: I feel sad cos it's blue. When my Gran's sad she says she feels blue.

Q: Why do you think Van Gogh used curling and swirling lines in the painting?

A: Because it was windy when he painted it.

Q: How do you think Van Gogh made the patterns and colours in the sky?

A: He mixed different colours on his paintbrush and then painted up and down and round and round.

SEND: Bipolar, Down syndrome.

Reflective Task 4.5

What can you learn about the pupils from their responses?

How do you think the teacher may have extended the pupils' thinking?

Can you identify the factual, process and personal questions and answers?

Practice

Links to the ITTECF 4.5

- **4.8 Learn that** practice is an integral part of effective teaching; ensuring pupils have repeated opportunities to practise, with appropriate guidance and support, increases success (DfE, 2024a, p. 19).

Pupils with SEND benefit from regular, purposeful practice. Agarwal et al. (2017) suggest that retrieval practice, with feedback during the learning process, benefits those pupils with lower working memory. Ofsted (2019) emphasise the importance of retrieval practice for all pupils:

> *Retrieval practice strengthens memory and makes it easier to retrieve the information later. Retrieval practice needs to occur a reasonable time after the topic has been initially taught and needs ideally to take the form of testing knowledge, either by the teacher (for example questioning using flash cards, a test or getting pupils to write a concept map) or through pupil self-testing. It is important that feedback on accuracy is provided either by the teacher or by the pupil checking accuracy for themselves. (p. 20)*

Although most of the research around retrieval practice has focused on the secondary phase, Jones (2022) examines the practical application of retrieval practice within the primary classroom, arguing how it can build confidence, motivation and impact progress. She highlights how it strengthens memory and recall while allowing the identification of gaps in pupil knowledge. Cattrall (2023) emphasises how games and practical activities, focused on retrieval practice, are more effective for younger pupils than testing. Although some tests are statutory, pupils with SEND need to be given opportunities to take part in activities which focus on the recall of specific areas of learning away from the 'high stakes' anxiety of testing. In this way, teachers can identify misconceptions early in the learning process.

Suggested Activities for Retrieval Practice

Cloze – missing words in the text can help check semantic knowledge of key concept vocabulary as well as grammatical understanding of vocabulary (nouns, verbs, adjectives).

Beat the teacher – quick quiz at the end of a topic. Teacher scores a point for every question not answered. Pupils aim to answer most questions correctly to beat the teacher.

Think-a-link – match card pairs to revise number bond links (6 + 4/7 + 3), vocabulary links (nouns, verbs, adjectives, synonyms, antonyms), form and function links (mug/cup, car/van, shoes/boots).

Who am I? – link clues to story characters, people in history, famous people.

Mnemonics – collect well-known or own mnemonics for retrieval of common exception words.

Mind Maps – compile prior knowledge or additional new learning of a specific topic as a mind map.

Yes/No – topic link similar to multiple choice questionnaire but with only a yes/no choice (A spider is an insect? Yes/No).

What am I? – link clues to science topics, geographical features, mathematics (shape, number), English (vocabulary).

Just a Minute – (group activity linked to prior learning) pupils pick a card and talk about the given topic for 20 or 30 seconds.

Many of the suggested activities can be prepared using Braille, signing, symbols and assistive technology. In addition, board games can be adapted for pairs and small groups to answer questions. Some additional support may be needed from the teacher or TA.

Flexible Grouping

Links to the ITTECF 4.6

- **4.9 Learn that** paired and group activities can increase pupil success, but to work together effectively pupils need guidance, support and practice.
- **4.10 Learn that** how pupils are grouped is also important; care should be taken to monitor the impact of groupings on pupil attainment, behaviour and motivation (DfE, 2024a, p. 19).

Flexible grouping is a way of organising pupils with SEND and giving them opportunities to work in different ways for different purposes. It can help promote positive behaviour if pupils are given guidance on how to work together. Adults need to:

- model positive behaviour within a cooperative learning situation;
- praise positive interactions while discouraging negative remarks;
- encourage pupils to recognise each other's individual strengths;
- set rules and routines for transitioning into groups (use visual grouping reminders);
- provide clear learning objectives and success criteria;
- allocate role responsibilities within the group.

Coe et al. (2014) show there is some evidence that the organisation of classroom space and resources, as well as good management of pupil behaviour, is necessary for effective teaching and learning to take place. Flexible grouping and adaptive teaching strategies need to be part of classroom organisation for pupils with SEND. A range of flexible grouping models are listed below.

- **Whole class** (mixed ability) can be used in all areas of the curriculum such as shared reading and writing, mental/oral maths, maths quizzes, introducing new concepts and skills, modelling new skills and techniques, circle time and PSHE activities.

- **Guided group work** (similar ability) can be used for guided reading and writing, synthetic phonic sessions, guided maths activities, IT coding and keyboard skills.
- **Cooperative learning groups** (mixed ability) can be used for science investigations, problem-solving activities, topic research, PE activities, role play, presentations and PSHE activities.
- **Group interventions** (similar ability) can be used for programs such as Catch-Up Literacy, Catch-Up Numeracy, Abracadabra (ABRA), Project X, Numicon, keyboard skills, board and card games for specific skills.
- **Think, Pair, Share** (mixed ability groups): Pupils are given time to think about a task before sharing their ideas with a partner in their group. At a given time, each pair can share their ideas with another pair and then with the group emphasising that all ideas are valuable.
- **Practical projects** (mixed ability groups) can be used for design and technology projects, music activities, educational visits, geography fieldwork and art projects.
- **Response partners** (similar ability): Pupils support each other through the writing process (plan, draft, edit, proofread, present).
- **Reading Buddies** (similar or mixed ability): The 'reading buddies' can be pupils with similar reading abilities, older/younger pupils, confident/not so confident reader, adult/pupil.
- **Individual** (targeted support): Activities will focus on individual needs and may be linked to the development of specific skills or ongoing therapies.

Flexible grouping, with a specific focus on pupils with SEND, is revisited in **5 – Adaptive Teaching.**

Homework

Links to the ITTECF 4.7

- **4.11 Learn that** homework can improve pupil outcomes, particularly for older pupils, but it is likely that the quality of homework and its relevance to main class teaching is more important than the amount set (DfE, 2024a, p. 19).

Little research has been undertaken on the impact of homework for pupils with SEND, but reports suggest that younger primary children lack the independent study skills needed for some homework tasks. It has also been argued that homework increases the inequalities between those from socioeconomically privileged backgrounds and those from socioeconomically disadvantaged backgrounds (EEF, 2021f). The EEF states that pupils from disadvantaged backgrounds:

> *...are less likely to have a quiet working space, are less likely to have access to a device suitable for learning or a stable internet connection and may receive less parental support to complete homework and develop effective learning habits. These difficulties may increase the gap in attainment for disadvantaged pupils. (2021f, para. 7)*

4.1 Did You Know?

In a 2018 study, Ofsted found more than a third of parents considered homework to be unhelpful to their children. Most parents (72%) thought that allowing pupils time to plan and get ready for lessons in school time was a better alternative to homework (Ofsted, 2018).

Many parents of pupils with SEND are concerned about the negative impact of homework. The school day can be tiring, and homework can be an added stress, detrimental to their health and self-esteem. In order to minimise difficulties with homework, teachers can:

- ensure pupils have adequate support at home through parent/teacher links and provide resources if necessary;
- organise homework hubs for those who have little or no home support;
- provide resources and time during school for regular reading sessions and games-based reading activities;
- ensure homework tasks are related to classwork;
- set short, focused tasks relevant to pupils' learning needs;
- pre-teach new learning with pupils and give them the choice to research at home and feedback to the class.

Durrant (2022) emphasises the importance of play-based literacy activities for all pupils and particularly those with SEND. Sharing the fun part of learning with pupils and their families can ensure homework is both meaningful and pleasurable for everyone.

5
Adaptive Teaching

Chapter Objectives

This chapter explores pupil differences including potential barriers to learning. It emphasises the importance of giving all pupils the same opportunities by adapting activities rather than creating completely different tasks for pupils with SEND. The chapter also explores the following:

- The principles and practice of adaptive teaching;
- Multisensory approaches to teaching;
- Flexible grouping for SEND;
- Interventions and targeted support;
- Using technology.

Pupil Differences

Links to the ITTECF 5.1

- **5.2 Learn that** pupils are likely to learn at different rates and to require different levels and types of support from teachers to succeed.
- **5.3 Learn that** seeking to understand pupils' differences, including their different levels of prior knowledge and potential barriers to learning, is an essential part of teaching.
- **5.6 Learn that** there is a common misconception that pupils have distinct and identifiable learning styles. This is not supported by evidence and attempting to tailor lessons to learning styles is unlikely to be beneficial (DfE, 2024a, pp. 20–21).

School populations encompass a variety of pupil differences including age, gender, culture, language, prior knowledge, ability, interests, motivation, self-efficacy and home and community factors. These all impact on the different ways in which pupils learn as they bring a range of personal experiences and strengths to the classroom. Although it's been argued that pupils are motivated if they are given opportunities to learn using their strengths (Galloway et al., 2020), there's no evidence to show that pupils have specific learning styles (EEF, 2021j). However, it's important that teachers are aware of the most effective types of support and teaching strategies needed to ensure all pupils with SEND are given opportunities to succeed.

To understand pupil differences, teachers need to practice the cycle of: assess, plan, do, review:

- **Assess** – use effective ongoing assessment strategies.
- **Plan** – plan for adaptive teaching within an inclusive environment.
- **Do** – deliver lessons using a variety of teaching strategies and resources.
- **Review** – regularly review teaching and learning outcomes and pupil progress.

The four areas of need and support, as outlined in the SEND Code of Practice (2015), show how particular barriers to learning may impact on pupil progress. Specific difficulties relating to each of the four areas are outlined in **9 - SEND Areas of Need and Support.**

Pupils with severe learning difficulties (SLD) and profound and multiple learning difficulties (PMLD) may have complex profiles across several categories with some needing therapies and tailored support in resource bases or special schools. However, in many mainstream primary classrooms, there are pupils who have moderate learning difficulties (MLD) and take longer than their peers to reach certain developmental milestones. Whatever their needs, individual pupils have strengths in certain areas. It's important for teachers to enhance those strengths and help pupils develop strategies to overcome, or at least minimise, their barriers to learning.

Case Study: A Love of Books

Coleen was a thoughtful member of a year 5 class. Her father worked at a local supermarket and her mother was a care assistant at a home for the elderly. Both parents had been educated at a special school and the whole family, including her younger brother, were given support from social services.

Coleen experienced difficulties with cognition and learning and was assessed as being nearly three years behind her peers in most areas of the curriculum. Despite her learning difficulties, Coleen loved school and made progress when taking part in practical, visual and tactile activities. She was an excellent mimic, and a popular member of role play groups. Always the first to arrive in the morning, Coleen helped her teacher organise resources in the classroom. It was during one of these sessions that the teacher

(Continued)

discovered Coleen's love of books. She loved everything about books, the smell, the feel, the pictures and print and, most of all, she loved sharing her reading book with her parents and brother at bedtime. Coleen was already part of a literacy intervention group, but the teacher felt she would benefit from being a school library monitor. With the help of her peer group, Coleen learnt how the fiction books were arranged in alphabetical order. She was particularly interested in the non-fiction section and regularly borrowed a variety of titles. During a parents' evening, Coleen's mother shared how proud she was of Coleen's reading skills and explained that Coleen was a volunteer reader at the retirement home where she worked. Although Coleen couldn't read the text in some of the books, she 'read' the pictures and used her role play talent to bring the information to life. As her confidence grew, Coleen made small steps in progress with her literacy skills and shared her love of books with everyone.

SEND: MLD (Moderate Learning Difficulties).

Reflective Task 5.1

Discuss with your colleagues or peers how Coleen's strengths could be used in other areas of the curriculum.

What do you think are the main differences between Coleen's educational experiences and those of her parents?

The Principles and Practice of Adaptive Teaching

Links to the ITTECF 5.2

- **5.1 Learn that** adapting teaching in a responsive way, including by providing targeted support to pupils who are struggling, is likely to increase pupil success.
- **5.4 Learn that** adaptive teaching is less likely to be valuable if it causes the teacher to artificially create distinct tasks for different groups of pupils or to set lower expectations for particular pupils.
- **5.8 Learn that** high quality teaching for all pupils, including those with SEND, is based on strategies which are often already practised by teachers, and which can be developed through training and support (DfE, 2024a, pp. 20–21).

In primary schools, where many pupils are taught in mixed ability mainstream classes, adaptive teaching is advocated rather than creating separate, differentiated tasks for pupils with SEND. Within adaptive teaching practices, Aubin (2023b) advocates flexible grouping where groups are allocated temporarily, based on current level of mastery, and are not fixed or set.

The main principles of adaptive teaching are to offer inclusive learning experiences and high-quality teaching to all pupils. Adaptive teaching should:

- recognise pupils' abilities and barriers to learning;
- plan for inclusive support with the help of the SENCo and other professionals;
- use formative assessment to inform next step planning;
- provide a supportive learning environment where pupils' cognitive, communication, social, emotional, sensory and physical needs are considered;
- use flexible grouping suitable for learning needs;
- activate pupils' prior knowledge and make explicit links to new learning;
- plan stepped tasks to help reduce cognitive load and model how to work through a task or solve a problem;
- adapt language and modify questioning to suit pupils with SEND;
- provide targeted support by using teaching assistants effectively and, where possible, provide real-time marking and feedback;
- use assistive technology, multisensory resources and graphic organisers to enhance and support the learning experience;
- provide guided group practice with concrete and visual scaffolds as support;
- adapt the classroom space to suit all needs.

Education South West (n.d.) have produced a useful one-page guide entitled *Understanding Adaptive Teaching* which provides examples of in-the-moment adaptions (see **References**).

Case Study: Ecosystems

A year 4 class were studying ecosystems in their school environment. The teacher planned a series of lessons to ensure spaced retrieval practice of concepts and skills. This example shows how the teacher built on previous year 2 work on living things and their habitats to develop a deeper understanding of specific ecosystems. Similarly, by reviewing pupils' prior knowledge of the importance of sunlight for plant growth and introducing a simple audio-visual explanation of the basic principles of photosynthesis, pupils were prepared for a more in-depth study of photosynthesis in key stage 3. Barriers to learning were identified and adaptive teaching strategies deployed.

Table 5.1 Barriers to learning with adaptive teaching strategies.

Lessons	**Barriers to learning**	**Adaptive teaching**
Class review of the word habitat. Introduce concept of ecosystems.	Semantic knowledge, working memory and word finding difficulties.	Visual/symbol resources to support understanding of concept vocabulary.
Visit pond, wildflower and tree area in school environment. Make drawings of creatures observed.	Difficulties with listening, attention and fine motor skills. Erratic and impulsive behaviour when outside.	Pupils identify creatures for TA to photograph in each area. Set rules for careful behaviour around wildlife, adult to monitor.
Using a variety of information resources, pupils to produce fact cards about different creatures in the three ecosystems (name, habitat, food, size).	Difficulties with reading and information retrieval skills. Problems with organisational and presentation skills.	Guided reading with adult, paired reading with more confident reader, use of visual and IT resources. Writing frame or assistive technology for presentation.
Pre-teach terms producer and consumer.	Semantic knowledge, working memory and word finding difficulties.	Visual, symbol and cue card resources to support understanding of concept vocabulary.
Class review of term producer and the importance of sunlight to producers.	Semantic knowledge, working memory and word finding difficulties.	Teacher to model constructing a mind map (sun at centre, producers around).
Watch short video on producers and a simple introduction to photosynthesis.	Semantic knowledge, working memory.	Pictures of different producers labelled and displayed (use of Widget Symbols).
Introduce the term food chains (most food chains start with a producer). Pupils to compile own food chains (pictorial or written).	Problems with organisational and presentation skills.	Show a worked example of a food chain. Provide pictorial fact cards on foods eaten by consumers. Provide food chain templates.
Class review term consumer. Introduce the terms carnivore, herbivore and omnivore.	Semantic knowledge, working memory and word finding difficulties.	Display poster for each consumer category using Widget Symbols.
Use a variety of information resources to identify creatures belonging to each category. Present information using a Venn diagram.	Difficulties with reading and information retrieval skills. Problems with organisational and presentation skills.	Adult or peer group support with reading fact cards. Provide a Venn diagram template. Can present information pictorially.

(Continued)

Table 5.1 (Continued)

Lessons	Barriers to learning	Adaptive teaching
Class review and discussion of the word ecosystem and why carnivores, herbivores, and omnivores may need specific ecosystems or may move between them.	Semantic knowledge, working memory and word finding difficulties.	What am I? (identifying creature and consumer category from oral clues). This can be a whole class or group plenary activity to assess conceptual understanding.
Class to visit the three ecosystems in the school environment. Pose questions about habitat change.	Difficulties with listening, attention. Erratic and impulsive behaviour when outside.	Modify questions, adult to help pupils focus on a specific way in which one habitat might change. Set rules for careful behaviour around wildlife.
Think, pair, share - What if the pond dried up? What if the trees were chopped down? What if the wildflower area was changed into a car park?	Difficulties with creative thinking skills.	Chunk the activity. Adult to scaffold each part of the task. Identify a creature and its habitat. Identify a possible problem and its effect on the creature.
Ask pupils to choose a creature, think about how habitat change might affect them. Choose a way to show how the creature is affected by change (story, news report, poster, etc).	Difficulties with creative ideas and presentation skills.	Choice of alternative ways of recording ideas on eco awareness and habitat change for one creature (comic strip, writing frame, poster, Clicker software).
Link ideas to an awareness of global climate change and loss of habitats for people and animals.	Difficulty in understanding thoughts and feelings of others globally.	Relate global ideas to personal experiences (how you feel when things change in your house).

SEND: Autism, ADHD, SLCN.

Reflective Task 5.2

Consider lessons experienced or taught where adapting responses to specific situations and needs has been necessary.

The ability to be adaptable in a range of situations is an important characteristic of being a teacher. Despite careful planning, motivating activities and enthusiasm for the subject, there is often an element of the unknown which can disrupt the smooth running of a lesson. Being able to make adaptions, alter responses, change teaching strategies and resources to meet the needs of all pupils is part of the everyday life of a teacher. Important adaptations to consider for pupils with SEND include the following:

- Adaptations to the classroom to ensure accessibility, mobility and suitable seating positions for sensory needs.
- Giving warning to pupils when changing layout of the classroom for specific purposes such as art, music or drama.
- Providing adapted resources and strategies for visual and hearing impairment such as Braille, speech technology and dictation software, scan recorder pens, signing, Cued speech and Visual Phonics by Hand.
- Visual timetables and task plans providing a visual reminder of daily lesson sequences.
- Allowing extra time for processing information, answering and completing tasks.
- Providing dyslexia friendly typeface, coloured overlays, reading rulers and highlighters.
- Giving opportunities to use assistive technology to support learning, communication and interaction.
- Providing visual resources such as pictures, diagrams, maps, charts, posters, mind maps, cue cards, prompt sheets, wall charts, books and computer graphics to support understanding.
- Using concrete materials to help pupils understand abstract ideas. Practical resources may include: maths apparatus, science investigation materials, constructional apparatus, individual whiteboards, highlighter pens, magnetic letters and numbers, IT control activities, art and design tools/media, musical instruments and language/word games.
- Using audio-visual resources, IT programmes and videos across all areas of the curriculum to support understanding within topics.
- Provision of tactile and sensory objects to help pupils respond to situations causing anxiety.
- Scaffolding – using visual aids, cue cards, prompt sheets, wall charts, visual task organisers, word mats, story starters, think-alouds, pre-teaching and writing frames.
- Modelling showing pupils how to solve a problem or complete a task by demonstrating and verbalising thought processes at each stage.
- Chunking – breaking longer tasks into smaller steps, each with its own clear learning objective and success criteria.

- Educational Visits related to specific topics and subjects – many museums and galleries provide access information adapted for pupils with SEND. The British Museum provides information on how to organise a visit and is an example of how many public places provide adapted access and information for visitors with SEND.

Case Study: The Crow and the Pitcher

A year 2 class read Aesop's fable *The Crow and the Pitcher* as a shared reading activity. The teacher left a solution to the crow's problem open-ended. Mixed ability groups were provided with narrow-necked containers, with a small amount of water at the bottom, and a variety of resources available to the crow (leaves, twigs, stones, grass). Pupils were asked to think, pair, share ideas for a solution to the crow's problem using only their thumb and finger, representing the crow's beak, to find ways to use the resources.

Several ideas were tried, but each time the children realised the crow would have to let go of the resource to drink the water. Max became frustrated with trying to pick up things using just his finger and thumb. The teacher reminded him of the story *Mr Archimedes Bath* by Pamela Allen, a story the class had read previously.

Max thought for a few minutes and then began to pick up some stones and put them in the container. 'Look! It's like Mr Archimedes,' he said, 'The water's getting higher.' The teacher asked Max to explain about the displacement of water which he did with confidence followed by a class discussion on the amazing ability of birds to find food and water and build nests with only their beaks and claws to help them.

SEND: Dyspraxia (Developmental coordination disorder).

Reflective Task 5.3

Why did the teacher feel it was necessary to give Max a clue to the solution?

Discuss with colleagues and peers how to recognise when to intervene during a problem-solving activity.

Multisensory Approaches to Teaching for Pupils With SEND

Cognitive overload often occurs when a task is complex. By organising the task into simpler chunks, and using a multisensory approach, the cognitive load can be reduced. Multisensory teaching strategies can be incorporated into most lessons and provide opportunities for pupils with SEND to develop learning skills and consolidate their conceptual understanding.

A multisensory approach is a way of teaching that engages more than one sense at a time. There is a diversity of ways in which pupils can experience learning in a multisensory way. Here are some ideas for activating the senses:

Visual (seeing) – learning through access to visual resources:

- Diagrams
- Photographs, paintings and pictures
- Television, visual IT resources
- Posters
- Mind maps
- Graphs and charts
- Picture/symbol cue cards
- Maps and plans

Auditory (speaking and listening) - learning through speaking and listening activities, using audio resources:

- Role play and drama
- Language and word games
- Puppets
- Listening books
- Music and songs
- Shared and guided reading/writing activities
- Think, pair, share activities.
- PSHE activities and circle time

Tactile (touch) – learning through tactile resources:

- Art and design using a range of media and materials
- Sand and water activities
- Activities using tactile letters and numbers
- Design and technology using a range of materials
- Constructional resources such as Lego

- Topic feely bag using objects of different shapes, size and textures
- Maths and science tasks using manipulatives
- Making and playing musical instruments

Kinaesthetic (movement) – learning through physical activity or body movement:

- Dance – music, movement and mime
- Role play and puppets
- PE and games activities
- Hydro experiences adapted to pupils physical and sensory needs
- IT control activities
- Practical science investigations
- Exploring the environment (history, science, geography walks)
- Gardening (indoors and outdoors)

Olfactory and gustatory (smell and taste) – learning through the senses of smell and taste:

- Cooking – focus on use of sense of taste and smell when cooking
- Scented playdough for multisensory activities
- Like or dislike – using semi covered containers, investigate popular and unpopular smells
- Comparisons – hard/soft, hot/cold, sweet/sour, chewy/crunchy taste
- Comparison – taste of chocolate bar with melted chocolate
- Smell walk, in a familiar environment
- Match the smell to a picture or photograph
- History – taste food from the past

Case Study: Silence

By the age of three, Ellie was considered to be a chatterbox delighting her family with her ability to entertain. However, while giving birth to Ellie's brother, her mother had a stroke and was hospitalised for several months. During that time, grandparents cared for the baby during the day while Ellie was sent to a nursery school.

(Continued)

At nursery school, the staff found that Ellie seemed unable to communicate orally though she followed instructions and was generally quiet and well-behaved. At home, Ellie communicated normally with the family but with less exuberance than before. When her mother returned home, Ellie refused to go to nursery school but enjoyed being a helper for her brother.

When Ellie started primary school, she made no protests about attending but, after a few weeks, her teacher queried her lack of oral communication. The teacher and parents decided the possible cause for her silence might be anxiety and agreed to several strategies to support Ellie. These included the following:

- Establishing relaxed and familiar classroom routines and using music as a calming technique.
- Ensuring the availability of a buddy and a trusted adult when needed.
- Providing visual timetables and task plans.
- Using a multisensory approach to learning.
- Encouraging attempts to communicate through non-verbal means (gestures, pictures and symbols, assistive technology), particularly for basic needs.

Ellie's parents did not want her to be referred to a Speech and Language therapist.

The first breakthrough for Ellie came at the end of year 1 when she began whispering to her friend and, after a while, to a trusted adult. Everyone agreed to let Ellie take things at her own pace and, by the time she was in year 4, she began to take a more active part in cooperative learning.

SEND: Selective mutism.

Reflective Task 5.4

Why do you think Ellie's parents didn't want her to be referred to a Speech and Language therapist?

How do you think the teachers were able to assess Ellie's academic progress?

Adaptive Teaching and Graphic Organisers

There is evidence to suggest that dual coding (providing pupils with verbal and visual materials together) can be effective in improving long-term memory (Clark and Pavio, 1991).

Dual coding can be enhanced by using graphic organisers which act as visual thinking tools. Research findings by Dexter et al. (2011) suggest that the use of graphic organisers can be associated with increases in vocabulary knowledge, comprehension and inferential knowledge. However, all pupils, and particularly those with SEND, should be taught clearly how to use graphic organisers for them to be effective.

Using graphic organisers as a visual reference or as an alternative method of organising and recording information can make reading and writing tasks not only accessible but also more enjoyable. Clickerboard (Crick Software) is a useful planning tool for the creation of a variety of graphic organisers and Widget symbols can support the development of semantic knowledge and word finding skills (see **11 – SEND Resources**). Graphic organisers can include:

- **Labelled pictures** as vocabulary cues for writing narratives or as part of a topic (label parts of an insect, a flower, a person, a building).
- **Word webs** compiled as vocabulary support related to a topic or subject.
- **Writing frames** as templates to provide structure for writing tasks. A writing frame provides an outline of what is expected with headings and sentence starters related to the genre (book review, news report, letter/postcard, storyboard).
- **Story maps** used as a pictorial map of events for a personal experience or for a story showing where the events took place and the sequence of events.
- **Comic strips** to help pupils organise a sequence of events such as a story or personal experience using pictures and simple speech bubble sentences. The speech bubble format can be used to introduce the use of question marks and exclamation marks.
- **Posters** to help relate information learnt in specific topic/subject areas, such as Amazing Animals, Wicked Weather. Posters can be shared with the class and act as a visual reminder of important facts and ideas.
- **Mind maps** to help pupils organise information visually in order to understand how new concepts can be linked with those already known.
- **Flow Charts** to help pupils with organising and sequencing their ideas when recording processes encountered across the curriculum.
- **Charts and graphs** such as bar charts, pie charts, pictographs and histograms to help pupils represent data by using symbols, lines, colours or pictures.
- **Tables** to help pupils represent data using words or numbers.
- **Diagrams** that show relationships and how things work together (water cycle, life cycles, electrical circuits). A Venn diagram is used to identify the relationship between sets of data. A Carroll diagram is used to separate and sort data into criteria.

- **Timelines** used to show events that happen over a period of time. They can be presented both horizontally and vertically. Timelines may relate to the chronology of personal events, historical events, journeys or events in a story.

Flexible Grouping

Links to the ITTECF 5.3

- **5.5 Learn that** flexibly grouping pupils within a class to provide more tailored support can support learning, but care should be taken to monitor its impact on attainment, behaviour, engagement and motivation, particularly for low attaining pupils (DfE, 2024a, p. 20).

Flexible grouping is an important element of high-quality teaching (EEF, 2021a). Pupils with SEND benefit from taking part in group activities but putting them in a group does not mean they will cooperate effectively. Johnson and Johnson (2014) point out, 'Not all group efforts are cooperative. Simply placing individuals in groups and telling them to work together does not in, and of itself result in cooperative efforts' (p. 845). Teachers need to monitor pupils' engagement and behaviour towards each other and initially some pupils with SEND may need to work with a trusted partner.

For many pupils with SLD and PMLD, in resource bases or special schools, the curriculum will be individualised and tailored support detailed in the pupil's EHCP. However, this should not mean that the pupil's learning environment is restricted. Although they receive a high level of adult support, they benefit from taking part in activities within small groups or in the wider community. Aubin (2023) notes that the way teachers organise groups should not perpetuate the belief that intelligence is fixed. Rather, groupings should be based on the idea that support is beneficial for all pupils some of the time.

Groupings can vary according to the subject or topic tasks and the nature of the pupils' barriers to learning. Below are some different ways in which teachers can use flexible grouping to support pupils with SEND in different contexts.

Whole Class (Mixed Ability)

Can be used in all areas of the curriculum, but for pupils with SEND, it's important to ensure clear, communication strategies are used, to suit their needs, including the use of assistive technology. Strategies such as activating prior knowledge, modelling and scaffolding for new learning, explicit instruction given in manageable chunks, making effective use of TAs as well as technology and audio-visual aids are all essential for supporting pupils with SEND during whole class teaching.

Guided Group Work (Similar Ability)

Useful when pupils need to practise similar levels of reading, writing, maths or IT skills.

Cooperative Learning Groups (Mixed Ability)

Useful for science investigations, PE activities, role play, PSHE activities and practical activities where pupils with SEND can contribute using their strengths while, at the same time, being able to access peer support. For some pupils with autistic or sensory difficulties, working with a partner initially may be necessary.

Group Interventions (Similar Ability)

Can be used for support groups when intervention programmes are needed to help pupils develop, consolidate, transfer and generalise knowledge, concepts and skills.

Think, Pair, Share (Mixed Ability Groups)

Helps pupils work together to solve a problem or answer a question. Pupils are given time to think before sharing their ideas with a partner in their group. At a given time, each pair can share their ideas with another pair and then with the group emphasising that all ideas are valuable. Some pupils with autism may wish to work with a partner but need adult support to interact with the group.

Practical Projects (Mixed Ability Groups)

Give all pupils opportunities to show their strengths in particular areas of the curriculum. This may be in design and technology projects, music activities, educational visits, geography fieldwork and art projects.

Response Partners (Similar Ability)

Pupils support each other through the writing process (plan, draft, edit, proofread, present). Some pupils with SEND may need the support of an adult response partner and scribe.

Reading Buddies (Similar or Mixed Ability)

The 'reading buddies' can be pupils with a similar reading ability, older/younger pupil, confident/not so confident reader, TA/pupil, volunteer/pupil. For this to be effective for pupils with SEND, a specific time during each day needs to be set aside for this activity (15–20 minutes is adequate).

Individual (Targeted Support)

Activities will focus on individual needs and may be linked to the development of specific skills or ongoing therapies.

Although pupils with SLD and PMLD need to access an individualised curriculum, flexible grouping will allow these pupils to benefit from spending time as part of a group within a classroom base or in the wider school environment. Activities can support the development of communication and interaction skills, structured turn-taking and the sharing of social and emotional responses, allowing pupils to develop a sense of community.

Interventions and Targeted Support

Links to the ITTECF 5.4

- **5.7 Learn that** pupils with SEND are likely to require additional or adapted support; working closely with colleagues, parents/carers, and pupils to understand barriers to learning and identify effective strategies is essential (DfE, 2024a, p. 21).

The term 'intervention' describes a short-term focused teaching approach offering a specific set of outcomes based on tried and tested practical research. Using assessment to gather information regarding individual pupils' progress, interventions should be focused on specific targets with close monitoring and evaluation of their effectiveness (EEF, 2021e).

Research evidence by the EEF (2021i) on making the best use of TAs identified features of effective interventions:

1. Sessions occur regularly during a week and have set times for delivery.
2. Sessions are timetabled and are sustained over a period of weeks.
3. Pupils are matched to the intervention according to need.
4. Training is given to the adults who will follow the structure and suggested delivery of the intervention.
5. Resources to support the intervention are readily available.
6. Pupil progress is tracked through formative assessment.
7. Connections are made between the intervention and classroom teaching.

Targeted support is an educational approach which personalises learning around the pupil's communicative, cognitive, social, emotional, physical and sensory needs. Where pupils have an EHCP, interventions or targeted support may be suggested by external advisors and therapists and shared with the pupil and family.

In resource bases and special schools, individual learning pathways may be developed. A pupil's EHCP details the interventions and targeted support which is reviewed regularly with the pupil and family including all those involved with supporting the individual. This may involve the input of a variety of professionals depending on the pupil's level of need (see Pupil Support Profiles in **9 – SEND Areas of Need and Support**).

Using Technology

Links to the ITTECF 5.5

- **5.9 Learn that** technology, including educational software and assistive technology, can support teaching and learning for pupils with SEND (DfE, 2024a, p. 21).

The 21st century has brought many changes in the use of technology in schools. Most mainstream schools have a dedicated space for IT lessons and resources as well as having whiteboards and other devices available in classrooms. Resource bases and special schools use technology for specific individual and group interventions and for some individualised learning. In special schools, technology is an integral part of the teaching and learning environment which helps to unlock opportunities for all pupils whatever their needs.

Inclusive Technology supplies a wide range of assistive technology for pupils with SEND including the following:

- Eye Gaze technology.
- Sensory technology.
- Communicate Symwriter V2.
- Adapted I-pads, keyboards, mouse controls and switches.
- Touch pads and touch screens.
- Boardmaker software.
- Go Talk speech output devices.
- Clicker.
- Helpkidzlearn app.

Augmentative and Alternative Communication (AAC)

Augmentative and Alternative Communication (AAC) incorporates the strategies and devices that can be used to communicate when pupils have difficulty using speech. They may have a developmental delay affecting their speech or a cognitive, emotional, physical or genetic disorder. AAC can include:

- **Facial expressions** – pupils may be able to convey some of their wishes and needs through their facial expressions.
- **Sign language** – Makaton is a language programme that uses signs and symbols to help pupils communicate. Makaton signs are very visual and concrete at the early levels.
- **Body language and gestures** – pupils may use body movements and gestures to convey specific messages and communicate wishes and needs. These may include head nodding and shaking, pointing and eye motion.
- **PECS (Picture Exchange Communication System)** – PECS is an augmentative, alternative training package. It is designed to help pupils with ASC and other communication difficulties to begin communicating through picture/symbol and object exchange.
- **Eye Gaze technology** – this is an electronic device that allows a pupil to control a tablet or computer by looking at words or commands on a screen. A camera picks up reflections from the pupil's cornea and retina.
- **Keyboards** – pupils may type in a message which is converted into speech. TextSpeak is a well-known provider of this type of AAC. TextAloud is a new iOS App developed by Ace Centre. It is a text-to-speech app which reads any text entered into it.
- **Symbol communication cards** – pupils with communication difficulties may benefit from using symbols across a range of learning experiences. Widget Online uses symbols to support text. It's useful for creating visual timetables, vocabulary cards, stories and other visual communication resources.
- **Go Talk speech output devices** – these are battery operated communication devices which can be used to convey pre-recorded messages for pupils who have speech difficulties. The messages can be pre-recorded by the pupil's support network.

The Ace Centre provides a range of AAC resources and downloads for teachers to use for adaptive purposes in the classroom.

6

Assessment

Chapter Objectives

This chapter examines the different types of assessment used in primary education. It explores the principles and purpose of assessment and how it provides teachers with information about pupils' knowledge, understanding, skills and barriers to learning. The chapter examines how assessment may be collected and used by schools and other agencies to support pupils with SEND. The chapter also highlights:

- the graduated approach;
- assessment without levels;
- the engagement model;
- feedback.

Principles and Purpose of Assessment

Links to the ITTECF 6.1

- **6.1 Learn that** effective assessment is critical to teaching because it provides teachers with information about pupils' understanding and needs.
- **6.2 Learn that** good assessment helps teachers avoid being over-influenced by potentially misleading factors, such as how busy pupils appear.
- **6.3 Learn that** before using any assessment, teachers should be clear about the decision it will be used to support and be able to justify its use (DfE, 2024a, p. 22).

Assessment is an integral part of teaching through which pupils with SEND can show their knowledge, skills and understanding of an area of learning. Assessment can also provide the teacher with further knowledge of the pupil's achievements and specific barriers to learning. As the *Final report of the Commission on Assessment Without Levels* (DfE, 2015) stated, 'A fully inclusive approach to assessment in all mainstream and specialist settings is one where policy and practice are designed to promote the outcomes of all pupils' (p. 38). For teachers in primary schools, the principles and purpose of assessment are to:

- Enable pupils to show what they know, understand and can apply, recognising positive achievements and continuing progress;
- Gather diagnostic information for specific pupils to identify their needs;
- Make use of formative assessments to check for prior knowledge, any pre-existing misconceptions and levels of understanding;
- Provide clear, reliable information, free from bias that supports curriculum planning, teaching and learning;
- Ensure the type of assessment used is time efficient, manageable, reliable and fair to all pupils;
- Support smooth transition as pupils move from class to class and from key stage to key stage;
- Provide information to be shared with pupils, families and school governors;
- Fulfil statutory requirements and ensure coverage of the national curriculum.

The Graduated Approach

When planning for inclusion, assessment of a pupil's areas of success as well as their barriers to learning is an essential element of effective teaching. The graduated approach (assess, plan, do, review) is a response tool which helps to identify and support pupils with SEND (see **Introduction**). The SEND Code of Practice 0 – 25 years (DfE & DoH, 2015) outlines ways in which assessment of pupils with SEND may take place. It clearly states that, in collaboration with the SENCo, the teacher should analyse a pupil's needs and identify the type of support needed. Initial information should be gathered from the teacher's ongoing formative assessments and possibly diagnostic assessment by the SENCo. If necessary, professional agencies may be involved in a pupil's assessment, discussing outcomes and the way forward, alongside the pupil, their family and the school staff.

Assessment Without Levels

In 2011, concern was expressed that the use of levels in both summative and formative assessment was inhibiting for pupils and teachers and particularly for pupils with SEND.

Inspections by Ofsted often resulted in schools being evaluated on assessment results with pupils being moved on at too fast a pace. Progression was not focused on the depth of pupils' understanding but rather moving through levels which, for some pupils, left gaps in their knowledge and skills development. Consequently, the *Commission on Assessment Without Levels* (DfE, 2015) concluded that the use of levels for assessment had adversely affected teaching. Assessments were not being used to identify pupil understanding but rather as a label which could impact motivation and enjoyment of learning.

By removing the assessment of pupils against national curriculum numerical levels, the government has allowed schools to focus on formative assessment where regular monitoring, feedback and interventions support pupils in their learning. Assessment without levels means that pupils can be assessed against the national curriculum age-related expectations for their year group using four categories:

- **Emerging:** Working below the year group expectations and in need of support and specific interventions.
- **Developing:** Working within the year group expectations but not yet secure in a number of areas, still needing some additional support.
- **Secure:** Have achieved the majority of the end of year expectations and are secure in most areas.
- **Greater Depth:** Are secure in all the end of year expectations and can begin adding more depth and breadth to their knowledge. They will also begin to use and apply the skills they have learnt in different contexts independently.

Case Study: Mechanisms

Amira was a friendly member of a year 5 class. She was able to communicate with her peer group using words and phrases learnt during the five months she had been in the UK. She was the eldest child of an asylum-seeking family with two younger siblings attending the same school. Amira was receiving EAL support with developing literacy skills and was keen to take part in group activities.

As an introduction to the understanding and use of mechanical systems in design and technology sessions, Amira's class were asked to investigate items from home and the ways in which they worked. Each group chose an item and prepared an illustrated talk to present to the class. Some chose simple mechanisms such as scissors, scales, a torch, a folding chair and a spray bottle. Amira's group were fascinated when she drew a diagram of the workings of a toilet system. Together the group prepared their presentation, and, on the day, Amira brought in a model of a working toilet system constructed with the help of her father. He had been a plumber and Amira had often helped him at work. Each member of the group supported Amira in giving a fascinating presentation to the class.

(Continued)

As the pupils continued with the project, and began designing and making their own mechanical models, the teacher was able to assess Amira as working at greater depth in design and technology. She also showed how well she could communicate her ideas using visual, verbal and tactile cues.

No SEND: EAL support.

Reflective Task 6.1

How do you think the teacher could share her assessment of Amira's knowledge and skills with her parents and help the family to integrate into the local community?

Types of Assessment

Currently, assessments used in schools may be summative, formative, diagnostic and self or peer assessed.

Summative Assessments

Summative assessments are usually given at the end of studying a unit of work. They are used to evaluate pupils' achievements and are often recorded as grades. Summative assessment may include the following:

- early years foundation stage profile assessment;
- reception baseline assessments;
- optional key stage 1 tests;
- phonics screening checks;
- statutory key stage 2 tests;
- year 4 multiplication table check;
- standardised reading, spelling or mathematics tests chosen by the school;
- written project or portfolio to show pupils' understanding of a topic;
- oral assessment (presentations);
- performance assessments used in subjects such as music and physical education.

Some summative tests may be norm-referenced which compare a pupil's performance to the performance of peers in a norm group, usually of similar age. Some tests are criterion-referenced and compare a pupil's performance to an objective standard. When choosing published summative tests, it's important they are relevant, appropriate and used for the purpose for which they were designed. It's also important to consider ways that test scores can be influenced by physical, social and emotional factors.

Formative Assessments

Formative assessments represent the ongoing monitoring of a pupil's learning to provide information for teachers to improve the learning experience. Wiliam (2018) highlights the importance of clarifying, sharing and supporting pupils in understanding learning intentions and success criteria as an effective formative assessment strategy.

Through feedback and the development of self-awareness, pupils with SEND can be guided into recognising their strengths and barriers to learning. Formative assessment may be undertaken through observations, verbal and written feedback, self and peer assessment against success criteria and end of topic projects which can be informal and fun. Assessment activities may include the following:

- **Quizzes**, in different formats – related to the topic or subject being studied.
- **Did you know?** Pupils compile fun facts related to a topic or subject and share them with others in the group or class.
- **Think-about Reading** – group reading tasks where pupils think about and discuss open-ended questions related to the text.
- **True or False** – identifying true facts related to a topic or subject.
- **Mind Maps**, written or pictorial – showing the main areas of knowledge both prior and after studying a topic or subject (using two colours to display progression).
- **Group or individual presentations** (subject-based or cross-curricular).
- **Reports** – pupils give a report in their chosen format to their group at the end of a project (teacher assessed).
- **Agree/Disagree** – teacher/support adult makes a statement relevant to the topic being studied, pupils respond with reasons for agreeing or disagreeing.
- **Teacher/adult observations** and discussions with pupils during guided group sessions.
- **Compositional writing/keyboarding/speech-to-text tasks** with clear learning objectives and success criteria.

- **Open-ended questioning** during group and class discussions with opportunities for verbal or non-verbal responses.
- **Problem solving or investigation tasks** alongside peers or adult facilitator.

Diagnostic Assessments

Diagnostic assessments are used as a way for teachers and other professionals to assess a pupil's strengths and weaknesses in specific areas of their development, and then plan ways in which to provide support. For example, diagnostic assessments can be used to analyse speech and language difficulties, dyslexia, reading comprehension, the understanding of numeracy concepts as well a range of key learning skills. For a pupil to be assessed as needing an Education, Health and Care plan (EHCP), professionals undertake diagnostic assessments alongside school-based formative and summative assessments to determine the specific level of difficulty and support provision required.

Self-Assessment

Self-assessment is a method of encouraging pupils to evaluate and assess their own work. This allows them to develop greater self-awareness and supports individual progress.

Peer Assessment

Peer assessment encourages pupils to work in partnership and evaluate each other's work against set learning objectives and criteria.

Case Study: Reading Beyond the Lines

Mia's parents were concerned she had not been identified as more or highly able. They pointed out she was able to read the newspaper, though not quite seven years old. The teacher explained that Mia could read the words by using her excellent phonemic and phonological skills but showed little understanding of the content. After some discussion, the parents agreed that Mia should be assessed using appropriate comprehension tests. The results showed that Mia needed support with developing her semantic knowledge, particularly with predicting unknown words using contextual cues. She also needed to develop prediction, deduction and inferencing skills.

The teacher praised Mia for her phonic skills and explained how, in addition, she needed to use her thinking skills when reading. Mia's parents agreed to play literacy games at home to improve Mia's levels of comprehension. After seeing how much Mia enjoyed interacting with the games, her parents became less anxious about her literacy development.

SEND: No specific need but encouraged to read for meaning and enjoyment.

Reflective Task 6.2

How do you think a diagnostic assessment helped Mia's parents understand her literacy development needs?

WALT and WILF

In mainstream classes, the two acronyms WALT and WILF have been developed to help teachers identify and share learning objectives, and the related success criteria, with pupils at the beginning of a lesson.

Visual displays of WALT and WILF at the beginning of an activity are useful reminders for both adults and pupils.

- **WALT – We Are Learning To:** Establishes, in child-friendly language, the aims and objectives of the learning activity.
- **WILF – What I'm Looking For:** Outlines, in child-friendly language, what the teacher expects to see in the pupils' work in order to achieve the learning goals.

The Rochford Review

Pupils with severe learning difficulties and profound and multiple learning difficulties may be able to take part in some summative assessments but, for pupils with complex needs, the *Rochford Review* (Standards and Testing Agency, 2016) recognised that age-related expectations were not appropriate for those pupils working below the standard of national curriculum assessments. The review made a number of recommendations, one of which emphasised that:

> *Initial teacher training (ITT) and Continuing Professional Development (CPD) for staff in educational settings should reflect the need for teachers to have a greater understanding of assessing pupils working below the standard of national curriculum tests, including those pupils with SEND who are not engaged in subject-specific learning.*
>
> (Standards and Testing Agency, 2016, p. 7)

The Engagement Model

For those pupils who have an EHCP, are working below the standard of national curriculum assessments and are not engaged in subject-specific study, the *Rochford Review* (Standards and

Testing Agency, 2016) recommended pupils should be assessed against aspects of cognition and learning which could be reported to families. Consequently, in 2020, the government introduced the engagement model as an assessment tool. This model replaced the use of the old P Scales and combined both a summative and formative approach. The model specifies five areas of engagement to assess a pupil's progress:

1. exploration;
2. realisation;
3. anticipation;
4. persistence;
5. initiation.

> *Progress through each of the 5 areas of engagement should be measured by identifying how established the pupil is against each of the areas of engagement. This will differ for each pupil according to their profile of needs as set out in their Education, Health and Care (EHC) plan. The model combines a formative and summative assessment approach. It should be used to assess pupils' progress and development regularly throughout the year.*
>
> (Standards and Testing Agency, 2020, p. 5)

The model allows teachers to observe the level of a pupil's engagement in learning during different activities, enabling 'assess, plan, do and review' to operate as a continuous cycle. This approach allows the progress of pupils with SEND to be measured over time.

Feedback

Links to the ITTECF 6.2

- **6.4 Learn that** to be of value, teachers use information from assessments to inform the decisions they make; in turn, pupils must be able to act on feedback for it to have an effect.
- **6.5 Learn that** high-quality feedback can be written or verbal; it is likely to be accurate and clear, encourage further effort, and provide specific guidance on how to improve.
- **6.6 Learn that** over time, feedback should support pupils to monitor and regulate their own learning (DfE, 2024a, p. 22).

Constructive feedback can support pupils with SEND in recognising what they have achieved and how to take the next step in their learning. Hattie (2012) emphasises that teachers should not combine feedback with praise, rather that praise should be part of a positive culture in the school environment and constructive feedback a part of a pupil's learning process. Hattie (2012) also points out that effective feedback helps pupils answer the questions: Where am I going? How am I going there? Where to next?

Hattie and Timperley (2007) highlight three levels of feedback:

1. **Task/product level** (for the novice) identifies whether the task has been completed correctly or incorrectly. The teacher/adult may model the task again for the pupil providing more information and direction.
2. **Process level** (for proficient level) is aimed at helping the pupil understand and improve the processes needed to complete a task. Feedback should support pupils in developing suitable learning strategies, recognise relationships and connections as well as understand and rectify their mistakes.
3. **Self-regulation level** (for the competent level) is about helping the pupil to monitor and evaluate their thinking. Feedback at this level needs to support the pupil in developing the ability to reflect on their choice of learning strategies and begin to make their own decisions on how to move forward.

Case Study: Digit Cards

A small group of year 2 pupils experienced difficulties when writing double digit numbers and frequently reversed the digit order. They were given opportunities to work in a targeted support group using digit cards to play number games. As they became more confident, they were asked to investigate the features of odd and even numbers. Leo became fascinated with numbers and began using the digit cards for his own personal investigations with larger numbers. By observing Leo, and encouraging him to demonstrate his findings, the teacher was able to assess the level of his ability and suggest ways in which he could make connections and recognise relationships between numbers. It soon became clear that Leo was able to act on feedback and make good progress when given the opportunity to show his findings using visual and tactile apparatus.

SEND: SLCN (Speech, Language and Communication Needs).

Reflective Task 6.3

Consider how manipulatives can be used to support formative assessment in mathematics.

The Education Endowment Foundation (2021g) makes six recommendations for teacher feedback to improve pupil learning:

1. Lay the foundations for effective feedback.
2. Deliver appropriately timed feedback that focuses on moving learning forward.
3. Plan for how pupils will receive and use feedback.
4. Carefully consider how to use purposeful, and time-efficient, written feedback.
5. Carefully consider how to use purposeful verbal feedback.
6. Design a school feedback policy that prioritises and exemplifies the principles of effective feedback (pp. 10–11).

Feedback in mainstream primary classrooms should be adapted to support pupils with SEND. Effective feedback should:

- make use of formative assessment and relate findings to learning objectives and success criteria;
- be relevant to the pupil's level of understanding with scaffolded prompts to correct any misconceptions;
- be given in real time, not as part of a later discussion;
- motivate pupils to develop what they do well and strengthen areas of difficulty;
- be delivered through verbal, signing, symbol or written responses using Augmentative and Alternative Communication (AAC) where necessary;
- allow time for pupils to respond to feedback;
- support pupils with choosing the strategies needed to complete the task and encourage next step targets;
- model peer group assessment and self-assessment strategies to encourage pupils to monitor and regulate their own learning;
- work with colleagues to identify efficient and alternative ways of providing feedback (oral and written).

Feedback and the Engagement Model

For those pupils who have an EHCP and are working below the standard of national curriculum assessments, feedback is an essential part of learning. Feedback helps pupils with SLD and PMLD to understand what is happening during the day and supports them in beginning to make sense of their learning environment. Feedback may need to be provided using AAC (Augmentative and Alternative Communication) and assistive technologies.

Feedback can be linked to assessment using the engagement model.

Exploration

> *This shows whether a pupil can build on their initial reaction to a new stimulus or activity; for example, whether they display more than an involuntary or startled reaction to the activity. Additionally, the pupil may be interested in and curious about the stimulus or activity; for example, they may notice it or reach out to it.*
>
> (Standards and Testing Agency, 2020, p. 5)

When a pupil shows an interest in exploring a group or class activity such as planting cress seeds, feedback can be given by scaffolding the task with the pupil individually. The nature and level of the scaffolding will depend on the cognitive and physical ability of the pupil. If the pupil's interest continues to be stimulated as the cress begins to grow, and they indicate a wish to explore the growing plants, they can be supported in giving the cress water. Feedback can indicate to the pupil that they have contributed to the growing process by giving water. Over time, further interest in the seed growing activity may be observed such as the pupil wanting to explore touching and smelling the cress culminating in the opportunity to eat a cress sandwich with the group or class. Feedback can be given by modelling a personal response to the experience and asking the pupil to give their individual response using AAC. Exploration can be identified when a pupil shows a curiosity and interest in an activity and wants to engage further. By giving appropriate feedback, exploration can become more established allowing the pupil to develop new knowledge and skills.

Realisation

> *This shows how the pupil interacts with a new stimulus or activity or discovers a new aspect of a familiar stimulus or activity. They will display behaviours that show they want more control of the stimulus or activity, for example by stopping it or trying to make changes to it. The pupil will often show what familiar adults consider to be 'surprise', 'excitement', 'delight', 'amazement' or 'fear'.*
>
> (Standards and Testing Agency, 2020, p. 5)

When a pupil is introduced to a new toy and shows a reaction (excitement, surprise, concern), they demonstrate whether they may like to play with the toy or not. By modelling how the toy works, the adult can encourage the pupil to explore ways in which they can play with it themselves. As the pupil realises the possibilities, the adult can give feedback by scaffolding the pupil's attempts. As realisation grows, the pupil may display behaviours that show they want more control of the toy. Realisation becomes more established when the pupil can use similar knowledge and skills with other toys or activities.

Anticipation

> *This shows how much the pupil predicts, expects or associates a stimulus or activity with an event. They may anticipate that a familiar activity is about to start or finish by interpreting cues or prompts such as auditory (what they hear), tactile (what they feel) and visual (what they see).*
>
> (Standards and Testing Agency, 2020, p. 5)

Anticipation is when a pupil is able to interpret different cues or prompts to anticipate an activity. For example, when a pupil observes preparations for a music therapy session, they may associate certain objects and aspects of the preparation with a previous musical activity and display a response. To encourage anticipation, an adult can present cues and prompts using a multisensory approach. Feedback can include providing opportunities for shared peer interaction where pupils can observe different ways of responding to music. Observing a pupil's ability to anticipate allows teachers to assess their understanding of cause and effect which, in turn, allows teachers to help them develop their memory skills.

Persistence

> *This shows whether the pupil can sustain their attention in a stimulus or activity for long enough that they can actively try to find out more and interact with it.*
>
> (Standards and Testing Agency, 2020, p. 5)

To encourage a pupil with PMLD to persist with an activity, it needs to be one which they will enjoy. It may be an activity involving tactile play such as sand and water or it may involve operating switches to interact with a game or toy. By observing activities that the pupil enjoys and giving feedback in the form of interactive encouragement, adults can motivate pupils to develop what they do well and strengthen areas of difficulty. Persistence in an activity helps a pupil develop knowledge and skills for other areas of development.

Initiation

> *This shows how much, and the different ways, a pupil investigates a stimulus or activity in order to bring about a desired outcome. The pupil will act spontaneously and independently during a familiar activity without waiting for direction.*
>
> (Standards and Testing Agency, 2020, p. 5)

A pupil will often act spontaneously when investigating a familiar activity particularly if it's one they enjoy. For example, a pupil may indicate they would like to take part in an interactive sensory story by reaching out to touch the sensory items or turn a page in the book. The teacher or supporting adult can give feedback by encouraging the pupil to take the next step in sharing the story. This may lead to the pupil sharing a story independently with another pupil or adult.

Assessment – The Way Forward

Links to the ITTECF 6.3

- **6.7 Learn that** working with colleagues to identify efficient approaches to assessment is important; assessment can become onerous and have a disproportionate impact on workload (DfE, 2024a, p. 23).

An up-to-date awareness of the current purposes, processes and principles relating to assessment is an important part of teaching. Despite the changes made to assessment procedures during the past few years, many educational professionals have serious concerns about the impact of high stakes statutory testing of primary age children, particularly those with SEND, as well as the onerous and disproportionate impact on teacher workload.

The Independent Commission on Assessment in Primary Education (ICAPE) was established to review assessment policies and practices in primary schools in England. ICAPE's (Butterfield et al., 2022) report on the future of assessment in primary schools concluded that policies and practices are in need of improvement. The report recommended twelve main principles, two of which are highlight below:

- Assessment is designed to support inclusive education for all children.
- Assessment of pupils provides a holistic picture of pupils' achievements that reflects the whole curriculum, encompassing a wide range of understanding including creative thinking (Butterfield et al., 2022, p. 34).

Moss et al. (2021) advocate removing high stakes, high pressure annual tests such as SATs and replacing them with a longitudinal sampling system. They argue how a more longitudinal approach would take greater account of pupil wellbeing, enjoyment in learning, socio-emotional outcomes and place more value on wider skills such as oracy. Similarly, the 2021 report produced by the 'More Than a Score' campaign questioned whether current statutory assessment is being used to measure school performance rather than as a diagnostic tool to support pupils. The report also highlights how much valuable learning time is lost to preparation for statutory tests, which is particularly damaging to pupils with SEND.

Developing a more holistic and inclusive approach to assessment for pupils with SEND, where all aspects of a pupil's development are considered, alongside careful consideration of pupil wellbeing is essential. Placing greater emphasis on personal achievement and the joy of learning will have a positive impact on the progress of all pupils. As teachers, it's important to remember that good assessment for pupils with SEND is good assessment for all.

7

Managing Behaviour

Chapter Objectives

This chapter examines ways in which schools can provide predictable and secure environments with established routines and positive behaviour modelled. It also explores:

- building effective relationships;
- behaviour for learning;
- supporting pupils to self-regulate emotions and develop an empathetic understanding of others;
- intrinsic and extrinsic factors affecting motivation;
- understanding and supporting pupil behaviour.

Establishing Predictable and Secure Learning Environments

Links to the ITTECF 7.1

- **7.1 Learn that** establishing and reinforcing routines, including through positive reinforcement, can help create an effective learning environment.
- **7.2 Learn that** a predictable and secure environment benefits all pupils, including younger pupils, but is particularly valuable for pupils with special educational needs (DfE, 2024a, p. 24).

Social learning theory (Bandura, 1977) suggests that individuals learn from each other through observation, modelling and imitation. By internalising what they observe, and being given opportunities to mirror modelled behaviour, pupils can be motivated to interact appropriately within a secure and positive environment. Carroll et al. (2017) state, 'it is clear that an environment in which students feel emotionally safe, in which there are clear rules, predictable consequences and positive goals, is good for those with and without SEND' (p. 15).

The needs of pupils with SEND may impact on their ability to cope in a variety of learning situations so it's important that all staff are aware of pupils' barriers to learning, social circumstances and any safeguarding issues on a day-to-day basis. It's important for teachers to recognise that some pupils' needs may be temporary, while others may experience needs such as social, emotional and mental health (SEMH) challenges in the long term. Continuing difficulties, requiring support from school staff as well as other professionals such as the Child and Adolescent Mental Health Services (CAMHS), should be provided on an ongoing basis.

A safe, comfortable physical environment is essential to ensure all pupils with SEND thrive. This may involve making sure:

- the school and classrooms are physically accessible;
- lighting and noise levels are suitable for sensory processing needs and resources such as noise cancelling headphones are provided;
- calm areas are established and modelled with pupils;
- learning materials are available for all needs (audio/visual, signing and symbols, assistive technology, multisensory resources);
- wall displays and visual timetables are clear, accessible and used appropriately;
- pop-up desk screens and quiet areas are available for pupils who need individual space;
- opportunities are provided for pupils to share their feelings verbally and visually;
- movement breaks and use of sensory objects are modelled.

Rules and Routines

Regular routines help pupils with SEND find order in complex situations. Rules are an explicit form of routine, understood by the whole school community (Bennett, 2017). Both rules and routines are part of effective school and classroom management. Coe et al. (2014) state that there is some evidence to suggest that learning can be maximised when teachers coordinate classroom resources and space and when clear rules are reinforced consistently. Some schools have found when pupils and families have an input into school and classroom rules, they are more willing to abide by them. Frequently used rules and routines include:

- **Greetings** – a friendly 'good morning' to each pupil as they enter the classroom, or at registration, ensures they feel valued and part of the school community.

- **Attention** – a clear attention signal, instantly recognised by all pupils, followed by the expectation that everyone responds to simple, precise directions.
- **Listening** – model good listening behaviour and recognise the different ways in which some pupils process language. For example, some pupils may need to hold a sensory object and be seated comfortably.
- **Transition times** – entering the classroom, changing from one activity to another and exiting the classroom are times when some pupils with SEND may experience confusion. Teach transitions through explicit verbal and visual explanations, regular routines, clear modelling and practice.
- **Collaborative and cooperative learning** – gives pupils opportunities to develop social skills such as active listening, taking turns, sharing ideas and showing respect for the feelings of others. Some pupils with SEND will need specific adult modelled support and feedback during activities, praising positive interactions and redirecting negative remarks.
- **Help** – some pupils, without TA support, may need help for academic or practical work and for physical needs. Modelling the use of a symbol card system can allow pupils to indicate needs.
- **Playground** – playground rules and routines are essential to maintain a safe and happy social environment. A playground buddy system can help in addition to the presence of a trusted adult.
- **Exit** – pupils with SEND are often tired at the end of a school day. Useful routines to establish include positive reflections on the day, story time and sensory regulation techniques such as finger breathing together.

Case Study: A Break in Routine

Riley, aged seven, was an anxious pupil, the youngest in a family known to social services as experiencing many challenges. Both the school and social services worked together to provide some stability for Riley by ensuring he was enrolled for breakfast club and after school care. The breakfast club staff noticed that Riley requested the same cereal each morning and became agitated if it was not available. The class teacher noted that Riley referred frequently to the visual timetable displayed each day, adhered rigidly to classroom rules and routines and became anxious if other pupils were less rigorous. This anxiety came to a head when Riley's class teacher was not in school, and a supply teacher took his place. Unable to cope with unexpected changes in routine, Riley became dysregulated, shouting and screaming at the teacher and running out of the classroom. After some time, Riley was able to go to a calm area with the SENCo and agreed to work with her until his own teacher returned.

(Continued)

At a meeting with Riley, his mother, class teacher, social services and a specialist SEMH support teacher, it was decided to implement a support plan with Riley to help him manage changes in routine. This was important as Riley would be in a different class the following term and needed to have emotional regulation strategies modelled with him.

Although Riley continued to have some SEMH needs, he began to confide in the mentor who had been assigned to support him, recognise his own difficulties and ask for help when necessary. As a result of his mother's involvement in the support plan, she also reached out for further support for the family.

SEND: SEMH (Social, Emotional and Mental Health).

Reflective Task 7.1

Why do you think Riley was anxious when other pupils didn't adhere to rules and routines?

Why were routines so important to Riley?

Building Effective Relationships

Links to the ITTECF 7.2

- **7.5 Learn that** building effective relationships is easier when pupils believe that their feelings will be considered and understood (DfE, 2024a, p. 24).

Developing a culture of mutual trust, concern for others and respect can help build effective relationships. When teachers consider pupils' goals and interests and provide a supportive learning environment, they are more likely to interact positively. Hattie (2008) argues that when teachers encourage the building of effective relationships early in the academic year alongside developing respect for others, pupils' behaviour and learning outcomes are better. The government statutory guidance on relationships (DfE, 2021) emphasises the importance of respecting others whatever their differences. Rathmann et al. (2018) indicate that pupils' attitudes to learning are influenced by teacher–pupil interactions as well as the behaviour and attitudes of their peer group. For pupils with SEND, negative attitudes from teachers or peer groups can create an additional barrier to learning.

Case Study: It's Not Our Fault!

At the beginning of a new academic year, a class of year 2 pupils had changed into their PE kit and were waiting to go outside. The teacher noticed that Ella was still struggling to get changed. Ella's parents were insistent she was given opportunities to become independent, especially with getting dressed and undressed. The teacher organised some indoor exercises with the class while they waited for Ella but some of the pupils became disruptive as they waited for the outdoor PE session to begin.

Once Ella was ready and the pupils were outside, the teacher explained that disruptive behaviour lessened the amount of time for PE. One pupil called out, 'It's not our fault. It's Ella's cos she's so slow and we're bored waiting'. The teacher decided to continue with the lesson and address the issue later.

The teacher organised support for Ella with developing her motor skills using timed activities. She also gave the rest of the class some specific timed warm-up activities to help them appreciate the physical difficulties Ella experienced when constrained by time.

SEND: Down syndrome.

Reflective Task 7.2

Why do you think the teacher did not confront the issue immediately?

Empathy, the ability to see things from the perspective of others, recognising their needs, is an important aspect of developing a caring, compassionate community. For some pupils with SEND, identifying the feelings of others needs to be taught explicitly through:

- adults modelling empathetic behaviour in their language and action;
- developing pupils' listening and attention skills through turn-taking games;
- teaching the identification of emotions though facial expressions and visual images;
- using role play and signing to help pupils recognise emotions via body language and other non-verbal communication;
- developing and sharing Social Stories.

Behaviour for Learning

Links to the ITTECF 7.3

- **7.3 Learn that** the ability to self-regulate one's emotions affects pupils' ability to learn, success in school and future lives.
- **7.8 Learn that** Teaching and modelling a range of social and emotional skills (e.g. how to recognise and understand feelings, manage emotions, and sustain positive relationships) can support pupils' social and emotional development (DfE, 2024a, pp. 24-25).

Behaviour for learning is a conceptual framework based on an approach developed by Powell and Tod (2004), further adapted by Ellis and Tod (2018). It's built on the idea that promoting learning and managing behaviour are not two separate issues. It explores ways in which positive behaviours can be developed that contribute towards successful learning. The behaviour for learning conceptual framework highlights three relationships that influence the behaviours necessary for learning within school and classroom settings.

1. **Relationship with self (emotional)** – for some pupils, emotional factors have a strong influence on their ability to develop positive learning behaviours. It's important for staff and families to support pupils to develop self-confidence, self-esteem and self-efficacy. By exploring their feelings, ideas and abilities within a supportive, scaffolded environment, pupils can be shown how learning from successes and mistakes can be a positive experience.
2. **Relationship with others (social)** – building positive social relationships can help pupils develop a shared understanding of each other's needs. Pupils need to be given opportunities to develop social skills such as active listening, taking turns, sharing ideas, showing respect for the feelings of others and valuing all opinions. Cooperative learning can help promote positive behaviour if pupils are encouraged and shown how to work together and recognise each other's strengths and barriers to learning.
3. **Relationship with the curriculum (cognitive/curricular)** – if pupils are unable to access the curriculum, they may display negative behaviours. It's important to ensure that any barriers to learning are recognised with lessons and activities adapted to engage and motivate learners.

The framework recognises that all three relationships can be influenced strongly by the school ethos. Other factors such as family, community, culture, services as well as school, local and national policies may also influence the development of positive learning behaviours. The teaching and modelling of social and emotional skills is an important aspect of helping pupils develop positive learning behaviours.

The report on *Improving Social and Emotional Learning in Primary Schools* (EEF, 2021b) outlines the core skills of Social and Emotional Learning (SEL):

- **Self-awareness** – able to identify own emotions, recognise strengths, develop self-confidence and self-efficacy.
- **Self-management** – able to control impulses, manage stress, develop self-discipline and self-motivation, set realistic goals and develop organisational skills.
- **Social awareness** – able to develop empathy/sympathy, appreciate diversity, develop respect for others and understand emotions.
- **Relationship skills** – able to communicate, engage socially, build relationships and work as part of a team.
- **Responsible decision making** – able to identify problems, analyse solutions, solve problems, evaluate and reflect and develop ethical responsibility.

The development of positive learning behaviour does not happen by chance. All pupils, including those with SEND, should be expected to abide by the ethos and behaviour rules of the school. Initially, all staff should be encouraged to use proactive behaviour management strategies but for some pupils there may be a need to use reactive or specific strategies (see Tables 7.1 and 7.2 for examples).

Table 7.1 Proactive behaviour management

Strategy	**Examples**
Model positive behaviour	• Stay calm, use positive, affirming language. • Use positive body language – smile and share enthusiasm for subjects taught and the pupils' personal interests. • Model positive interactions needed for cooperative learning activities.
Develop social awareness skills	• Introduce 'getting to know you' activities and continue using them to build relationships. • Take time to listen to pupils' concerns and empathise with their feelings. • Encourage pupils to listen to each other by using cooperative activities and games requiring turn-taking and sharing of ideas. • Use role play, stories and games to help manage anxieties and emotions.

Table 7.1 (Continued)

Strategy	Examples
Have a well organised and structured classroom	• Arrange spaces, furniture, visual displays and lighting to suit all learning needs. • Have well-labelled storage areas so pupils know where to find equipment. • Organise rotas for classroom tasks to support the movement of pupils and aid transitions.
Establish regular rules and routines in the classroom	• Build class rules on the foundations of whole school behaviour policies. • Emphasise classroom rules using a positive voice. • Use specific visual or auditory signals to gain attention. • Use visual cues as reminders for levels of noise in the classroom. • Provide regular routines for transition times.
Establish fair and consistent expectations with positive affirmation	• Express empathy rather than anger. • Praise positive attitudes and actions when pupils are working together. • Praise achievements of individual pupils rather than in comparison with the group or class. • Any consequences for behaviour should be part of an agreed whole school behaviour policy and take account of pupils' needs.
Practise early intervention and prevention	• Provide privacy screens, classroom spaces and quiet areas for pupils with specific needs. • Use role play to help pupils understand social situations. • Implement visual timetables for pupils. • Develop Social Stories to help pupils understand specific social situations. • Note context and trigger points for behaviour to facilitate a proactive rather than reactive approach.
Provide explicit task explanations to support understanding	• Model tasks and offer guided practice before independent use of a skill. • Provide visual and written guides as a reminder. • Set small step targets within each task.

Table 7.2 Reactive behaviour management

Strategy	**Examples**
Conflict resolution activities	• Take 10 - encourage pupils to count to 10 when feeling frustration or anger. • Conflict resolution cards for both group and class discussion can be downloaded from several websites. Choose those with scenarios most applicable to the class. • Social skills role play - encouraging resolutions as part of the activity.
Develop awareness of positive and negative feelings associated with behaviour	• Explain calmly the positive reasons for following an instruction and remind pupils of the agreed rules and classroom routines. • Be consistent with agreed actions when a pupil becomes dysregulated and ensure there is time to talk when the pupil is ready.
Use distraction techniques to guide pupils away from confrontational situations	• Intervene in an argument by asking questions or giving information related to a task. • Give the pupil a task away from the situation emphasising the positive things happening in the classroom.
Adapt task expectations to prevent task avoidance	• Organise tasks into small chunks. Set small step targets within the task. • Use prompt, positive praise for small step achievements.
Use of agreed physical interventions, adhering to school policy, when there is danger of injury or damage	• Physical interventions should only be carried out by trained adults. • Interventions may include leading a pupil away from a confrontational situation or taking a pupil to a quiet area to talk about the situation with a trusted adult.

Motivation

Links to the ITTECF 7.4

- **7.4 Learn that** teachers can influence pupils' resilience and beliefs about their ability to succeed, by ensuring all pupils have the opportunity to experience meaningful success.
- **7.6 Learn that** pupils are motivated by intrinsic factors (related to their identity and values) and extrinsic factors (related to reward).
- **7.7 Learn that** pupils' investment in learning is also driven by their prior experiences and perceptions of success and failure (DfE, 2024a, pp. 24-25).

Pupils' enthusiasm for learning can be influenced by a number of factors. Some may centre around both home and school experiences. Teachers cannot change a pupil's home environment, but they can endeavour to provide positive and supportive classroom environments where all pupils are valued and have opportunities to experience meaningful success as well as failure. Teachers can influence pupils' resilience and beliefs about their ability to achieve success as well as helping them learn from their failures. Motivation for learning may be extrinsic (influenced by external factors) or intrinsic (influenced by internal feelings of personal satisfaction).

Teachers can support the development of intrinsic motivation by:

- considering pupils' interests – pupils who are intrinsically motivated want to be successful in tasks which relate to their own interests (Theobald, 2006);
- helping pupils to develop ownership of their work by encouraging their personal interest and involvement in activities (Ferlazzo, 2015; Stearns, 2013);
- ensuring that technology and interactive formats are integrated into some lessons including assistive technology for pupils with SEND;
- ensuring that some elements of the curriculum are relevant to pupils' needs and everyday lives (Ferlazzo, 2015);
- providing a range of multisensory resources to enhance personal interests and abilities;
- encouraging pupils' autonomy by allowing them to set some of their own learning objectives and be responsible for their own learning (Theobald, 2006).

Teachers can support the development of extrinsic motivation by:

1. recognising and praising pupils' efforts when undertaking a task;
2. showing enthusiasm for a topic or subject and conveying this positivity to their pupils which, in turn, affects pupil motivation (Schiefele & Schaffner, 2015);
3. giving positive feedback and recognising pupils' strengths (Theobald, 2006);
4. recognising that pupils who are praised for their efforts rather than their ability are more likely to see intelligence as variable and something they can be in control of and be motivated to attain (Willingham, 2009).

Case Study: Maths Motivation

At the age of nine, Oliver arrived at a language resource base, attached to a large primary school, with a diagnosis of autism. Having waited for some time for Oliver to be given an EHCP, his parents were keen for him to receive the support he needed.

(Continued)

(Continued)

Initially, Oliver spent most of his time in the resource base with targeted support organised by the resource base teacher and input from a speech and language therapist. He refused to interact with other pupils, avoided any physical contact and spent much of the day in his own space.

Each day Oliver was given a visual timetable using Widget symbols and, as he began to make progress with his expressive language, he was encouraged to take part in some paired maths tasks. With the help of Social Stories, Oliver and his partner began to learn social conventions, such as turn-taking, when playing maths games and using IT resources.

After a while, it became clear that Oliver was making exceptional progress in maths but what surprised his teacher was his ability to convey his interest to others. Gradually, Oliver was given opportunities to work with his peer group on maths investigations in the classroom. The think, pair, share strategy was used to give Oliver individual thinking time before sharing his ideas with a partner. The class teacher noted that he was intrinsically motivated by his love of maths and extrinsically motivated by having the opportunity to impart his knowledge to others. Oliver continued to need support with developing his social communication skills, but his interest in maths was a key part of his motivation to work with others.

SEND: Autism.

Reflective Task 7.3

Consider other areas of the curriculum where Oliver might have been able to use his knowledge and skills to interact with his peer group.

Understanding and Supporting Pupil Behaviour

Links to the ITTECF 7.5

- **7.9 Learn that** teaching typically expected behaviours will reduce the need to manage misbehaviour.
- **7.10 Learn that** pupils who need a tailored approach to support their behaviour do not necessarily have SEND and pupils with SEND will not necessarily need additional support with their behaviour.
- **7.11 Learn that** a key influence on a pupil's behaviour in school is being the victim of bullying (DfE, 2024a, p. 25).

It's important to recognise that many pupils with SEND develop positive behaviour when given opportunities to be part of an inclusive learning environment where barriers to learning are minimised. The Department for Education states:

> *Creating a culture that promotes excellent behaviour requires a clear vision of what good behaviour looks like. Schools' circumstances will vary but every culture should ensure pupils can learn in a calm, safe, and supportive environment and protect them from disruption.*
>
> (DfE, 2024c, p. 6)

The EEF report, *Improving Behaviour in* Schools (2019) highlights six main recommendations:

1. Know and understand your pupils and their influences.
2. Teach learning behaviours alongside managing misbehaviour.
3. Use classroom management strategies to support good classroom behaviour.
4. Use simple approaches as part of your regular routine.
5. Use targeted approaches to meet the needs of individuals in your school.
6. Consistency is key.

The need to model and teach positive learning behaviours alongside understanding the context of a pupil's negative behaviour should be part of everyday classroom management strategies.

Behavioural Concerns

Lockdown, during the covid pandemic, has been blamed for some deterioration in pupil behaviour and social skills. Despite efforts by teachers to help pupils develop positive learning behaviours, the teachers' union NASUWT (2023) reports that low level disruption and rudeness were the most common behaviours cited by members. Some examples of low-level behaviour are:

- deliberately making noises during a quiet time;
- procrastinating when starting a task;
- continually chatting and distracting others in the group;
- occasionally making disruptive remarks to other children or support staff;
- causing a distraction by trying to make others laugh.

Low level behavioural concerns may be disruptive but can usually be minimised by using proactive behaviour management strategies.

Here are some examples of what schools may view as a moderate behavioural concern:

- being rude and unkind to other pupils or staff;
- refusal to follow instructions and arguing with pupils and staff;
- task avoidance tactics such as pencil sharpening or frequent toilet breaks;
- being generally disruptive and calling out to others across the room.

Moderate level behavioural concerns need to be noted, and the underlying reasons explored alongside support for the pupil. Support ideas can be taken from both proactive and reactive behaviour management strategies (see Tables 7.1 and 7.2 for examples).

Some pupils may display challenging behaviour which cannot be minimised by proactive or reactive management strategies. This may include:

- swearing, shouting and temper tantrums;
- withdrawn behaviours such as staring, avoidance of eye contact, rocking, hand flapping;
- kicking, biting, punching and breaking equipment;
- bullying and aggressive behaviour towards other pupils and adults;
- sexual and suggestive actions both to self and others.

An individual behaviour support plan should be developed with advice from the SENCo for challenging and potentially harmful behaviours such as these. Planned responses for specific behaviours can be implemented by the teacher, support adult or SENCo.

A behaviour support plan should include:

1. a description of the behaviour using evidence from observations;
2. identification of possible triggers for the behaviour;
3. possible ways to eliminate or minimise triggers;
4. any home, school or personal challenges recorded;
5. the setting of clear, positive behaviour targets;
6. implementing teaching strategies to support behaviour targets;
7. collaborating and reviewing the support plan with all concerned (pupil, parent, SENCo and all staff involved with the pupil).

Reasons for Negative Behaviour

There are a number of reasons why some pupils with SEND have difficulty in overcoming challenging behaviour. Possible causes may be temporary or ongoing, including:

- changes at home such as a new baby, moving house or school, divorce, bereavement, being put into care;
- adapting to living in a new country with different customs and language;
- difficulties coping with the curriculum if tasks are not adapted for specific barriers to learning;
- lack of regular routines at home making it more challenging to cope with structure in school;
- learnt negative behaviour from the home environment such as shouting, swearing, arguing or physical aggression;
- physical, mental or sexual abuse at home or in the community;
- physical or mental health challenges;
- learning goals which are not challenging enough

Table 7.3 provides examples of specific behaviour management strategies schools may adopt.

Table 7.3 Specific behaviour management strategies

Behaviour	Support strategies
Frustration or anger when experiencing difficulty with a task	• Redirect the pupil into a more manageable activity linked to the task. • Give the pupil time and space to calm down and talk about difficulties and feelings with a trusted adult.
Refusing to interact socially or take part in group activities and discussion	• Help the pupil develop social skills through parallel partner activities such as playing or working alongside each other without forcing interaction. • Paired card and board games which involve taking turns. • Reading buddies. • Social stories with a partner.
Refusing to conform to classroom rules, routines and instructions	• Be consistent when modelling and practising agreed class rules and routines. • Use a visual symbol system to allow pupils to communicate how they are feeling in that moment. • Offer pupils a choice between two specific options. • Use circle time (group or class) to discuss behaviour challenges without attributing them to specific pupils.

(Continued)

Table 7.3 (Continued)

Behaviour	Support strategies
Shouting or swearing at adults and other pupils	• If possible, intervene and use distraction strategies before frustration becomes out of control. • Encourage pupils to handle sensory objects when they feel angry or dysregulated. • Practice mindful breathing techniques with pupils on a regular basis and help them use it when they feel frustrated. • Note context and trigger points for challenging behaviour. Allow pupils to share these with a mentor. • Ask pupils to share the reason for their anger and the effect it has on others. This can be done using a visual sign system.
Aggressive and violent behaviour to both adults and other pupils	• Stay calm and ensure all pupils in the class are put into a safe position. • Employ school policy behaviour strategies which may include sending for help from the SENCo and trained support staff. • Allow pupils to calm down before investigating triggers and organising a behaviour plan with the SENCo. • Document aggressive behaviour and discuss behaviour plans with pupils, families and staff.

Case study: Rights and Responsibilities

Mason and his twin brother Preston joined a year 4 class in a rural school after the family moved from the city. Initially, the brothers appeared to settle well but, after the second week, reports of bullying at playtime became more frequent. Mason was found to be using a compass to threaten pupils who didn't follow his orders. Although a few incidents of bullying had been reported at his previous school, Mason had not been considered a safeguarding threat to others. When confronted with his actions, Mason became angry and defiant. The SENCo led him away from the situation and spoke calmly to him, reassuring him that she was there for him to talk to. The compass was confiscated, and Mason responded by screaming that the SENCo had no right to take his compass. He threatened he would send his big brother to 'sort her out'.

Later that week a meeting was arranged with Mason, his parents, class teacher and SENCo. It was noted that not only did Mason display bullying behaviour at school but also towards

(Continued)

his brother at home. His mother explained that when his father was away, she had difficulty controlling the boys.

It was agreed that the SENCo would produce an individual behaviour plan with Mason. The aim was to use a consistent, positive approach to show Mason that everyone had the right to feel safe at school and everyone was responsible for making sure this happened. Short, clearly defined targets were set with praise given when Mason displayed positive interactions.

Mason continued to receive school-based behaviour support but was also referred to the Educational Psychologist, where he was later diagnosed with Oppositional Defiant Disorder (ODD). He was also referred to CAMHS and was offered support with cognitive behavioural therapy.

SEND: ODD (Oppositional Defiant Disorder).

Reflective Task 7.4

During your time in the classroom, explore ways in which proactive, reactive and specific behaviour management strategies are used.

Negative behaviour not only affects the individual but also the family, peer group and school community. There has been ongoing concern about the increase in negative behaviour in schools since the pandemic and the breakdown of everyday routines (DfE, 2024c). The reasons for an increase in negative behaviours are complex. They reflect a mixture of the impact of poverty, parenting challenges, anti-social behaviour in the community, SEND needs not being met and disturbing social media content. Schools cannot provide all the answers to the wider problems in society. However, if resources are made available for school-based nursery places, parenting groups, pastoral care and timely specialist support for pupils with SEND, then pupils and their families can grow more confidently within a safe, positive and caring community.

8

Professional Behaviours

Chapter Objectives

This chapter looks at ways in which trainee teachers can develop effective and mutually supportive relationships with colleagues. It explores the different types of Continuing Professional Development (CPD) available in primary schools including those related to SEND and inclusive education. Ideas for working collaboratively with colleagues and reflecting on practice via observation and feedback are suggested. The chapter also examines ways in which primary teachers may:

- build effective relationships with parents, carers and families;
- use teaching assistants effectively within an inclusive classroom;
- liaise with SENCos and other SEND professionals;
- explore and use educational research in the classroom.

Developing Supportive Relationships With Colleagues

Links to the ITTECF 8.1

- **8.3 Learn that** teachers can make valuable contributions to the wider life of the school in a broad range of ways, including by supporting and developing effective professional relationships with colleagues (DfE, 2024a, p. 26).

Building good working relationships is the key to enjoying a fulfilling career in any occupation, but it's particularly important in education where positive everyday interactions affect the well-being of everyone in the school community. The Department for Education states:

> *Teaching really is a "people profession". Building relationships with other people, including pupils, colleagues, parents, carers and other specialist professionals, is key to the job. Relationships matter and we can build and nurture these proactively (n.d.).*

Teaching is also about teamwork, particularly when supporting pupils with SEND, where a team of people work together to meet pupils' needs. The team may include families, teaching colleagues, support staff and other professionals. Working as part of a team requires a number of skills including being an interactive listener, that is, listening carefully and making considered responses to develop a deeper understanding of a pupil's needs.

Teaching can be all encompassing, leaving very little spare time for other contributions to school life, yet these can enhance both staff and pupil wellbeing. Co-curricular activities give teachers and pupils opportunities to get to know each other in more informal settings. Sharing a personal interest outside of the academic curriculum can also enhance and develop supportive relationships. For example, volunteering to help run a sport or art-based club builds a positive community atmosphere. In some schools, homework hubs are an essential part of the day for many pupils. By taking part in these, teachers can gain an understanding of the barriers to learning many pupils face.

Student and early career teachers receive guidance from experienced practitioners to support their progression and development throughout the initial years of training. During this time, sharing experiences, both successes and failures, can help build effective professional relationships. Contributing to the wider life of the school in a range of ways ensures integration into a supportive and rich learning community.

Reflective Practice

Links to the ITTECF 8.2

- **8.2 Learn that** reflective practice, supported by feedback from and observation of experienced colleagues, professional debate, and learning from educational research, is also likely to support improvement (DfE, 2024a, p. 26).

A school environment that encourages reflective practice, peer observation and constructive feedback from leaders and colleagues, is an environment where the development of professional relationships and the sharing of knowledge and skills can take place successfully. Peer observation and feedback can be linked to teacher self-efficacy when a teacher is able to replicate successful strategies observed in a colleague's classroom (Hendry et al., 2012). Peer observation can also provide teachers with opportunities to share expertise and discuss ways in which techniques can be adapted and modified to suit pupils in their own classrooms (Wiliam, 2016).

The *SEND Reflection Framework* (Knight, 2020) supports school improvement helping teachers evaluate the degree to which they meet pupils' additional needs. It provides a structure which allows school leaders and teachers to critically consider the cultures and practices in their schools relating to provision for pupils with SEND. In the framework, Knight states, 'Reviewing SEND attitudes and practice can have a beneficial impact on the wider pupil population, as it supports the development of teaching practice that is not only limited to those with a designation of SEND' (2020, p. 6). In relation to knowledge of the learners in the class, statements include the following:

- I describe the requirements of all learners in my classroom, particularly those with SEND, in accordance with the SEND Code of Practice broad areas of need.
- I demonstrate a range of adaptations to my practice that enable me to address their requirements effectively.
- I evaluate critically the potential impact of the interventions which are provided by the setting I work in. I explore alternatives to establish whether better outcomes for the learner can be achieved with different approaches.
- I understand the importance of evaluating the impact of any additional provision and reviewing this with home and school.

(Knight, 2020, p. 11)

Although the framework has statements which capture contributions from learners, families, education professionals and academic researchers, they are not meant to be a checklist of competencies for teachers. They are provided to highlight opportunities to stimulate professional debate, develop knowledge and skills related to SEND and have a positive impact on pupil outcomes.

Continuing Professional Development

Links to the ITTECF 8.3

- **8.1 Learn that** effective professional development is likely to be sustained over time, building knowledge, motivating staff, developing teaching techniques and embedding practice.
- **8.7 Learn that** engaging in high quality professional development can help teachers improve (DfE, 2024a, pp. 26-27).

CPD refers to the continuing commitment of teachers to acquiring an up-to-date understanding of reliable best practices. Testing relevant educational theories and new technology, developing approaches and strategies for teaching all pupils, as well as adapting to changes in the curriculum, are all part of a teacher's professional development. In its guidance report, *Effective Professional Development* (2021h), the EEF identifies the mechanisms of professional development as building knowledge, motivating teachers, developing teaching techniques and embedding practice.

With the large numbers of pupils now being recognised as having additional needs, it's necessary for all teachers and support staff in mainstream schools to be skilled in working with pupils who have barriers to their learning. Regular CPD, sustained over time, can support staff in developing their knowledge, skills and understanding of using adaptive teaching strategies within inclusive classrooms.

CPD can be delivered in several ways, but each school needs to identify areas for improvement and ongoing development. CPD related to SEND may include the following:

- Courses accredited online or attended.
- Conferences, seminars and workshops.
- School-based academic research projects.
- Classroom-based action research projects.
- INSET (in-school training) led by SENCos or other professionals.
- School visits to observe best practice in action.
- Mentoring – receiving or giving support.
- Project working parties for joint planning and observation of school needs.

Providing all pupils, including those with SEND, with a high quality, inclusive education requires both teachers and support staff to have strong curriculum knowledge and an understanding of effective teaching strategies that can be adapted to support all pupils. The report, *Supporting SEND* (Ofsted, 2021), emphasises the importance of the development of teacher knowledge in relation to SEND.

Building Effective Relationships With Parents, Carers and Families

Links to the ITTECF 8.4

- **8.4 Learn that** building effective relationships with parents, carers and families can improve pupils' motivation, behaviour and academic success (DfE, 2024a, p. 26).

When parents and carers are encouraged to engage with their child's education, it can have a positive impact on the pupil's attitude to learning and attainment. Hattie (2008) highlighted a two-to-three-year difference in a pupil's progress when families were engaged in their learning. In addition, the SEND Code of Practice (2014) makes it clear that parents and carers should be given a clear role to play in discussions and decisions regarding the provision for their children.

Building effective relationships with parents, carers and families requires clear lines of communication. If parents are kept informed regularly of school and class activities, they feel part of a community of learning. Most schools use the school website, social media, emails and messaging services to keep parents up to date. However, regular face-to-face contact between families and class teachers is the most effective way of giving individual feedback and allowing parents to share concerns informally.

Case Study: Bump on the Head

A year 3 teacher encouraged parents to talk to her informally at the end of the school day. One afternoon, she noticed Grant and his mother waiting anxiously in the reading corner as she chatted to other parents. When everyone left, Grant's mother explained her concerns. Grant had arrived home the previous day with a lump on the back of his head. He told his mother the teacher had banged his head against the wall. She was worried because she thought Grant was lying, something which he'd never done before, and wondered if he was being bullied at school.

Together, the teacher, mother and Grant began to chat about the bump on his head. It transpired that, in a roundabout way, the teacher had been the cause of the accident. The pupils had returned to the classroom after a PE lesson in a disruptive manner and were asked to line up again, quietly. In the process, Grant had been pushed to the end of the line and bumped the back of his head against the wall. The teacher apologised to Grant and explained how he should tell an adult if he was hurt. Grant's mother went away relieved that the incident had been resolved.

SEND: SLCN (Speech, Language and Communication Needs).

Reflective Task 8.1

How do you think Grant's barriers to learning affected his response to the accident?

Developing effective relationships with families relies on effective communication across a range of needs. The more teachers know and understand about pupils and their families, the more they can build successful partnerships between school and home.

The Education Endowment Foundation's (2018b) guidance report on *Working with Parents to support Children's Learning* makes four recommendations for schools.

1. **Critically review how you work with parents** – this involves being honest about how well current strategies are working, realising that different approaches are needed for different ages and abilities, and involving all parents in suggesting the support they would find most helpful.
2. **Provide practical strategies to support learning at home** – these may include providing resources and guidance on using reading material, language and mathematics games as well as guidance on how to promote good homework habits for older pupils.
3. **Tailor school communications to encourage positive dialogue about learning** – this may involve regular communication via termly letters and weekly messages to celebrate personal and collective successes, consultation about school activities and encouragement to take an active part.
4. **Offer more sustained and intensive support where needed** – this may include organising group-based parenting initiatives (such as regular workshops on supporting pupils with barriers to learning), building relationships with those parents who struggle to attend meetings by being available for after school chats both at school and online.

Some parents struggle with becoming involved in school activities for a number of reasons. They may:

- have had negative experiences of school themselves;
- work long hours and be unable to attend functions and meetings;
- have a first language other than English;
- feel they have nothing to offer to the life of the school;
- have little interest in education and place all responsibility on the school.

However, with perseverance and encouragement parents can be valuable assets to a school. They can be invited to share their knowledge and skills across several aspects of school life. By involving them and listening to their voice, a school is more able to meet the needs of its community.

Using Teaching Assistants Effectively

Links to the ITTECF 8.5

- **8.5 Learn that** teaching assistants (TAs) can support pupils more effectively when they are prepared for lessons by teachers, and when TAs supplement rather than replace support from teachers (DfE, 2024a, p. 26).

The changing nature of school populations and the development of inclusive classrooms has seen a change in the way many TAs are deployed. *Use of Teaching Assistants in Schools* (DfE, 2024d) found that the roles and responsibilities of TAs has increased significantly in recent years.

> *Leaders, TAs and teachers reported that the increased role of TAs is largely driven by the changing characteristics of the pupils they support. They describe a rise in the number of pupils with SEND in mainstream settings as well as the increased social, emotional and mental health (SEMH) needs of pupils further to the COVID-19 pandemic more broadly.*
>
> (DfE, 2024d, p. 2)

The report also found that training for teachers on how to deploy TAs effectively in the classroom was limited.

Some schools provide time for teachers and TAs to plan co-teaching approaches in the classroom. Others deploy TAs strategically by training them to deliver specific interventions and then continue working with pupils in the classroom to ensure transfer of knowledge and skills across the curriculum. Some schools provide training for TAs to work in a specialist area of SEND, usually in an area where they show a particular interest.

The types of TA support observed frequently in classrooms are as follows:

- **Helicopter support** – the TA is deployed to respond to requests for support when needed by observing and working with the whole class.
- **Facilitator support** – the TA supports a small group, helping them recall prior knowledge, develop the key concepts and skills needed for a task and modelling cooperative learning when necessary.
- **Velcro support** – the TA works closely with an individual pupil. This may be needed if there is a medical risk or safeguarding issue but, for most pupils with SEND, this is not necessary as it encourages them to rely on adult support.

The Education Endowment Foundation guidance report, *Making the Best Use of Teaching Assistants* (2021i), makes seven recommendations based on research evidence. They are as follows:

1. TAs should not be used as an informal teaching resource for low-attaining pupils.
2. Use TAs to add value to what teachers do, not to replace them.
3. Use TAs to help pupils develop independent learning skills and manage their own learning.
4. Ensure TAs are fully prepared for their role in the classroom.

5. Use TAs to deliver high-quality one-to-one and small group support using structured interventions.
6. Adopt evidence-based interventions to support TAs in their small group and one-to-one instruction.
7. Ensure explicit connections are made between learning from everyday classroom teaching and structured interventions.

The evidence in the report shows that poor TA deployment has a negative impact on pupils' attainment, but effective TA deployment can have a positive impact.

Perhaps the most difficult recommendation for primary teachers to fulfil is to 'ensure TAs are fully prepared for their role in the classroom'. This requires a whole school approach to TA deployment where time is allocated:

- For teachers and TAs to meet regularly for planning and preparation.
- For TAs to be part of INSET days where teaching approaches and strategies are disseminated.
- For the SENCo or other professionals to train TAs to deliver interventions.
- For TAs to be part of the graduated approach (assess, plan, do, review).

When working with TAs, effective communication skills and a shared sense of purpose are essential. Teachers need to:

- provide clear learning objectives and success criteria for lessons;
- identify pupils with barriers to learning and model adaptive teaching strategies for both pupils and TAs;
- ensure TAs can make effective use of resources;
- share feedback with both pupils and TAs as part of a team.

A scaffolding framework for TA and pupil interactions developed by Bosanquet et al. (2016) outlines a system which aims to support pupils to develop key learning skills and strategies, gradually moving towards self-scaffolding. The framework includes the following:

- **Correcting** – TAs may need to provide answers occasionally, particularly when they observe pupil misconceptions.
- **Modelling** – TAs may need to demonstrate a new skill or strategy verbalising their thought processes at each stage.

- **Clueing** – TAs may ask questions that stimulate pupils' thinking and provide a clue to the next step needed to continue with a task.
- **Prompting** – TAs provide prompts when pupils have some difficulties with self-scaffolding. Prompts should encourage pupils to think about their own prior knowledge of learning strategies.
- **Self-scaffolding** – TAs allow pupils thinking and processing time, observing how well they manage a task independently.

By recognising the interests and personal qualities of their TAs, schools can ensure they are not only deployed effectively but also given opportunities to make progress in their careers. Some may wish to take on extra training and become a Higher-Level Teaching Assistant (HLTA) if funding allows. TAs are not just additional classroom helpers but an integral part of a school that strives to be truly inclusive.

Liaise With SENCos and Other SEND Professionals

Links to the ITTECF 8.6

- **8.6 Learn that** SENCos, pastoral leaders, careers advisors and leaders and other specialist colleagues also have valuable expertise and can ensure that appropriate support is in place for pupils.
- **8.8 Learn that** teacher attitudes towards inclusion and SEND are a key determinant in the school experience of pupils with SEND (DfE, 2024a, p. 27).

There is a need to provide the right support in schools and classrooms to enhance the progress of all pupils with SEND. Pupils who have supportive learning experiences will have positive views of school. Losberg and Zwozdiak-Myers (2024) found that, although teachers are broadly in favour of inclusion, they face daily challenges when trying to implement inclusive practices successfully. Managing neurodiverse classrooms, without the necessary resources and support staff in place to help manage the workload, has been cited as being the main cause of stress for teachers (Warnes et al., 2022).

The impact of teacher wellbeing on pupil progress is highlighted by Glazzard and Rose. They noted that, 'children learned more when their teacher was happy and performing well' (2019, p. 40). So, it's important for school leaders to provide a working environment where:

- everyone feels valued for their individual knowledge and skills;
- school infrastructure is adapted according to pupil needs;

- a positive attitude towards inclusion is encouraged;
- staff and other resources are organised to make inclusive teaching practices manageable;
- teachers support each other rather than work in isolation;
- work-life balance is valued;
- a quiet area for teachers to relax and unwind is provided;
- recognition and appreciation of contributions to school life are given frequently;
- early career teachers are given additional support and guidance, particularly with understanding how to minimise pupils' barriers to learning.

The attitude towards teaching pupils with SEND in mainstream classes can be more positive if teachers feel they have the active support of school leaders, the SENCo and other professionals. Active support involves providing suitable staff and resources as well as demonstrating how to use specific teaching strategies and approaches, not just giving a verbal or written explanation.

- **The SENCo** is usually the first person to talk to when looking for help and advice, but other professionals may also have an input. For pupils with an EHCP, there will be regular multi-agency team meetings to review pupil progress. The class teacher is part of that team. Depending on local authority organisation, a variety of different professionals will be able to offer support, advice and resources.
- **Behaviour Support** teams identify and support pupils with behavioural, emotional and social difficulties. They work alongside other support teams to develop positive behaviour and emotional well-being in pupils who may be at risk of social exclusion.
- **CAMHS** (Child and Adult Mental Health Service) covers most types of provision, interventions and care for pupils with mental health difficulties.
- **Community Paediatricians** are based in hospitals or community care trusts. Pupils who have physical or medical difficulties may be referred to a paediatrician for general assessment. The community paediatrician will refer the pupil to other expert professionals but continue to monitor their overall progress.
- **Educational Psychologists** (EPs) may be responsible for several schools so work with pupils across school phases. They are involved in the statutory assessment and early identification of pupils' learning difficulties, observe and report on barriers to learning, advise on resources, assistive technology and interventions, liaise with other professionals and attend annual reviews for pupils with EHCPs.
- **Education Welfare Officers** (EWOs) are employed by the local authority. Their main responsibilities are to ensure pupils attend school regularly. They make home visits when

there are concerns about attendance, working jointly with social services especially when there are concerns about bullying, school avoidance and safeguarding issues.

- **Health Visitors** visit all homes where there are children under five. They carry out health and developmental checks at regular intervals. They identify and refer children who may have SEND, supporting the parents by explaining the process of applying for an assessment.
- **Occupational Therapists** (OTs) work with those who have physical disabilities, dyspraxia, medical or traumatic difficulties, perceptual barriers to learning such as visual-spatial relationships as well as working with pupils who have congenital problems. OTs may provide and advise on the use of a range of equipment or adaptations designed for specific disabilities.
- **Physiotherapists** work with pupils whose conditions require treatment on a regular basis. They devise programmes of exercise to help maintain a range of movement and functional ability. These programmes may also be implemented by parents, TAs and others. Physiotherapists liaise regularly with OTs.
- **Sensory Impairment Advisers** are usually employed by the local authority and are specialists in their field. They work with pupils, parents, teachers and TAs to monitor the needs of pupils with specific sensory impairments. They provide advice on classroom adaptations, assistive technology and the use of other resources necessary to minimise pupil's barriers to learning.
- **Social Workers** are employed by the local authority and have responsibility for child protection issues, children in need and looked after children. Social workers are responsible for maintaining a register of children considered to be at risk.
- **Speech and Language Therapists** (SALTs) assess pupils as having a receptive language impairment (difficulty in understanding language) and expressive language impairment (difficulty in using language). SALTs devise therapy plans which may offer support for phonology, prosody, dysfluency, articulation, syntax, semantics and pragmatics. Some elements of a therapy plan may be implemented by a TA, trained by the SALT.

Using and Exploring Educational Research in the Classroom

Links to the ITTECF 8.7

- **8.8 Learn that** research evidence can vary in its level of reliability, which is determined by how the research was conducted and other factors that might introduce bias, such as the level of independence. High quality research communicates methods and limitations transparently (DfE, 2024a, p. 27).

The concept of reliability in research describes how well a study can be replicated. When making observations, conducting interviews and testing theories, researchers need to standardise procedures to avoid bias. Previous educational theories accepted by teachers as reliable such as the theory that pupils have specific learning styles, and need to learn using those styles, is not supported by research evidence. Although we know pupils process information in different parts of the brain, systematic research reviews and meta-analyses have examined the validity of utilising learning styles in education but have found no reliable evidence to support this approach.

Meta-analysis, as used by Hattie (2008) in *Visible Learning*, is a statistical analysis that combines the results of several studies, similar in nature, and explores relationships between findings. By comparing findings from different studies, researchers can advise on how some of the results might be generalised across learning situations.

Due to the nature of academic research, which is rigorous in applying its study methods to specific participants and situations, it's often difficult to apply this rigour in everyday classroom environments. Mainstream class teachers must consider the diverse needs of large classes, making it more challenging to implement research findings from controlled studies. For reliable educational research to have an impact in the classroom, it needs to be practically accessible to busy teachers. Researchers have a responsibility to ensure their findings are utilised rather than developing their field of research solely for peer review. Cancer research findings inform practice in the saving of lives. In the same way, educational research should inform practice which can be used in busy mainstream classrooms to improve outcomes for all pupils, including those with SEND.

It's important for schools to find reliable evidence for using an intervention or teaching approach before investing in new resources. Obsolete materials can be found in many classroom cupboards, a testament to the limitations of some educational theories and their practical application.

Case Study: A Breakthrough Experience

I was introduced to the Breakthrough to Literacy materials in the 1970s and used them enthusiastically. Based on the sociolinguistic theory that reading matter for children should be linked to their own spoken language, it used a system of sentence makers and word makers to introduce children to compositional language and the rules of grammar and syntax. The programme was evaluated and found to produce some successful teaching strategies (Reid, 1974). However, the effect of introducing children, at an early stage in their language development, to the form and function of written language, and the differences between oral and written language, was not investigated further.

The practical aspect of using materials where each pupil collected, and often lost, a range of individual words for the sentences they composed, soon became onerous in busy classrooms. Despite some clear indications of improvement in pupils' use of grammar and

(Continued)

(Continued)

syntax as they progressed through school, the Breakthrough materials were used less frequently. Gradually, they became part of small group intervention programmes for pupils with literacy difficulties. Now they have long been destroyed, a casualty of the mismatch between educational theory and everyday classroom practicalities. However, the idea of giving pupils the opportunity to manipulate tactile phonemes and words into sentences before developing formal writing skills can still be found in a number of resources available today (see SEND Resources).

Teachers need to be able to identify, use and evaluate evidence-based approaches suitable for all pupils but, to do this, they need access to academic research via support agencies that present information in an accessible way. The Educational Endowment Foundation (EEF) is an initiative which:

- reviews research evidence on teaching and learning and presents it in a clear, accessible way;
- aims to raise the attainment of pupils from disadvantaged backgrounds by funding independent evaluations of programmes and teaching approaches;
- supports all those involved in the education of children and young people to use research evidence that improves teaching and learning.

The EEF (2024) has also produced a short guide entitled *Using Research Evidence* which gives an overview of evidence-based research in education, noting its reliability and limitations. The foundation looks at different forms and uses of research evidence and how it can help teachers develop effective practice. Quigley (2023) highlights ways in which the foundation tries to provide a bridge between educational research and practice in schools while acknowledging that this transfer can be challenging. Nevertheless, evidence-based research, founded not only on rigorous scientific and peer-reviewed studies but also on regular, practical classroom monitoring, can help ensure that suggested teaching strategies are successful in inclusive educational settings. Research and real classroom experience should work together to ensure good teaching for pupils with SEND is good teaching for all.

Part 2

9
SEND Areas of Need and Support

The areas of need and support as defined by the SEND Code of Practice (2015) are as follows:

- communication and interaction;
- cognition and learning;
- social, emotional and mental health;
- sensory or physical needs.

They are not organised in order to place individuals into a specific category but rather to show how these particular difficulties impact on a child's learning. Many children and young people with severe learning difficulties (SLD) and profound and multiple learning difficulties (PMLD) have complex profiles across several categories (see **Pupil Support Profiles** in Tables 9.1 to 9.4 at the end of this chapter). Some disabilities or conditions listed can be found under more than one category.

Communication and Interaction

The *SEND Code of Practice 0 to 25 years* (2015) describes the area of need for pupils with communication and interaction difficulties.

> *Children and young people with speech, language and communication needs (SLCN) have difficulty in communicating with others. This may be because they have difficulty saying what they want to, understanding what is being said to them or they do not understand or use social rules of communication. The profile for every child with SLCN is different and their needs may change over time. They may have difficulty with one, some or all of the different aspects of speech, language or social communication at different times of their lives.*
>
> (2015, p. 97)

> *Children and young people with ASD, including Asperger's Syndrome and Autism, are likely to have particular difficulties with social interaction. They may also experience difficulties with language, communication and imagination, which can impact on how they relate to others.*
>
> (2015, p. 97)

Pupils with communication and interaction needs may have:

Difficulties with phonology

- Being able to detect similarities and differences between sounds (auditory discrimination).
- Processing speech sounds often confusing or substituting sounds.
- Articulating sounds when trying to communicate.
- Combining sounds into longer words.
- Stammering or stuttering resulting in sounds, words or parts of words being repeated frequently.
- Have differences in intonation so the meaning is unclear.

Difficulties with grammar (syntax and morphology)

- Organising words into sentences, using the correct grammatical structure.
- Pupil's speech is below their chronological age in the way sentences are formed.
- Verb tenses may be muddled and inflectional endings (ed, ing, s) used incorrectly.
- Poor understanding of conjunctions and prepositions.
- Difficulty in sequencing ideas, events or information (when retelling events or stories, information may be given in the wrong order or elements missed out).

Difficulties with word finding

- Difficulty with recalling the right word when needed, describing the word rather than naming it (It's hot. You make tea. You put water in it for the word 'kettle').
- Making connections between prior knowledge and new learning experiences.
- Learning and remembering new topic/subject specific vocabulary.
- Processing language and needing longer thinking time.
- Need visual and symbol cues.

Difficulties with semantics

- Understanding the meanings of words and the way they relate to each other.
- May have poor auditory memory skills.
- Difficulty understanding and recalling key concept vocabulary.

- Confusing words with similar meanings.
- Difficulty with drawing inferences and making deductions.
- Making inappropriate responses to questions, instructions and directions.

Difficulties with listening and attention

- May not be able to screen out what is unimportant from what they hear around them, so listen to everything.
- May lack skill at controlling attention and therefore miss large chunks of information.
- Difficulty following discussions during cooperative learning sessions.
- Responding to questions, often repeating what has been said.
- Sustaining attention during whole class sessions.

Difficulties with pragmatics

- The way that language is used to convey thoughts and feelings in social situations.

Some pupils may show signs of **semantic pragmatic disorder**. This is a communication disorder which crosses the boundaries of both specific language impairment and autism. Although each pupil is unique, elements of the characteristics of semantic pragmatic disorder and autism are as follows:

- **Communication** – language impairment, which may include speech, intonation, gesture, body language and/or facial expression, limited non-verbal communication skills.
- **Social interaction** – difficulties such as lack of empathy and perception, sharing and taking turns, following social rules and routines, inappropriate eye-contact, poor grasp of timing or some sensory perception difficulties.
- **Imaginative thought** – inflexible or over-literal thought-processes, which may include obsessional behaviours or repetitive movements and a resistance to change.
- May have some sensory processing integration difficulties.

Communication and Interaction – Information Contacts

You may have pupils in your class identified with the following disabilities or conditions:

Aphasia

- British Institute for Brain Injured Children (BIBIC) www.bibic.org.uk

- Cerebra www.cerebra.org.uk

Autistic spectrum condition (ASC)

- National Autistic Society www.autism.org.uk

Cerebral palsy

- Scope www.scope.org.uk
- Cerebra www.cerebra.org.uk
- Action Cerebral Palsy www.actioncp.org

Cleft Lip and Cleft Palate

- Cleft Lip and Palate Association (CLAPA) www.clapa.com

Developmental verbal apraxia

- Speech Teach www.speechteach.co.uk
- The Brain Charity www.thebraincharity.org.uk

Fragile X syndrome

- Fragile X Society (UK) www.fragilex.org.uk

Global Developmental Delay (GDD)

- Brainwave www.brainwave.org.uk
- Mencap www.mencap.org.uk

Moderate Learning Difficulties (MLDs)

- Mencap www.mencap.org.uk

Pragmatic Language Impairment

- Speech and Language UK www.speechandlanguage.org.uk

Selective mutism

- SmiRA www.selectivemutism.org.uk

Specific Language Impairment

- AFASIC www.afasic.org.uk

Stammering

- The British Stammering Association (BSA) www.stamma.org

Verbal dyspraxia

- Dyspraxia Foundation www.dyspraxiafoundation.org.uk

Cognition and Learning

The *SEND Code of Practice 0 to 25 years* (2015) characterises the area of need for pupils with cognition and learning difficulties.

> *Support for learning difficulties may be required when children and young people learn at a slower pace than their peers, even with appropriate differentiation. Learning difficulties cover a wide range of needs, including moderate learning difficulties (MLD), severe learning difficulties (SLD), where children are likely to need support in all areas of the curriculum and associated difficulties with mobility and communication, through to profound and multiple learning difficulties (PMLD), where children are likely to have severe and complex learning difficulties as well as a physical disability or sensory impairment.*
>
> (2015, p. 97)

This includes pupils with specific learning difficulties (SpLD) including dysgraphia.

> *Specific learning difficulties (SpLD), affect one or more specific aspects of learning. This encompasses a range of conditions such as dyslexia, dyscalculia and dyspraxia.*
>
> (2015, p. 98)

You may observe pupils in your class who may be working at below age-related expectations and have difficulties with:

- listening and attention skills;
- auditory memory skills;
- visual memory skills;
- verbal and non-verbal reasoning skills;

- making connections between prior knowledge and new learning experiences;
- understanding key concept vocabulary;
- verbal reasoning skills;
- developing visual perception skills (the ability to understand, process and make use of visual information);
- remembering and using the correct sequence of muscle movements in order to write;
- structuring and organising written work;
- sorting and classifying information;
- acquisition and use of language, literacy and numeracy skills;
- phonemic and phonological awareness;
- organisational skills;
- drawing inferences and making deductions;
- independent working and may sometimes need the support of an adult and a modified curriculum;
- difficulties in some aspect of cognitive processing (slow phonological processing, poor working memory, and difficulties with auditory and visual processing);
- poor self-esteem and motivation.

Cognition and Learning – Information Contacts

You may have pupils in your class with the following disabilities or conditions:

DAMP (deficits in attention, motor control and perception)

- ADDers www.adders.org.uk

Down syndrome

- Downs Syndrome Association www.downs-syndrome.org.uk

Dyscalculia

- British Dyslexia Association www.bdadyslexia.org.uk
- Dyslexia Action www.dyslexiaaction.org.uk

Dysgraphia

- British Dyslexia Association www.bdadyslexia.org.uk
- Dyslexia Action www.dyslexiaaction.org.uk

Dyslexia

- British Dyslexia Association www.bdadyslexia.org.uk
- Dyslexia Action www.dyslexiaaction.org.uk

Dyspraxia

- Dyspraxia Foundation www.dyspraxiafoundation.org.uk

Fragile X syndrome

- Fragile X Society UK www.fragilex.org.uk

Global Developmental Delay (GDD)

- Brainwave www.brainwave.org.uk
- Mencap www.mencap.org.uk

Meares-Irlen syndrome

- Irlen Institute (USA) www.irlen.com
- Irlen UK www.irlenuk.com

Moderate Learning Difficulties (MLDs)

- Mencap www.mencap.org.uk

Prader-Willi syndrome

- Prader-Willi Syndrome Association www.pwsa.co.uk

Social, Emotional and Mental Health (SEMH)

The *SEND Code of Practice 0 to 25 years* (2015) describes the area of need for pupils with social, emotional and mental health difficulties.

> *Children and young people may experience a wide range of social and emotional difficulties which manifest themselves in many ways. These may include becoming withdrawn or isolated, as well as displaying challenging, disruptive or disturbing behaviour. These behaviours may reflect underlying mental health difficulties such as anxiety or depression, self-harming, substance misuse, eating disorders or physical symptoms that are medically unexplained. Other children and young people may have disorders such as attention deficit disorder, attention deficit hyperactive disorder or attachment disorder.*
>
> (2015, p. 98)

You may observe pupils in your class who may:

- be quiet and withdrawn;
- be overly worried about making mistakes;
- be vulnerable and easily led;
- have mood swings with high levels of anxiety;
- have low self-efficacy;
- be bullied or have characteristics of being a bully;
- have difficulty in building and maintaining friendships;
- have difficulty in recognising cause and effect in actions;
- have poor self-control over emotions;
- display some verbal or physical aggression;
- have difficulty working collaboratively and taking part in group discussion;
- have difficulty in conforming to class/school rules and routines;
- display lethargy and apathy, often daydreaming;
- have some eating issues;
- become agitated during transition times or unexpected changes in routines.

Social, Emotional and Mental Health – Information Contacts

You may have pupils in your class with the following disabilities or conditions:

ADD/ADHD

- ADD/ADHD Family Support Group www.addcontact.org.uk

- ADD Information Services (ADDISS) www.addiss.co.uk

Social, Emotional and Mental Health (SEMH)

- SEBDA (Social, Emotional and Behavioural Difficulties Association) www.sebda.org
- Young Minds www.youngminds.org.uk

Bipolar disorder

- MDF (The Bipolar Organisation) www.mdf.org.uk
- Young Minds www.youngminds.org.uk

Eating disorders

- ABC (Anorexia and Bulimia Care) www.anorexianulimiacare.co.uk
- Beat (beat eating disorders) www.b-eat.co.uk

Fragile X syndrome

- Fragile X Society UK www.fragilex.org.uk

Obsessive compulsive disorder (OCD)

- OCD UK www.ocduk.org

Oppositional defiant disorder (ODD)

- Young Minds www.youngminds.org.uk

Pathological demand avoidance syndrome (PDA)

- PDA Contact Group www.pdacontact.org.uk

School phobia

- Anxiety Care www.anxietycare.org.uk
- No Panic www.nopanic.org.uk

Tourette syndrome

- Tourettes Action www.tourettes-action.org.uk

Young carers

- Young Carers Initiative www.youngcarers.net

Sensory and/or Physical Needs

The *SEND Code of Practice 0 to 25 years* (2015) describes the area of need for pupils with sensory and/or physical needs.

> *Some children and young people require special educational provision because they have a disability which prevents or hinders them from making use of the educational facilities generally provided. These difficulties can be age related and may fluctuate over time. Many children and young people with vision impairment (VI), hearing impairment (HI) or a multi-sensory impairment (MSI) will require specialist support and/or equipment to access their learning, or habilitation support. Children and young people with an MSI have a combination of vision and hearing difficulties. Information on how to provide services for deafblind children and young people is available through the Social Care for Deafblind Children and Adults guidance published by the Department of Health. Some children and young people with a physical disability (PD) require additional ongoing support and equipment to access all the opportunities available to their peers.*
>
> (2015, p. 98)

You may observe pupils in your class who have disabilities including visual impairment, hearing impairment, physical difficulties and sensory integration difficulties.

Pupils with **visual impairment** may have mild, moderate or severe vision but with a visual acuity worse than 3/60 they would be registered as blind. Pupils with visual impairment may:

- hold objects or text close to their face to see better;
- squint at objects when trying to focus;
- react to variations in lighting;
- tilt head to one side to focus better;
- bring objects to one eye rather than using both eyes;
- might not be able to recognise some colours;
- have poor hand-eye coordination;
- appear clumsy when moving around the classroom;

- need the support of braille books, specially designed screen reading software, listening books, speech technology and dictation software, portable recorders and other assistive technology.

Most pupils with **hearing impairment**, in mainstream classrooms, have a moderate to severe hearing loss. The term 'deaf' usually refers to a hearing loss so severe that there is little or no functional hearing. Pupils with hearing impairment may:

- have frequent ear infections;
- appear dreamy or distracted;
- have difficulty following instructions;
- watch people's faces and lips intently;
- frequently ask for repetition;
- watch what others are doing before doing it themselves;
- have difficulty in controlling tone and volume of voice;
- become frustrated easily;
- appear socially isolated at times;
- have difficulty in taking an active part in group discussion;
- need the support of visual systems (signing, symbols, assistive technology).

You may observe pupils in your class who have **physical disabilities**. They may have difficulty with:

- accessing the physical learning environment;
- taking part in specific practical tasks;
- using support equipment safely;
- developing self-care skills;
- working independently;
- communicating and interacting with their peer group;
- managing pain and fatigue;
- developing self-efficacy;
- building self-esteem;

- developing gross motor skills;
- developing fine motor skills;
- developing perceptual-motor skills (includes hand-eye coordination, body-eye coordination, auditory language skills and visual-auditory skills);
- developing visual perception skills (the ability to understand, process and make use of visual information);
- structuring and organising written work without the use of assistive technology.

You may observe pupils in your class who have **sensory integration difficulties**. They may:

- be over-sensitive or insensitive to specific sights, sounds, smells, tastes or tactile materials;
- show signs of fatigue or distress as a result of sensory overload;
- dislike being touched without warning;
- need regular access to particular sensory experiences;
- have difficulty defining sights and sounds;
- have difficulty controlling and co-ordinating movements;
- have some listening and attention difficulties.

Sensory and/or Physical Needs – Information Contacts

You may have pupils in your class with the following disabilities or conditions:

Arthritis

- Arthritis Care www.arthritiscare.org.uk
- Children's Chronic Arthritis association (CCAA) www.ccaa.org.uk

Asthma

- National Asthma Campaign www.asthma.org.uk

Brittle bones

- Brittle Bone Society www.brittlebone.org

Cerebral palsy

- Scope www.scope.org.uk

Cleft lip or palate

- Cleft Lip and Palate Association (CLAPA) www.clapa.com

Cystic fibrosis

- Cystic Fibrosis Trust www.cftrust.org.uk

Diabetes

- Diabetes UK www.diabetes.org.uk

Epilepsy

- British Epilepsy Association www.epilepsy.org.uk

Fragile X syndrome

- Fragile X Society UK www.fragilex.org.uk

Global Developmental Delay

- Brainwave www.brainwave.org.uk
- Mencap www.mencap.org.uk

Hearing impairment

- British Deaf Association (BDA) www.bda.org.uk
- Deaf Education through Listening and Talking (DELTA) www.deafeducation.org.uk
- Royal National Institute for the Deaf (RNID) www.rnid.org.uk

Heart disorders

- Children's Heart Association www.heartchild.info

Human immunodeficiency virus (HIV)

- National AIDS Trust (NAT) www.nat.org.uk

Hydrocephalus

- The Association for Spina Bifida and Hydrocephalus (ASBAH) www.asbah.org

Leukaemia and cancer

- CLICSargent (Cancer and Leukaemia in Childhood Trust) www.clicsargent.orf.uk
- Leukaemia Care www.leukaemiacare.org

Myalgic encephalomyelitis (ME)

- Action for ME (AfME) www.afme.org.uk
- Association of Young people with ME (AYME) www.ayme.org.uk

Muscular dystrophy

- Duchenne Family Support Group www.dfsg.org.uk
- Duchenne UK Guide for Teachers https://www.duchenneuk.org/wp-content/uploads/2021/06/Duchenne-UK-Guide-for-Teachers.pdf

Sickle cell disorder (SCD)

- Sickle Cell Society www.sicklecellsociety.org

Sensory integration disorder (SID)

- Sensory Integration Network www.sensoryintegration.org.uk

Spina bifida

- Association for Spina Bifida and Hydrocephalus (ASBAH) www.asbah.org

Turner syndrome

- The Child Growth Foundation www.childgrowthfoundation.org
- The Turner Syndrome Support Society UK www.tss.org.uk

Visual impairment

- LOOK www.look-uk.org
- Royal National Institute for the Blind (RNIB) www.rnib.org.uk
- Visual Impairment Centre for Teaching and Research (VICTAR) www.education.bham.ac.uk/research/victar

Pupil Support Profiles in Different Educational Settings

*Table 9.1 Support profile for a child with Duchenne Muscular Dystrophy supported in a **mainstream** primary school classroom*

Physiotherapist Individual therapy sessions with Aadan in designated space. Setting up programmes of exercise to be implemented by teaching assistant.	**Class teacher** Planning and delivering the curriculum, adapting according to need. Organising weekly timetable to include additional support from medical professionals and teaching assistant. Ensuring classroom organisation is suitable for Aadan's physical disability.	**Occupational therapist** Advising and providing equipment and adaptations to support learning. Training of support staff to help Aadan with mobility and self-help skills using physical adaptations.
SENCo Liaising with all professionals. Organising and overseeing implementation and review of Aadan's ECHP and PLP. Planning and delivering INSET for both teachers and teaching assistants relating to learning difficulties experienced by children with physical and sensory needs.	**Aadan (aged 9)** **Eldest of two children, sister (aged 7) at the same school, very supportive family. Aadan has a cheerful, outgoing personality and a supportive group of friends.**	**Teaching Assistant** Supporting Aadan with classroom learning activities using computer programmes and some assistive technology. Supporting Aadan with mobility and self-help skills using physical adaptations. Implementing physiotherapy exercises in designated space.
Educational Psychologist Liaising with SENCo and parents and attending annual review of Aadan's needs.	**SEND assessment:** • Duchenne Muscular Dystrophy • Respiratory difficulties	**Neurologist** Regular visits to hospital to monitor degenerative muscle loss and related health problems.

*Table 9.2 Support profile for a child with severe learning difficulties (SLD) supported in a **resource base** (RB) as part of a **mainstream** primary school*

Educational Psychologist Liaise with resource base teacher, SENCo, class teacher, parents and all professionals involved with Sam. Observe, assess and advise on pro-active management of Sam's behavioural difficulties. Attending annual review of needs.	**Class teacher** Planned integration for Sam to take part in mainstream classroom-based lessons where he is cognitively capable. Organise quiet learning spaces for Sam and be aware of sensitivity to certain sensory triggers (specific smells, bright light and colours).	**Speech and Language Therapist** Activities to help Sam with sensory integration difficulties. Therapy sessions to help Sam with grammatical, semantic and pragmatic understanding of language. Advise RB teacher and TA on the use of Social Stories.

(Continued)

Table 9.2 (Continued)

SENCo Liaise with RB teacher and all professionals to organise integration into some classroom-based lessons and gifted support. Organise and oversee review of Sam's ECHP.	**Sam (aged 10)** **An only child in a one parent family. Mother very keen to support son in all aspects of his development. Sam likes to work in a contained space. Over-sensitive to light, bright colours and specific smells.**	**Teaching Assistant** Supporting Sam with integration in mainstream classroom using assistive technology when necessary. Work with RB teacher to develop Sam's grammatical, semantic and pragmatic skills in literacy sessions.
Resource Base Teacher Provide a weekly and daily visual timetable for Sam. Organise supported and unsupported classroom integration for science, maths, DT, art, PE, topic, IT and music. Small group and individual learning activities in resource base covering areas where specific support is needed.	**SEND Assessment:** • Autism • Sensory integration difficulties • Identified as more and most able in music (singing and piano) and etymology, high score on BPVS (British Picture Vocabulary Scale).	**Teacher responsible for more and most able support** Provide opportunities for Sam to take part in musical activities with TA support (choir, concerts) Devise word challenges, quizzes and crosswords for small, high-attaining group and encourage Sam to become a library monitor.

Table 9.3 Support profile for child with profound and multiple learning difficulties (PMLD) supported as a day pupil in a ***special*** *school*

Occupational Therapist Advise on postural alignment and supportive sitting. Advise on how to support complex movements such as self-help skills (going to the toilet, getting dressed). Advise on mobility aids and the use of assistive technology in liaison with SLT and physiotherapist.	**Class Teacher** Plan, produce and coordinate a daily visual timetable for Jemma in liaison with all professionals involved. Provide individualised learning experiences which can be assessed using the engagement model. Review EHCP regularly providing ongoing updates to parents and professionals.	**Speech and Language Therapist** Regular speech and language therapy sessions to help Jemma improve verbal communication skills including strengthening muscles and increasing breath support to help improve articulation. Teaching sign language and use of widget software.

Nurse Practitioner Support during and after seizures. Advise on rest sessions. **Counsellor** Individual and small group counselling sessions using assistive technology to help Jemma communicate her concerns more easily.	**Jemma (aged 8)** **Jemma is the eldest of three children, siblings are at a mainstream school. Family needs a great deal of support from social services and other professionals.**	**Teaching Assistant** Support with curriculum activities using sign language and assistive technology. Develop self-help skills using physical adaptations. Implement physiotherapy exercises. Liaise with class teacher and parents.
Physiotherapist Individual therapy sessions with Jemma to encourage movement, increase strength and stop muscles becoming weak. Advise on mobility aids with occupational therapist. Set up programmes of exercise to be implemented by teaching assistant.	**SEND Assessment:** • Cerebral palsy • Epilepsy • Moderate hearing loss • Dysarthria • Anxiety and depression	**Hearing impaired sensory services** Regular assessment of Jemma's hearing loss with provision and advice on any specialist equipment needed to support communication needs. Provide advice and support to all those working with Jemma.

Table 9.4 Personal profile template

Things I am good at	**Name and Photo**	**Things I need help with**
What makes me happy	**My family**	**What makes me sad**
My best friends are	**My favourite food is**	**Something important**

10 Key Learning Skills

This section focuses on the key learning skills mentioned frequently in assessment reports. For some pupils, activities may need to be adapted using different types of assistive technology, multisensory resources and graphic organisers. Most activities can be adapted for class, group, paired or individual learning situations.

Auditory Discrimination

Auditory Discrimination is the ability to detect similarities and differences between sounds, both larger sounds such as those made by animals, vehicles or musical instruments as well as being able to discriminate between phonemes (units of sounds in words).

Pupils with difficulties in this area may have problems with:

- identifying similarities and differences between sounds;
- identifying speech sounds and have poor articulation of sounds and words;
- discriminating between similar sounds and words, especially when there is a background noise.

Auditory Discrimination Support Activities

- **Transition times** (cross curricular) – use specific musical phrases to indicate different transition times (breaktime, lunchtime).
- **Sound journey** (cross curricular) – use recorded sounds to activate prior knowledge for a topic with visual resources as cues.
- **Making music** (design and technology, music) – making musical instruments, identifying and experimenting with pitch, tempo and volume (high/low, fast/slow, loud/soft).
- **Sound walks** (cross curricular, geography) – identify sounds heard on a walk, link to a study of the local environment.
- **Tune into environmental sounds** – Yellow Door Education uses photo cards and audio sound effects as a targeted support activity.

- **Same/Different** (English) – identify pairs of words that are the same or different (bat/bad, sing/sing).
- **Sound effects** (music, drama) – use a variety of materials to create sound effects for a puppet show or role play sequence.
- **Odd one out** (English) – identify the non-rhyming word (ring/sing/song).
- **Patterns of sound** (science, music) – find patterns between the volume of a sound and the strength of the vibrations that produce it. Identify and describe sound volume (loud/louder/loudest, high/higher/highest).
- **Tongue twisters** (English) – identify the initial sound used in the tongue twister.

Auditory Memory

Auditory Memory is the ability to retain and recall information that has been presented orally. This information may be retained for a short while and be in active use (working memory), processed, rehearsed and retained for a longer period of time (long-term memory) or retained and recalled in the correct sequence (auditory sequential memory).

Pupils with difficulties in this area may have problems with:

- recalling information given verbally;
- retaining information over a period of time;
- recalling information in the correct sequence.

Auditory Memory Support Activities

- **Songs and rhymes** (English, maths) – recall, recite and sing action rhymes, raps and songs.
- **Alphabet and number sequences** (English, maths) – recall sequences of given letters and numbers from different starting points using multisensory resources.
- **Actions** (PE) recall two or three actions – clap your hands, bend your knees, touch your shoulders.
- **Mnemonics** (English) – pupils learn and recall how to spell specific common exception words using mnemonics as a memory aid.
- **I went shopping and I bought** (maths) recall two, three or four items – can be played as a practical shopping activity.

- **Messages** (English) – remember a message to take to another class.
- **Repeating rhythms** (music) – repeat rhythms using a variety of different instruments.
- **Flow chart** (science, maths) – organise and sequence ideas or processes discussed verbally using a prepared template.
- **Tell a memory** (English, PSHE) – show an object, photo or drawing relating to a memory, then relate memory to partner or group.

Creative Thinking

Creative thinking requires pupils to use their imagination to generate new ideas, to evaluate and improve ideas leading to original solutions to problems, to make innovative connections and find new and interesting ways to approach tasks.

Pupils with difficulties in this area may have problems with:

- making imaginative responses to stimuli;
- using visualisation techniques (creating pictures in the mind);
- making connections and drawing inferences.

Creative Thinking Support Activities

- **Making models** (art and design, cross curricular) – use modelling clay, playdough and other materials to create models linked to a topic or theme.
- **Music and movement** (PE, music) – create a series of movements to music, can be related to a topic (water, animals in a rainforest).
- **Build a raft** (design and technology, science) – choose materials to build a raft that will float and carry a given object.
- **Story chains** (English) – oral storytelling where each pupil adds a new sentence to the story.
- **Create a garden** (science) – use an understanding of how plants grow to create a garden either as a window box or a part of the school environment.
- **Collage** (art and design) – use a range of materials and media to design a collage.
- **Puppets** (drama) – use puppets to dramatise familiar stories.

- **What if ....?** (cross curricular) – pose scenarios related to topic or subject. Pupils to consider possible outcomes and think of creative ideas for solutions to problems.
- **Mouse maze** (design and technology) – create a maze for a toy mouse using given materials (wooden bricks, Lego, straws).

Critical Thinking

Critical thinking requires pupils to think and reason logically to make decisions and solve problems. Critical thinking activities encourage individuals to analyse information from a variety of sources, make connections between ideas, make deductions, give reasoned explanations and evaluate conclusions.

Pupils with difficulties in this area may have problems with:

- making connections and comparisons between different types of information;
- making deductions from given clues;
- giving reasons for their ideas and evaluating their decisions.

Critical Thinking Support Activities

- **Form and function** (history) – pupils handle artefacts and make deductions about their possible use. Adult offers simple verbal clues making links to prior knowledge.
- **Carroll diagrams** (maths, science) – sorting shapes (4 sides//more than 4 sides, red//blue), sorting minibeasts (insects//not insects, fly//not fly).
- **Odd one out** (science, cross curricular) using pictorial cards – animal groupings (lion, tiger, fox, cheetah), clothing (socks, hat, shoes, slippers).
- **Where am I?** (geography) map skills – using simple letter/number coordinate clues for pupils to identify a location. Pupils can also make up clues as a paired activity.
- **Logic trees** (science) – Amphibian or fish? (Does it have lungs/gills? Does it have fins and scales/smooth skin? Does it have limbs/no limbs?)
- **Fact or opinion** (English, history, art and design) – pupils discuss and decide which statements are fact or opinion (The tortoise was tired after his race with the hare. Henry VIII had six wives).
- **The answer is... What is the question?** (cross curricular) – The answer is green. The answer is water. The answer is 5. What is the question?

- **Comparisons** (maths, science, music, history) – pupils identify similarities and differences between 2D and 3D shapes, between plants, between musical instruments, between toys used then and now.

Enquiry Skills

Enquiry skills enable pupils to ask relevant questions, pose and define problems, observe and measure, identify and classify, predict outcomes and test conclusions.

Pupils with difficulties in this area may have problems with:

- asking relevant questions relating to an investigation;
- identifying and classifying information;
- making predictions about possible outcomes;
- interpreting, evaluating and communicating results.

Enquiry Skills Support Activities

- **Hot seat** (English, history) – pupils devise questions to ask an historical character or a character in a story. Teacher/adult gives answers ensuring that pupils know whether it's a fact or opinion answer.
- **Yes or no** (English, science, geography) – multisensory questionnaire or quiz related to topic or subject studied. Pupils asked to give yes or no answers.
- **Concept cartoons** (science, maths) – the cartoons represent everyday situations visually and show the characters discussing different viewpoints about a particular scientific or mathematical concept. Pupils are encouraged to think about and discuss the different ideas and give reasons for their viewpoints.
- **Investigations** (cross curricular) – Which material is the strongest? Why does the weather change? Pupils work in cooperative learning groups to explore ideas and possible answers.
- **Classification** (maths, science) – pupils sort shapes, objects, materials, living things into specific groups according to given criteria.
- **Why? Because** (science) – pupils make predictions about outcomes, giving reasons, before testing ideas (predicting what might happen to specific materials when put in water, what might happen to seeds under different conditions).

- **Flow chart** (science, geography) – pupils draw, write or use assistive technology to show the correct order of a process.
- **Posters** (cross curricular) – pupils discuss and evaluate topic findings and communicate findings via a poster (A World of Water, Amazing Animals, Wicked Weather).

Fine Motor Skills

Fine motor skills make use of smaller muscles in the body for precise tasks. These movements may also require the use of perceptual motor skills including body awareness, spatial awareness, directional awareness and temporal awareness. Fine motor skills require eye-hand co-ordination and precise manipulative skills.

Pupils with difficulties in this area may have problems with:

- self-help skills such as dressing and undressing;
- hand-eye coordination (using scissors, throwing and catching a ball);
- precise hand movements for writing, drawing and constructional activities.

Fine Motor Skills Support Activities

- **Patterns** (maths, art and design) – pupils copy patterns using beads, peg boards and shapes, investigate tessellating shapes.
- **Sensory writing** (English) – pupils copy writing patterns using fingers in coloured sand or paste paint and form letters using Play-Doh.
- **Pencil and paper** (English, art and design) – pupils create shapes and patterns using free pencil movements, maze and tracking activities, tracing, line links (mouse to cheese).
- **Sorting** (maths) – pupils sort small objects (paper clips, buttons, counters, tiles, coins) to encourage precise finger movements.
- **Sky Writer** (Top Marks) – this is an aeroplane-themed handwriting computer tool supporting the development of correct letter formation.
- **Dot to Dot** (English, maths) – pupils follow number or alphabetical sequences to form pictures or shapes.
- **Construction apparatus** (design and technology) – topic themed or open-ended activities using a variety of construction apparatus.

- **Musical instruments** (music) – pupils use precise finger movement to play an instrument (recorder, triangle, xylophone, finger cymbals).
- **Scissor control** (art and design, cross curricular) – pupils cut and paste paper shapes for patterns and collage pictures, cut and paste pictures for project scrapbooks.
- **Threading, lacing and sewing** (art and design) with a variety of sized laces, beads and sewing materials.

Grammar, Syntax and Morphology

Grammar, syntax and morphology – Grammar is the organisation of words into sentences using correct grammatical structure. Syntax is the way in which words are sequenced to convey meaning. Morphology refers to the way words are formed. A morpheme represents the smallest unit of meaning in a word.

Pupils with difficulties in this area may:

- have poor receptive language (difficulty in understanding past, present and future tenses, in understanding different sentence structures and the use of pronouns, prepositions and conjunctions);
- have poor expressive language (use a limited vocabulary and poor sentence construction, muddle word order in sentences, use verb tenses and inflectional endings such as 'ed' and 'ing' incorrectly).

Grammar, Syntax and Morphology Support Activities

- **Model correct grammar** (English) – pupil says, 'I seed my gran yesterday.' Teacher remodels, 'You saw your gran yesterday. What did you do together?'
- **Tell me** (English, cross curricular) – encourage pupils to think and speak in sentences by describing objects, pictures, story characters for a group to guess (It has a long point. It's made of wood.).
- **Sort a sentence** (English) – pupils use common exception words and words that can be decoded phonetically to organise into a sentence, recognising that the word with a capital letter starts the sentence and a full stop ends the sentence. Cards using Widget Symbols or published resources can be used for this activity.
- **Rebus sentences** (English, cross curricular) – write a simple sentence relating to a topic using pictures for the nouns.

- **Sentence completion** (English, cross curricular) – pupils to complete open-ended sentences orally or written (The cat was looking at... The tadpole changed into...).
- **Beginnings and endings** (English, cross curricular) – pupils match beginnings and endings of sentences using sentence meaning as well as punctuation clues. Sentences can be subject- or topic-related.
- **Questions and answers** (English, cross curricular) – pupils to match sentence questions to answers related to a story or topic.
- **Actions** (English, cross curricular) – introduce verbs both oral and written. Using Widget software, make a visual display of verbs familiar to pupils (look, walk, help, eat, sing, fly, run). Pupils to match actions to a subject (A cat can... The bird can...).
- **Now and then** (English, history) – link simple verb tenses to a history project using a 'then' and 'now' board (Victorian children played ball games. We play ball games).
- **Cloze** (English) – pupils choose a suitable word to complete a sentence (A cat/crow/crab had a nest in the tree.). Cloze procedure sentences can also be open-ended with pupils asked to complete by using nouns, adjectives, verbs, adverbs or prepositions (The old dog was asleep ________ the table.).

Gross Motor Skills

Gross motor skills make use of the large muscles of the body. These movements may also require the use of perceptual motor skills including body awareness, spatial awareness, directional awareness and temporal awareness involving the coordinated effort of the large muscle groups.

Pupils with difficulties in this area may:

- appear clumsy and un-coordinated when trying to control their movements for physical activities such as running, hopping, jumping, skipping, balancing or riding a bike;
- have difficulty in judging distances and the position of objects in space such as in ball games involving throwing, catching and kicking;
- have difficulty with directional awareness such as in differentiating between left and right, up and down, forward and back.

Gross Motor Skills Support Activities

- **Stepping stones** (PE) – pupils use small hoops as stepping stones, crossing the water by jumping from one to the other without falling in.

- **Balancing** (PE) – pupils use a range of small and large apparatus for balancing activities. Individual therapy targets can be incorporated into activities.
- **Dodgems** (PE) – this can be a warm-up activity with pupils running in different directions, dodging out of the way of each other. When teacher calls 'change', pupils change direction.
- **Parachute games** (PE, PSHE) – choose games that help develop gross motor skills and teamwork.
- **Ball Games** (PE) – pupils take part in a variety of ball games involving rolling, throwing, catching kicking, dribbling and batting.
- **Music, movement and mime** (PE, drama) – dance and drama can help develop different types of gross motor movements. Individual therapy targets can be incorporated into activities.
- **Climbing** (PE) – use a range of large apparatus to support the development of specific gross motor skills.
- **Obstacle course** (PE) – using a range of apparatus to design an obstacle course which encourages pupils to practise running, jumping, crawling, balancing and climbing.

Listening and Attention

Listening is the ability to attend to sounds across a range of stimuli. Attention is the ability to listen carefully and sustain attention.

Pupils with difficulties in this area may:

- be easily distracted by noise and movement;
- often have constant movement of hands and feet;
- be unable to focus on cooperative learning tasks;
- have difficulty with following instructions and attending to detail in a task.

Listening and Attention Support Activities

- **Sensory stories** (English) – encourage pupils to listen to stories, experience new vocabulary and respond to thoughts and feelings through the senses.
- **Follow the leader** (PE) – pupils watch the actions of the group leader and copy them.

- **Name game** (English) – I came to school, and I saw... Group activity encouraging pupils to listen and recall names.
- **Mrs T says** (cross curricular) – similar to Simon Says with teacher/adult giving instructions.
- **Parachute activities** (PE, PSHE) – pupils listen to instructions as part of a team activity.
- **Tap a rhythm** (music) – pupils listen to a rhythm being tapped out then repeat the rhythm using a range of instruments.
- **Listen and Do** (cross curricular) – pupils listen carefully and follow one and two step instructions to complete an activity.
- **Circle Time** (PSHE) – the pupil who is speaking holds an object indicating others must listen.
- **Messages** (cross curricular) – pupils recall verbal messages containing one or two elements (a) requiring a yes or no reply; (b) requiring a simple sentence reply.

Organisational Skills

Organisational skills involve pupils in following, planning and sequencing everyday routines, developing independence in self-care, gathering and organising information for learning tasks, managing homework.

Pupils with difficulties in this area may:

- have poor self-help skills such as getting dressed and brushing teeth;
- frequently lose personal items;
- lack awareness of time frames or organisation of materials needed for a task;
- have difficulty using language in an ordered and logical way.

Organisational Skills Support Activities

- **Visual timetables** (cross curricular) – create class and group timetables using Widget Symbols.
- **Visual task sequences** (cross curricular) – create individual and group task sequences using Widget Symbols.
- **Routines** (cross curricular) – establish regular routines such as morning greetings, using signs and symbols to indicate time for listening or cooperative learning and entering and exiting the classroom.

- **Checklists** (cross curricular) – provide visual checklists as reminders for items needed at specific times such PE kit or items needed for homework hubs and after school clubs.
- **Personal diary** (English, PSHE) – encourages the use of a diary as a reminder of personal problems and activities.
- **Tidy Up** (cross curricular) – ask pupils to tidy specific classroom items using sorting, classifying and grouping.
- **Graphic organisers** (cross curricular) – pupils can be supported with organising information and narrative writing using suitable graphic organisers such as mind maps, storyboards, comic strips, charts, diagrams, tables, graphs, writing frames, timelines and posters.
- **Organising materials** (design and technology, art and design, science) – encourage pupils to make visual checklists of the materials, media and items needed before beginning a design project or science investigation.

Phonemic and Phonological Awareness

A phoneme is a single speech sound and can be represented by one or more letters. Phonemic awareness is the ability to identify and use these speech sounds in spoken and written words. Phonological awareness is the ability to identify and manipulate parts of words, including syllables, onset–rime and phonemes.

Pupils with difficulties in this area may:

- have poor articulation of sounds and difficulty discriminating between similar sounds and words;
- have problems identifying and blending phonemes;
- have problems identifying syllables in polysyllabic words.

Phonemic and Phonological Awareness Support Activities

- **Magnetic letters** (English) – pupils can use magnetic letters and phonemes to learn letter and phoneme recognition and phoneme blending.
- **Lego Braille bricks** (English) – these can be used for a number of phonological awareness activities with ideas and guidance given.
- **Talking Phonics Flashcards** (Carter's Yard) – are a set of 32 interactive, augmented reality 'talking' flashcards featuring English phonics sounds, powered by the Zappar App.

- **Vowel change** (English) – use magnetic letters to show how CVC words can change (bat/but, cup/cap, top/tip).
- **Sense or nonsense** (English) – identify the words that make sense when phonemes are blended (hat/top/hin, moon/foon/spoon, brick/trick/smick).
- **Blends and ends** (English) – collect beginnings and endings of words (bl/ack, gr/een, th/en, th/ink).
- **Odd word out** (English) – asks pupils to identify the words that do not rhyme (sat/mat/dad, ring/sing/song).
- **Syllable count** (English, cross curricular) – clapping, tapping, syllables in pupils' names, high frequency words (today, everyone, yesterday, animals) and in key concept vocabulary.
- **Rhyming Snap, Pelmanism, Families** (English) – using published resources or resources produced using Widget Symbols play these well-known games to encourage identification of rhyming words.
- **Validated Systematic Synthetic Phonic programmes** (English) – a list of programmes can be found on the government website.

Semantic Knowledge

Semantics refers to the meanings of words and how they relate to each other. This includes the ability to understand the meanings of words in different contexts, as well as understanding the meaning of relationships between words (categories, opposites, synonyms, word functions and word associations).

Pupils with difficulties in this area may:

- have difficulty with developing more than a literal understanding of a text;
- have word finding problems and need time to process information;
- need new concept vocabulary to be taught explicitly and have time for repetition and practice.

Semantic Knowledge Support Activities

- **Colourful Semantics** (Routledge. Integrated Treatment Services) is a method of teaching children how to understand and build sentences using colour coding. It's aimed at helping children to understand the meanings of words (semantics) and develop their grammar skills.

- **Lotto** (cross curricular) – picture/word baseboards linked to a topic/subject (toys, food, minibeasts, vehicles). Widget Symbols can be used or other published resources.
- **Comparisons** (maths, science) – using visual and tactile materials, introduce pupils to comparative language (taller than, heavier than, colder than).
- **Identifying and describing** (Black Sheep Press) is a series of activities and games designed to develop semantic skills in pupils at key stage 1.
- **Opposites** (English, cross curricular) – use everyday objects to introduce key concept vocabulary (long/short pencils, old/new shoes, full/empty containers, sweet/sour food).
- **What is it?** (art and design, English) – pupils describe a specific part of a work of art giving verbal clues. This can be a cooperative learning activity to develop descriptive language.
- **Compound word pairs** (English) – pupils to match individual words to form compound words such as foot/ball, bed/room, to/day, pan/cake.
- **Odd one out** (English, science, maths, history, geography) – pupils to identify key concept vocabulary related to a topic/subject and recognise which one does not belong to a specific category, giving reasons why (river, lake, hill, stream).
- **Homophone pelmanism** (English) – pupils collect word pairs (see/sea, for/four, blue/blew, meet/meat). Widget Symbols can be used for this activity.

Social Communication (Pragmatics)

Pragmatics refers to the ability to understand how to communicate in social situations.

Pupils with difficulties in this area may:

- have problems in interpreting both verbal and non-verbal communication (tone of voice, facial expression, gestures);
- have difficulty in understanding how to use language in a range of social situations and can make inappropriate remarks;
- have problems understanding other points of view and in taking turns when involved in cooperative learning activities.

Social Communication Support Activities

- **Role play** (English) – adults to role play specific social situations alongside pupils, in small groups, exploring possible reactions.
- **Social Stories** (PSHE) – this is a well-researched and published approach to help pupils with autism cope with certain social situations they find difficult.
- **Tell me** (English, PSHE) – pupils to talk about topics of interest to the group. Subtle adult questioning should support the pupil in keeping to the topic and giving relevant background information.
- **Circle time** (PSHE) – provide opportunities for pupils to develop the ability to listen to other children's points of view and begin to express their own.
- **Comic Strip Conversations** (Carol Gray) – these help individuals with autism to develop greater social understanding. They also provide an insight into the individual's perception of particular situations.
- **Puppets** (English) – pupils with social communication difficulties can be encouraged to take an active part in puppet activities after watching modelled situations.
- **Making faces** (English) – group miming activities, showing pupils how to portray feelings through facial expressions. Scenes from well-known stories can be enacted where character's feelings are expressed.
- **Positive Pragmatic Game Boards** (Super Duper Publications) are ten laminated board games to help pupils improve their social communication skills.
- **Time to Talk** (LDA) is a programme of activities to develop oral language and social interaction skills. It includes the skills of turn-taking, giving and following instructions, eye contact, listening and attention.

Spatial Awareness

Spatial awareness is the ability to be aware of oneself in space within the environment and to see objects in relation to each other. It includes knowing about shapes, space, position, direction and movement.

Pupils with difficulties in this area may:

- have some visual perception problems and difficulties with positional language used across the curriculum;
- have difficulty with presentation skills, structuring and organising written work;

- have problems with abstract maths concepts in the areas of shape, space and measure and in using comparative language (taller than, shorter than).

Spatial Awareness Support Activities

- **Action songs and games** (cross curricular) to develop an awareness of different parts of the body (head, shoulders, knees and toes, one finger one thumb keep moving).
- **Catch the croc** (PE) – pupils to walk along a chalk line with cardboard pictures of crocodiles either side. Adult calls 'right' or 'left' and pupils jump in correct direction. Those who jump on a croc keep it. Aim to collect a certain number of crocs.
- **Treasure hunt** (English, geography) – pupils to follow directional instructions (forward three steps, turn right) or use simple map skills to follow directions.
- **Robotics and coding** (computing) – pupils to learn how to input directional coded instructions into a robotic device.
- **Puzzles** (cross curricular) – pupils to complete puzzles of varying degrees of difficulty which may be related to a topic.
- **Tangrams** (maths) are useful for developing spatial awareness, for exploring size, perimeter, the properties of shape and other geometric concepts.
- **Model making** (design and technology) using a range of materials, including construction apparatus, pupils can build models following simple pictorial and diagrammatic instructions.
- **Tessellation** (maths, art and design) – pupils can arrange 2D magnetic shapes into tessellating patterns or choose 2D shapes they think will tessellate, draw round them as a design for a floor pattern.

Verbal Reasoning

Verbal reasoning is the process by which our brains make sense of what we hear and read. It's the ability to listen to or read information, develop an understanding and use this in various problem-solving activities.

Pupils with difficulties in this area may:

- have problems understanding some instructions and information without visual and concrete cues;
- have difficulty following group and class discussions;

- need multisensory support with understanding key concept vocabulary;
- have difficulty making connections between ideas and developing inferencing skills.

Verbal Reasoning Support Activities

- **Connections** (English, cross curricular) – published games can be used or topic cards made using Widget Symbols. Pupils make links between cards giving reasons for the connections (pizza, balloons, cake – a party). If linked to a topic, these cards can support pupils with activating prior knowledge and compiling mind maps.
- **Criss cross** (English) – pupils to complete simple two-word crosswords following across and down clues. These can be completed using magnetic letters.
- **Who am I?** (English) – pupils to read or listen to clues and then identify a story character.
- **True or false** (cross curricular) – pupils to hold up true or false cards after listening to a statement. This activity can act as an interim assessment of pupils' understanding of topic/subject knowledge.
- **My number is** (maths) – each pupil in the group picks a number card. They take turns to give three clues to help their group identify the number card they've picked (It's an odd number. It's larger than 8. It's smaller than 12.).
- **I wonder why**... (English) – pose questions about character motivation to encourage pupils to use inferencing skills.
- **Wanted** (English) – this is a paired activity to support pupils in developing descriptive skills. Pupils draw and describe a story book character's face with a partner copying their description.
- **Bedtime at the wildlife park** (English) – pupils use the clues to arrange the animals in the correct bedtime order (The giraffes went in last. The tigers went in before the bears. The lions went in first. The elephants went in after the bears. The monkeys went in before the giraffes. The bears went in third.).

Visual Discrimination

Visual discrimination is the ability to recognise similarities and differences between visual images. These images could be objects, pictures, symbols, letters and could vary in shape, pattern, colour and size.

Pupils with difficulties in this area may:

- have problems with identifying shapes, symbols, objects, letters and words that look similar;
- reverse words in both reading and spelling (was/saw) and have difficulty with letter and number orientation;
- find simple scanning activities difficult (wordsearches, word banks, dictionaries, contents, index);
- have problems with interpreting and organising diagrams, charts, graphs, maps and other visual methods of recording information.

Visual Discrimination Support Activities

- **Sorting** (maths, science, art and design) – pupils to sort items for colour, shape, size, material, media and texture.
- **Silhouettes** (English, art and design) – pupils to match shape, object or story character to silhouette. High frequency word silhouettes can be used to support pupils in identifying word shape.
- **Ordering** (maths, cross curricular) – pupils to order shapes, objects and household items in order of size.
- **Spot the difference** (English) – Winslow Resources produce colourful picture sequences for pupils to identify similarities and differences.
- **Sentence bingo** (English) – pupils collect words that match to a sentence strip, then read the sentence when all the correct words are collected.
- **Missing numbers/letters** (English, maths) – pupils to arrange specific magnetic numbers in order and identify the missing number (4, 5, 6, _ 8, 9). Similarly, magnetic letters can be arranged in alphabetical order (d, e, f, _ h).
- **Environmental patterns** (cross curricular) – observational activities where pupils look for patterns in nature, buildings, soft furnishings and clothing.
- **Where is it?** (English, art and design) – pupils search a picture or photo for a specific detail or feature.

Visual Memory

Visual memory is the ability to retain and recall information that has been presented visually. This information may be retained for a short while and be in active use (working memory), be processed, rehearsed and retained for a longer period of time (long-term memory) or retained and recalled in the correct sequence (visual sequential memory).

Pupils with difficulties in this area may:

- have immature drawing skills (drawings lack detail);
- have difficulty with recalling patterns, shapes, designs and letter and number orientation;
- have problems recalling and spelling high frequency words.

Visual Memory Support Activities

- **Memory patterns** (maths) – pupils to recall repeating patterns using manipulatives (red, blue, green counters; red, yellow, red, yellow cubes).
- **Memory sequences** (English, maths) pupils to (a) – Recall a series of three or four coloured shapes. (b) Recall a series of three or four everyday pictorial sequences. (c) Recall alphabet and number sequences using magnetic letters and numerals.
- **Kim's game** (cross curricular) – place five or six objects, related to a topic, on a tray. Pupils to talk about the form and function of the objects and name them. Cover the objects and ask pupils to name as many as possible. One object can be taken away and pupils identify the missing object.
- **Pelmanism** (English, maths, cross curricular) – pictorial or word cards are placed face down. Pupils take turns to pick up two cards with the aim of finding two that match. Pupils need to use visual memory to recall pairs. Cards can be related to a topic or numerals, shapes, letters and words.
- **Memory skills board games (LDA)** – six board games to develop visual memory skills including matching and spot the difference.
- **Complete the shape** (maths) – show pupils a 2D shape. Give them an incomplete drawing of the same shape. Ask pupils to complete the shape from memory.
- **Visual memory spelling games** (English) – using specific word cards, related to individual needs, and a baseboard, pupils need to spell words correctly to move around the board.
- **Story maps and storyboards** (English) – pupils recall the main points and sequence of a story then present it as a story map or storyboard.

Word Finding

Word finding is the ability to understand and access vocabulary from the long-term memory. A pupil may have difficulty in retrieving and using a word.

Pupils with difficulties in this area may:

- have difficulty naming everyday items, people or places;
- need to describe the form and function of a word rather than naming it;
- substitute words that have a similar meaning (cup/mug).

Word Finding Support Activities

- **Tell me** (English, cross curricular) – pupils handle objects in a box. Each pupil in the group describes an object by feature and function for others in the group to name.
- **Labelled pictures** (cross curricular) – pupils to label a picture (person, animal, insect, vehicle, street scene) naming the different parts.
- **Miming** (cross curricular) – pupils choose a picture of an object, related to a topic, then mime how it is used for others in the group to name.
- **It's on the tip of my tongue** (Black Sheep Press) – A range of word finding activities for key stage 1 pupils.
- **Habitats** (science) – pupils match an animal to its habitat and name both animal and habitat (pictorial).
- **Word/picture web** (English, cross curricular) – pupils to draw pictorial reminders around the name of an item they have difficulty in remembering; can use Rebus symbols if necessary.
- **Semantic links** (English) – using published cards or Widget Symbol cards ask pupils to make links and explain reasons for choices (hen/eggs, foot/shoe, pencil/paper).
- **What am I?** (cross curricular) – pupils to use prior knowledge to guess an answer from the sentence clues given.

11
SEND Resources

The resources listed below represent some of those available to support pupils with SEND but can also be used with pupils in mixed ability classrooms. Many have been developed from practical research and have been tried and tested in schools. The resources are organised under the four government identified categories of SEND.

Communication and Interaction

Ace Centre is a registered charity providing Assistive Technology and Augmentative and Alternative Communication services for people with communication difficulties and complex needs.

Black Sheep Press produces a range of resources to support pupils with speech, language and communication difficulties. The resources can be used by speech and language therapists for specific interventions as well as teachers and TAs to reinforce learning.

Blank's Levels of Questioning was developed by Blank, Rose and Berlin in 1978 by analysing levels of comprehension required by year 1 pupils for the classroom. The four levels of questioning are as follows:

- Level 1 – naming things (What is it? Who is this?).
- Level 2 – describing things (What is the cat doing?).
- Level 3 – talking about stories and events (What might happen next? What happened to the mouse in the story?).
- Level 4 – problem solving, reasoning, inferencing (How do you know that? Why do you think that happened?).

ColorCards (Winslow): 'Cause and Effect' and 'Decisions' are visual cards designed to help develop verbal reasoning skills. The cards also help pupils to develop pragmatic language and social skills as they begin to understand why things happen and predict possible outcomes.

Colorcards: Everyday Objects (Winslow): These cards can be used to assess pupils' prior vocabulary knowledge and understanding of the function of everyday items. Used for individual or small group speech and language intervention activities.

Colourful Semantics (Routledge. Integrated Treatment Services): Colourful Semantics is an approach created by Alison Bryan, a Speech and Language Therapist. It's a method of teaching children how to understand and build sentences using colour coding. It's aimed at helping children to understand the meanings of words (semantics) and develop their grammar skills.

Comic Strip Conversations (Future Horizons) is a technique developed by Carol Gray (1994) to assist individuals with autism to develop greater social understanding. Comic Strip Conversations provide visual representations of the different levels of communication that take place in a conversation, using symbols, stick figure drawings and colour. By seeing the elements of a conversation visually presented, some of the abstract aspects of social communication such as recognising the feelings and intentions of others are made more concrete and are therefore easier to understand. Comic Strip Conversations can also provide insight into the pupil's perception of a particular situation.

Eddie's Book of Idioms (2021), Nikki Saunders: This is a useful story for introducing pupils to the confusing world of idioms.

Find the Link (Speechmark Publishing Ltd. Routledge) is an interactive board game designed to develop word finding and categorisation skills suitable for all key stages. The game can be played individually with adult support or in groups of two to five players.

Go Talk speech output devices (Inclusive Technology) are battery operated communication devices which can be used to convey pre-recorded messages for pupils who have speech difficulties. The messages can be pre-recorded by the pupil's support network.

Identifying and Describing (Black Sheep Press): Identifying and Describing is a series of activities and games designed to support pupils develop semantic skills.

InPrint 3 (Widgit Software) is a useful resource for creating and printing a range of visual communication resources such as posters, timetables and activity sheets suitable for all literacy levels and key stages.

It's on the Tip of my Tongue (Black Sheep Press): A range of word finding activities for key stage 1 pupils.

Makaton (The Makaton Charity): Makaton is a language programme that uses signs and symbols to help individuals communicate. Makaton signs are very visual and concrete at the early levels. The Makaton resources available in the UK use some signs from the British Sign Language. When using Makaton, each country uses their own sign language.

PECS (Picture Exchange Communication System) (Pyramid Educational Consultants UK Ltd): PECS is an augmentative, alternative training package. It's designed to help pupils with autism and other communication difficulties to begin communicating through picture/symbol and object exchange.

Positive Pragmatic Game Boards (Super Duper Publications): These are 10 laminated board games to help pupils improve their social communication skills.

Rainbow Parachutes (WF Education Group): Parachute activities help to improve spatial awareness, social skills, communication and interaction through a wide range of games.

Sensory App House produces software for reading support, communication, therapy and early learning suitable for pupils with SLD and PMLD.

TACPAC (Tacpac) is a sensory approach to developing communication through an integrated experience of touch, sound, pattern and relationship. TACPAC was developed for pupils with sensory impairment, developmental delay and complex learning difficulties involving pre-verbal levels of communication. It involves combining music with textured objects and movement.

The New Social Story Book – by Carol Gray (Future Horizons): Social Stories are short descriptions of particular situations, events or activities written by a supportive adult for an individual with autism. Each story includes specific information about what to expect in certain situations and how to respond appropriately.

Time to Talk Book and Game (LDA): Time to Talk is a programme of activities to develop oral language and social interaction skills. It includes the skills of turn-taking, giving and following instructions, eye contact, listening and attention.

Tune into Environmental Sounds (Yellow Door Education) uses photo cards and CD sound effects as a targeted support activity.

Visuals2Go is an all-in-one app to support pupils with communication and learning difficulties.

Widget Online (Widget Software): This is a useful for creating visual timetables, vocabulary cards, stories and other visual communication resources.

Widget Symbols (Widget Software) form a complete visual language of over 20,000 symbols representing more than 55,000 words to help pupils understand new words and develop their vocabulary.

Cognition and Learning

Bee-Bot (TTS) is a programmable floor robot which can be used to develop a pupil's ability to give a sequence of instructions using directional language.

Carter's Yard Phonics (ednology): These flashcards are a set of 64, interactive talking flashcards.

Clicker Board (Crick Software) provides pupils with a planning and mind-mapping tool. Pupils can combine text, images and sounds to help plan their written work as well as helping them understand links between concepts.

Clicker 8 (Crick Software) Clicker 8 is a talking word-processor where pupils can click on a word or picture and the word is spoken aloud. Clicker uses a multi-sensory approach suitable for pupils with specific learning difficulties.

ColorCards (Winslow): Categories, Sequences, Odd One Out, Prepositions, Familiar Verbs and Adjectives are cards designed to develop cognitive language skills including auditory memory, visual memory, sequencing, classification and problem-solving across all key stages.

Concept Cartoons in Science and Maths (Millgate House Education Ltd): Concept Cartoons are designed to stimulate mathematical and scientific thinking and provoke discussion. The cartoons represent everyday situations visually and show the characters discussing different viewpoints about a particular scientific or mathematical concept. Pupils are encouraged to think about and discuss the different ideas and give reasons for their viewpoints. Each Concept Cartoon includes ideas for finding out about the scientific or mathematical concept in question.

Foam Magnetic Phonics (TTS Resources): These are cursive style letters which are colour coded to help pupils recognise the most common phoneme groupings.

Geoboards (tts): Using elastic bands to create shapes across the geoboards supports pupils in recognising the properties of 2D shapes and orientations.

Go Bananas (LDA**)**: Go Bananas encourages the development of auditory and visual sequential memory skills. It also helps with the understanding of positional language and gross motor skills.

HelpKidzLearn (Inclusive Technology Ltd): HelpKidzLearn provides accessible educational software specially designed for a fun and inclusive learning experience.

Identifying and Describing (Black Sheep Press): Identifying and Describing is a series of activities and games designed to support pupils develop semantic skills.

InPrint 3 (Widgit Software): InPrint 3 is a useful resource for creating and printing a range of visual communication resources such as posters, timetables and activity sheets suitable for all literacy levels and key stages.

Letter formation (Top Marks): This is a handwriting demonstration tool which demonstrates correct letter formation and can be used on an interactive whiteboard.

Memory Skills Board Games (LDA): Six board games to develop visual memory skills including matching and spot the difference.

Nessy Learning Ltd is a publisher of educational software, originally developed to support pupils with dyslexia.

NRICH – Millennium Mathematics Project (Cambridge University) provides free maths education resources for all pupils aged 3 – 18. The resources are designed to challenge, inspire and engage pupils as well as including support for teachers and families.

Numicom (Oxford University Press): Numicom is a multisensory and interactive way in which to teach a variety of maths concepts and skills. The different shapes, colours and numbers can be used for creating patterns, counting, ordering and calculating.

See and Learn (Speech, Language and Reading): This is a programme designed to teach children with Down syndrome early vocabulary, sight words, simple phrases and sentences, and grammar rules. Learning to read offers the children concrete, visual representations of language concepts to support the development of their spoken language skills.

Spot the Difference: Winslow Resources (Literacy) Colourful picture sequences for pupils to identify similarities and differences.

Stile maths (LDA) covers a number of areas and provides self-checking activities.

Storybook Puppets (TTS Resources) encourages pupils to retell familiar stories and interact with the characters from those stories.

Sound Linkage (Wiley Blackwell) is a reading and phonological programme designed to support dyslexic pupils and those with a reading delay. The materials can be used for both individual and group teaching.

Stile Dyslexia (LDA) is a structured self-checking programme which helps pupils with the rules of spelling and grammar.

SymWriter 2 (Widget Software) Symwriter 2 is a symbol supported word processor which can be used to create documents suitable for all literacy levels.

Tune into Environment Sounds (LDA): This resource uses photo cards and CD sound effects for auditory discrimination.

Visual Memory Skills (LDA): The book is divided into sections, each of which is designed to improve a different aspect of visual memory, such as remembering objects, object details and elements of objects like colour and pattern. It also explores sequential memory for objects, letters and digits; and object details such as orientation and size.

Wordshark and Numbershark are interactive computer programmes using a wide range of games to support the development of word recognition, spelling and mathematical skills.

Behavioural, Emotional and Social Development

Any Game Cards (Incentive Plus): This product has over 200 question cards for use with any popular board or card game. The sentence questions can be asked as part of the game moves. There are six sets of cards, each covering a different type of behaviour. The cards can be used in adult/pupil, pupil/pupil or small group sessions.

ABC Model of Behaviour: ABC stands for **antecedent** (A), **behaviour** (B) and **consequence** (C). It is an observation tool that therapists and teachers can use to analyse what happened before, during and after specific behaviour.

Circle time (Jenny Mosley Consultancies): This is a whole school approach to building positive relationships and behaviour. It aims to help enhance the self-esteem of all pupils.

Colorcards: Emotions (Winslow Resources) – These photo cards are divided into three categories exploring emotions in individual people, in difficult situations and in enjoyable situations.

Colorcards: Emotions and Expressions (Winslow Resources) – These photo cards explore the idea of recognising the emotions, feelings and social behaviour of others and responding appropriately.

Colour Away Your Worries (Winslow Resources): This is a colouring, doodling and drawing book, for children and young people that offers strategies showing how to cope with worries and fears.

Conflict Resolution Discussion Cards (Incentive Plus): This resource has 20 cards with scenarios showing an activity leading to conflict. The cards aim to encourage discussion about positive ways of dealing with conflict situations.

Expandaball (Hope Education) is a rainbow-coloured expansion ball for indoor and outdoor games. The ball becomes bigger when thrown and if it falls to the ground or hits an object, it will automatically decrease. It can be used in a sensory setting to demonstrate calming breathing techniques with children to release anxiety, stress, anger or fear.

Good Behaviour Book – Taming Little Monsters (Incentive Plus): This book explains how positive reinforcement techniques can give pupils positive goals to work towards rather than negative ones to overcome.

Let's Talk Behaviour Book (LDA): Let's Talk Behaviour aims to help pupils recognise emotions and expressions, support anxieties about separation and attachment as well as giving ideas for creating positive praise and strategies for calming unsettled children.

Puppets: Puppets can be used to address specific emotional and behavioural issues using adult/pupil interaction through the puppets. Puppet play with other pupils allows children to express their thoughts and feelings, learn conversational skills and act out difficult social scenarios without stress.

Rainbowchute (Winslow Resources): This resource helps to improve positive social interaction as well as spatial awareness through a number of games.

Stress balls (Sensory Direct) are soft balls which can be squeezed and manipulated using one or both hands. By applying pressure to the ball, pupils can release energy and help themselves to calm down in a stressful situation.

Superhero Behaviour Mission Cards (Imprint Educational): This is a card game to promote positive behaviour and to encourage responsibility, self-control and respect for others.

The Anger Alphabet (Sage Publications): This is an emotional development programme which aims to help pupils manage their own anger and cope effectively with the anger of others.

The Little Book of Big Anger (Winslow Resources): This book provides 48 pages of stories, drama activities and art ideas to help pupils learn to recognise and cope with anger.

What's got into you? (LDA): This is a game that will help pupils explore their emotions as well as recognise and manage them through role play and discussion.

Sensory and/or Physical Needs

Angled Writing Aid (Hope Education): This writing accessory is effective for both left and right-handed users. It helps prevent neck, shoulder and back strain, is light and portable and is ideal for pupils who struggle with pressure when using a pencil.

Boardmaker 7 (Inclusive Technology) helps teachers and parents create on-screen and printed symbol-based learning activities for pupils with SEND.

ChatBox (Saltillo) is a voice output communication device which combines the use of pictorial images with the latest technology to enable people who cannot speak to communicate easily and quickly.

ClearVision (Clearvision Project) is a postal lending library of mainstream children's books with added braille, making them suitable for visually impaired and sighted children and adults to share, as well as tactile board books.

Come Alive Stories (Yellow Door) bring traditional stories to life in a multisensory way through story books, wooden characters, story apps, games and activities.

Cued speech UK is a system which helps deaf pupils see what someone is saying. It uses a system of eight handshapes in four positions near the mouth which help to clarify the lip patterns of speech turning spoken language into a visual language.

CustomEyes Books (Guide Dogs for the Blind Association) produces large print books for children with vision impairment. These are tailor-made for each child or young person, charging only the recommended retail price.

Developmental Dyspraxia (Madeline Portwood) provides practical information for both parents and professionals on a range of exercises and strategies to support pupils with developmental motor coordination disorder.

Dough Disco is a fine muscle exercise which involves moulding play dough in time to music and performing different actions. Shonette invented the idea when she realised the children in her class were struggling to write letters. She discovered the fingers are one of the last things the brain controls during child development.

Eye Gaze technology (Inclusive Technology) is an electronic device that allows a pupil to control a tablet or computer by looking at words or commands on a screen. A camera picks up reflections from the pupil's cornea and retina.

Large Ultra Pencil Grip (Hope Education): A carefully researched design of a larger, softer and more comfortable pencil grip, offering more control. It shows where to position the thumb and denotes the letters R and L.

Lego Braille Bricks allow sighted and blind children to play and learn together using the bricks which have Braille letters and numbers on them. Several suggested literacy activities can be found on the website.

Listening Books is a national charity providing a postal and internet-based audiobook service to members who find it difficult to read the printed word in the usual way.

Living Paintings (The Living Paintings Trust) publishes 'Touch to See' books that bring the visual world to life for blind and partially sighted people.

Makaton (The Makaton Charity): Makaton is a language programme that uses signs and symbols to help people communicate. Makaton signs are very visual and concrete at the early levels. The Makaton resources available in the UK use some signs from the British Sign Language. When using Makaton, each country uses their own sign language.

Multisensory Resources (Sensory Education Ltd) supplies a wide range of resources and equipment including balance and movement resources, construction toys as well as fine and gross motor resources.

Popoids (ROMPA) is a snap together construction system. It helps develop fine motor skills, sequencing and coordination.

RNIB Library offers a wide choice of fiction and non-fiction books in audio, braille and giant print for adults and children.

Rotation Board (Space Kraft) is a balance board that helps to improve coordination and motor skills for pupils with limited mobility.

Sandpaper letters (The Dyslexia Shop) help pupils learn the shape of the letters by means of motor and visual memory.

Sensory Stories convey simple narratives using a mixture of text and linked sensory experiences. Each part of the story is accompanied by a sensory experience to help bring the story to life. Multisensory experiences are particularly stimulating for pupils with PMLD and SLD.

Shut the Box (Braille Superstore) is a popular dice game with numbers in braille for the visually impaired.

Signalong the communication charity is a key word sign-supporting system based on British sign language which uses speech, body language facial expression, voice tone and signing.

Sky Writer (Top Marks) is an aeroplane-themed handwriting demonstration tool to support pupils with developing fine motor skills.

Teaching Tac–Tiles (Hope Education) encourage tactile awareness, reinforces shape identification through touch and develops fine motor skills through games.

Write From the Start (Hope Education) helps children gain the necessary control to form letter shapes and create appropriate spaces between words, alongside the development of hand-eye co-ordination, spatial organisation, figure-ground discrimination and orientation.

Visual Phonics by Hand is designed to support the most profoundly deaf pupils. It's a system of visual hand cues for teaching and using phonics. Although we associate phonological awareness with the ability to hear sounds, lip reading, visual systems, finger spelling and the written alphabet can be used to build up a visual knowledge of spelling patterns.

References

Agarwal, P. K., Finley, J. R., Rose, N. S., & Roediger, H. L. (2017). Benefits from retrieval practice are greater for students with lower working memory capacity. *Memory (Hove)*, 25(6), 764–771.

Ainscow, M., & Sandill, A. (2010). Developing inclusive education systems: The role of organisational cultures and leadership. *International Journal of Inclusive Education*, 14(4), 401–416.

Alexander, R. J. (2020). *A Dialogic Teaching Companion*. Routledge.

Aubin, G. (2023a). *EEF Blog: What Exactly is Explicit Instruction?* EEF. https://educationendowmentfoundation.org.uk/news/eef-blog-what-exactly-is-explicit-instruction

Aubin, G. (2023b). *EEF Blog: Flexible Grouping: What Is It and Why Use It?* EEF. https://educationendowmentfoundation.org.uk/news/eef-blog-flexible-grouping-what-is-it-and-why-use-it

Bandura, A. (1977). *Social Learning Theory*. Englewood Cliffs.

Barnett, S. M., & Ceci, S. J. (2002). When and where do we apply what we learn? A taxonomy for far transfer. *Psychological Bulletin*, 128(4), 612–637.

Bass, R. V., & Good, J. W. (2004). Educare and Educere: Is a balance possible in the educational system? *The Educational Forum* (West Lafayette, Ind.), 68(2), 161–168.

Bennett, T. (2017). *Creating a Culture: How School Leaders can Optimise Behaviour*. https://assets.publishing.service.gov.uk/media/5a7506e4ed915d3c7d529cec/Tom_Bennett_Independent_Review_of_Behaviour_in_Schools.pdf

Bloom, B. S. (1956). *Taxonomy of Educational Objectives: The Classification of Educational Goals. Handbook I, Cognitive Domain*. Longman.

Bloom, B. S. (1968). Learning for Mastery. *Evaluation Comment*, 1(2), 1–12.

Blume, H. (1998). On the neurological underpinnings of geekdom. *The Atlantic*. https://www.theatlantic.com/magazine/archive/1998/09/neurodiversity/305909/

Booth, T., & Ainscow, M. (2002). Index for inclusion developing learning and participation in schools. https://www.eenet.org.uk/resources/docs/Index%20English.pdf

Bosanquet, P., Radford, J., & Webster, R. (2016). *The Teaching Assistant's Guide to Effective Interaction: How to Maximise Your Practice*. Routledge.

Bowlby, J. (1969). *Attachment and Loss: Volume 1*. Random House.

Breadmore, H. L., Vardy, E. J., Cunningham, A. J., Kwok, R. K. W., & Carroll, J. M. (2019). *Literacy Development: Evidence Review*. Education Endowment Foundation. https://d2tic4wvo1iusb.cloudfront.net/production/documents/guidance/Literacy_Development_Evidence_Review.pdf?v=1713540023

Bruner, J. S. (1960). *The Process of Education*. Harvard University Press.

Butterfield, H., Earle, S., Jones, K., Lucas, B., Maine, F., Marks, R., Lee Moncrieffe, M., Murray, M., Quinn, M., Robinson, L., & Richardson, M. (2022). *The Independent Commission on Assessment in*

Primary Education Final Report. https://www.icape.org.uk/reports/NEU2762_ICAPE_final_report_A4_web_version.pdf

Carroll, J., Bradley, L., Crawford, H., Hannant, P., Johnson, H., & Thompson, A. (2017). SEN support: A rapid evidence assessment. https://assets.publishing.service.gov.uk/media/5a822e2c40f0b6230269b43a/DfE_SEN_Support_REA_Report.pdf

Cattrall, R. (2023). *EEF Blog: Retrieval practice: a game of "hide and seek."* EEF. https://educationendowmentfoundation.org.uk/news/retrieval-practice-a-game-of-hide-and-seek

Chandler, P., & Sweller, J. (1992). The split-attention effect as a factor in the design of instruction. *British Journal of Educational Psychology*, 62(2), 233–246.

Clark, C., Picton, I., & Galway, M. (2023a). *Children and Young People's Reading in 2023.* National Literacy Trust. https://nlt.cdn.ngo/media/documents/Reading_trends_2023.pdf

Clark, C., Bonafede, F., Picton, I., & Cole, A. (2023b). *Children and Young People's Writing in 2023.* National Literacy Trust. https://nlt.cdn.ngo/media/documents/Writing_in_2023.pdf

Clark, J. M., & Pavio, A. (1991). Dual coding theory and education. *Educational Psychology Review*, 3(3), 149–170.

Clark, R. C., Nguyen, F., & Sweller, J. (2006). *Efficiency in Learning: Evidence-Based Guidelines to Manage Cognitive Load.* Pfeiffer.

Coe, R., Aloisi, C., Higgins, S., & Major, L. (2014). *What Makes Great Teaching? Review of the Underpinning Research* (p. 2). The Sutton Trust. https://www.suttontrust.com/wp-content/uploads/2014/10/What-Makes-Great-Teaching-REPORT.pdf

Collins, P. H. (2019). *Intersectionality as Critical Social Theory.* Duke University Press.

Cowan, N. (2005). *Working Memory Capacity: Essays in Cognitive Psychology.* Taylor & Francis.

Cowan, N. (2008). What are the differences between long-term, short-term, and working memory? *Progress in Brain Research*, 169(07), 323–338.

Crenna-Jennings, W. (2018). *Key Drivers of the Disadvantage Gap – Literature Review.* Education in England Report. Education Policy Institute. https://epi.org.uk/wp-content/uploads/2018/07/EPI-Annual-Report-2018-Lit-review.pdf

Crenshaw, K. (1994). Demarginalizing the intersection of race and sex: A black feminist critique of antidiscrimination doctrine. In A. M. Jaggar (Ed.), *Feminist Theory, and Antiracist Politics* (1st ed., pp. 39–52). Routledge.

Davies, K., & Henderson, P. (2021). *Special Educational Needs in Mainstream Schools.* https://d2tic4wvo1iusb.cloudfront.net/production/eef-guidance-reports/send/EEF_Special_Educational_Needs_in_Mainstream_Schools_Guidance_Report.pdf?v=1721824006

Department for Education and Department of Health. (2015). *SEND code of practice: 0 – 25 years.* https://assets.publishing.service.gov.uk/media/5a7dcb85ed915d2ac884d995/SEND_Code_of_Practice_January_2015.pdf

Department for Education. (2013). *National Curriculum in England: framework for key stages 1 to 4.* GOV.UK. https://www.gov.uk/government/publications/national-curriculum-in-england-framework-for-key-stages-1-to-4

Department for Education. (2015). *Final report of the Commission on Assessment without Levels.* https://assets.publishing.service.gov.uk/media/5a808bf9ed915d74e33fb0c7/Commission_on_Assessment_Without_Levels_-_report.pdf

Department for Education. (2019). *Character Education Framework Guidance*. https://assets.publishing.service.gov.uk/media/5f20087fe90e07456b18abfc/Character_Education_Framework_Guidance.pdf

Department for Education. (2021). *Relationships Education, Relationships and Sex Education (RSE and Health Education*. https://www.gov.uk/government/publications/relationships-education-relationships-and-sex-education-rse-and-health-education

Department for Education. (2023a). *Special Educational Needs and Disabilities (SEND and Alternative Provision (AP Improvement Plan)*. https://assets.publishing.service.gov.uk/media/63ff39d28fa8f527fb67cb06/SEND_and_alternative_provision_improvement_plan.pdf

Department for Education. (2023b). *The Reading Framework*. https://assets.publishing.service.gov.uk/media/664f600c05e5fe28788fc437/The_reading_framework_.pdf

Department for Education. (2024a). *Initial Teacher Training and Early Career Framework*. https://assets.publishing.service.gov.uk/media/661d24ac08c3be25cfbd3e61/Initial_Teacher_Training_and_Early_Career_Framework.pdf

Department for Education. (2024b). *Special Educational Needs in England*. Explore-Education-Statistics.service.gov.uk. https://explore-education-statistics.service.gov.uk/find-statistics/special-educational-needs-in-england

Department for Education. (2024c). *Behaviour in Schools Advice for Headteachers and School Staff*. https://assets.publishing.service.gov.uk/media/65ce3721e1bdec001a3221fe/Behaviour_in_schools_-_advice_for_headteachers_and_school_staff_Feb_2024.pdf

Department for Education. (2024d). *Use of Teaching Assistants in Schools: Research Report*. https://www.gov.uk/government/publications/use-of-teaching-assistants-in-schools

Department for Education. (n.d.). *Understanding the Evidence – Support for Early Career Teachers*. https://support-for-early-career-teachers.education.gov.uk/education-development-trust/year-1-a-people-profession/summer-week-1-ect-evidence/

Dexter, D. D., & Hughes, C. A. (2011). Graphic organizers and students with learning disabilities: A meta-analysis. *Learning Disability Quarterly*, 34(1), 51–72.

Donaldson, J. (1999). *The Gruffalo*. Macmillan.

Durrant, G. (2022). *How to Boost Reading and Writing through Play: Fun Literacy-Based Activities for Children*. Jessica Kingsley Publishers.

Ebbinghaus, H. (1885). *Memory: A Contribution to Experimental Psychology*. Teachers College.

Ebbinghaus, H. (2013). Memory: A contribution to experimental psychology. *Annals of Neurosciences*, 20(4), 155–156.

Education Act 1981. (1981). *Legislation.gov.uk*. https://www.legislation.gov.uk/ukpga/1981/60/enacted

Education Endowment Foundation. (2018a). *Guidance Report Metacognition and Self-Regulated Learning*. EEF. https://d2tic4wvo1iusb.cloudfront.net/production/eef-guidance-reports/metacognition/EEF_Metacognition_and_self-regulated_learning.pdf?v=1719829260

Education Endowment Foundation. (2018b). *Working with Parents to Support Children's Learning*. https://educationendowmentfoundation.org.uk/education-evidence/guidance-reports/supporting-parents

Education Endowment Foundation. (2019). *Improving Behaviour in Schools: Guidance Report.* EEF. https://educationendowmentfoundation.org.uk/education-evidence/guidance-reports/behaviour

Education Endowment Foundation. (2021a). *Special Educational Needs in Mainstream Schools: Guidance Report.* EEF. https://educationendowmentfoundation.org.uk/education-evidence/guidance-reports/send

Education Endowment Foundation. (2021b). *Improving Social and Emotional Learning in Primary Schools.* EEF. https://educationendowmentfoundation.org.uk/education-evidence/guidance-reports/primary-sel

Education Endowment Foundation. (2021c). *Cognitive Science Approaches in the Classroom: A Review of Evidence.* EEF. https://d2tic4wvo1iusb.cloudfront.net/documents/guidance/Cognitive_science_approaches_in_the_classroom_-_A_review_of_the_evidence.pdf?v=1684304682

Education Endowment Foundation. (2021d). *Mastery Learning.* EEF. https://educationendowmentfoundation.org.uk/education-evidence/teaching-learning-toolkit/mastery-learning

Education Endowment Foundation. (2021e). *Targeted Academic Support.* EEF. https://educationendowmentfoundation.org.uk/support-for-schools/school-planning-support/2-targeted-academic-support

Education Endowment Foundation. (2021f). *Homework.* EEF. https://educationendowmentfoundation.org.uk/education-evidence/teaching-learning-toolkit/homework

Education Endowment Foundation. (2021g). *Teacher Feedback to Improve Pupil Learning.* Education Endowment Foundation. https://educationendowmentfoundation.org.uk/education-evidence/guidance-reports/feedback

Education Endowment Foundation. (2021h). *Effective Professional Development Guidance Report.* https://educationendowmentfoundation.org.uk/education-evidence/guidance-reports/effective-professional-development

Education Endowment Foundation. (2021i). *Making the Best Use of Teaching Assistants: Guidance Report.* EEF. TA_Guidance_Report_MakingBestUseOfTeachingAssistants-Printable_2021-11-02-162019_wsqd.pdf

Education Endowment Foundation. (2021j). *Learning Styles.* EEF. https://educationendowmentfoundation.org.uk/education-evidence/teaching-learning-toolkit/learning-styles

Education Endowment Foundation. (2024). *Using Research Evidence: A Concise Guide.* https://educationendowmentfoundation.org.uk/support-for-schools/using-research-evidence

Education South West. (n.d.). *Understanding Adaptive Teaching.* https://d2tic4wvo1iusb.cloudfront.net/production/documents/Understanding-Adaptive-Teaching-v11.pdf?v=1723971749

Ellis, S., & Tod, J. (2018). *Behaviour for Learning: Promoting Positive Relationships in the Classroom* (2nd ed.). Routledge.

Ellis, P., Kirby, A., & Osborne, A. (2023). *Neurodiversity and Education.* SAGE.

Equality Act 2010. (2010). *Legislation.gov.uk.* https://www.legislation.gov.uk/ukpga/2010/15/schedule/10

Ferlazzo, L. (2015, March 25). *Strategies for Helping Students Motivate Themselves*. George Lucas Educational Foundation. https://www.edutopia.org/blog/strategies-helping-students-motivate-themselves-larry-ferlazzo

Galloway, R., Reynolds, B. & Williamson, J. (2020). Strengths-based teaching and learning approaches for children: Perceptions and practices. *Journal of pedagogical research*, 4(1), 31–45.

Gathercole, S., & Alloway, T. (2007). *A Classroom Guide*. https://pdnet.org.uk/media/WM-classroom-guide.pdf

Gibb, N. (2021, July 21). *The Importance of a Knowledge-Rich Curriculum*. GOV.UK. https://www.gov.uk/government/speeches/the-importance-of-a-knowledge-rich-curriculum

Glazzard, J., & Rose, A. (2020). The impact of teacher well-being and mental health on pupil progress in primary schools. *Journal of Public Mental Health*, 19(4), 349–357.

Glazzard, J., & Stones, S. (2020). A rigorous approach to the teaching of reading? Systematic synthetic phonics in initial teacher education. *Frontiers in Education (Lausanne)*, 5.

Gordon, D., Meyer, A., & Rose, D. (2016). *Universal Design for Learning: Theory and Practice*. CAST.

Guerriero, S. (Ed.). (2017). *Pedagogical Knowledge and the Changing Nature of the Teaching Profession*. OECD Publishing.

Hattie, J. (2008). *Visible Learning: A Synthesis of over 800 Meta-Analyses Relating to Achievement*. Routledge.

Hattie, J. (2012). *Visible Learning for Teachers: Maximizing Impact on Learning*. Routledge.

Hattie, J., & Timperley, H. (2007). The power of feedback. *Review of Educational Research*, 77(1), 81–112.

Hattie, J., & Yates, G. (2014). *Visible Learning and the Science of How We Learn*. Routledge.

Hendry, G. D., Oliver, G. R., & of Sydney, U. (2012). Seeing is believing: The benefits of peer observation. *Journal of University Teaching and Learning Practice*, 9(1), 87–96.

Howard-Jones, P., Ioannou, K., Bailey, R., Prior, J., & Jay, T. (2018). Applying the science of learning in the classroom. *Impact: Journal of the Chartered College of Teaching*, 2, 9–12.

Jay, T., Willis, B., Thomas, P., Taylor, R., Moore, N., Burnett, C., Merchant, G., & Stevens, A. (2017). *Dialogic Teaching Evaluation Report and Executive Summary Independent Evaluators*. https://d2tic4wvo1iusb.cloudfront.net/production/documents/projects/Dialogic_Teaching_Evaluation_Report.pdf?v=1720110920

Johnson, D. W., & Johnson, R. T. (1994). *Learning Together and Alone: Co-operative, Competitive, and Individualistic Learning* (4th ed.). Allyn & Bacon.

Johnson, D. W., & Johnson, R. T. (2014). Cooperative learning in 21st century. [Aprendizaje cooperativo en el siglo XXI]. *Anales de psicología (Murcia, Spain)*, 30(3), 841–851.

Jones, K. (2022). *Retrieval Practice: Primary: A Guide for Primary Teachers and Leaders*. John Catt Educational Ltd.

Knight, S. (2020). *SEND Reflection Framework*. NASEN. https://asset.nasen.org.uk/send_reflection_framework_web.pdf

Krathwohl, D. R., Bloom, B. S., & Masia, B. B. (1964). *Taxonomy of educational objectives: The classification of educational goals, Handbook II: Affective Domain*. Longman.

Krathwohl, D. R., & Anderson, L. W. (2001). *A Taxonomy for Learning, Teaching and Assessing: A Revision of Bloom's Taxonomy of Educational Objectives: Complete Edition*. Longman.

Leatherman, J. M., & Niemeyer, J. A. (2005). Teachers' attitudes toward inclusion: Factors influencing classroom practice. *Journal of Early Childhood Teacher Education*, 26(1), 23–36.

Losberg, J., & Zwozdiak-Myers, P. (2024). Inclusive pedagogy through the lens of primary teachers and teaching assistants in England. *International Journal of Inclusive Education*, 28(4), 402–422.

Martin, A. J., & Malmberg, L.E. (2019, August 8). Teachers' expectations help students to work harder but can also reduce enjoyment and confidence – New research. *The Conversation*. https://theconversation.com/teachers-expectations-help-students-to-work-harder-but-can-also-reduce-enjoyment-and-confidence-new-research-119761

McNess, E., Broadfoot, P., & Osborne, M. (2003). Is the effective compromising the affective? *British Educational Research Journal*, 29(2), 243–257.

Molbaek, M. (2018). Inclusive teaching strategies – dimensions and agendas. *International Journal of Inclusive Education*, 22(10), 1048–1061.

Montgomery, D. (2015). *Teaching Gifted Children with Special Educational Needs: Supporting Dual and Multiple Exceptionality*. Routledge.

Moss, G., Goldstein, H., Hayes, S., Munoz Chereau, B., Sammons, P., Sinnott, G., & Stobart, G. (2021). *High Standards, not High Stakes*. BERA.

Mould, K. (2020, August 28). *EEF Blog: Five Evidence-Based Strategies to Support High-Quality Teaching for Pupils with SEND*. Education Endowment Foundation. https://educationendowmentfoundation.org.uk/news/five-evidence-based-strategies-pupils-with-special-educational-needs-send

MTAS. (2021, July 2). Drop SATs for good: The case for recovery without high-stakes assessment. *More than a Score*. https://www.morethanascore.org.uk/drop-sats-for-good-the-case-for-recovery-without-high-stakes-assessment/

Murdock-Perriera, L. A., & Sedlacek, Q. C. (2018). Questioning Pygmalion in the twenty-first century: The formation, transmission, and attributional influence of teacher expectancies. *Social Psychology of Education*, 21(3), 691–707.

NASEN. (2022, April 8). *NASEN Responds to the SEND and Alternative Provision Green Paper*. NASEN. https://nasen.org.uk/news/sendgreenpaper

NASUWT. (2023). *Behaviour in Schools*. https://www.nasuwt.org.uk/static/357990da-90f7-4ca4-b63fc3f781c4d851/Behaviour-in-Schools-Full-Report-September-2023.pdf

NASEN. (2024). *Teacher Handbook: SEND*. https://asset.nasen.org.uk/Teacher%20SEND%20handbook%2030th%20January%202024.pdf

National Literacy Trust. (2017). *What is literacy?* National Literacy Trust. https://literacytrust.org.uk/information/what-is-literacy/

National Literacy Trust. (2022, October 5). *Role Models and Their Influence on Children and Young People's Reading*. National Literacy Trust. https://literacytrust.org.uk/research-services/research-reports/role-models-and-their-influence-on-children-and-young-peoples-reading/

Ofsted. (2018). *Parents Panel Annual Report*. https://assets.publishing.service.gov.uk/government/uploads/system/uploads/attachment_data/file/691220/REPORT_Parents_Panel_Annual_Report_2016-2017.pdf

Ofsted. (2019). *Education Inspection Framework: Overview of Research*. https://assets.publishing.service.gov.uk/media/6034be17d3bf7f265dbbe2ef/Research_for_EIF_framework_updated_references_22_Feb_2021.pdf

Ofsted. (2021, 13 May). *Supporting SEND*. https://www.gov.uk/government/publications/supporting-send/supporting-send

Ofsted. (2023). *Coordinating Mathematical Success: The Mathematics Subject Report*. https://www.gov.uk/government/publications/subject-report-series-maths

Packer, N. (2019, 29 October). Delivering inclusive high quality teaching strategies for SEND pupils. *Schools and Academies Show*. https://blog.schoolsandacademiesshow.co.uk/quality-send-teaching

Perkins, D. (1993). *Smart Schools*. Simon & Schuster.

Perkins, R., Moran, G., Shiel, G., & Cosgrove, J. (2009). Reading literacy in PISA 2009: A guide for teachers. https://www.erc.ie/documents/p09teachersguide.pdf

Piaget, J., & Cook, M. T. (1952). *The Origins of Intelligence in Children*. International University Press.

Powell, S., & Tod, J. (2004). *A Systematic Review of How Theories Explain Learning Behaviour in School Contexts*. EPPI-Centre. https://eppi.ioe.ac.uk/cms/Portals/0/PDF%20reviews%20and%20summaries/BM(CCC_2004review.pdf?ver=2006-03-02-125203-580

Quigley, A. (2023, 18 October). *Bridging the Gap between Research and Practice*. EEF Blog. https://educationendowmentfoundation.org.uk/news/eef-blog-bridging-the-gap-between-research-and-practice

Rathmann, K., Herke, M. G., Hurrelmann, K., & Richter, M. (2018). Perceived class climate and school-aged children's life satisfaction: The role of the learning environment in classrooms. *PloS One*, 13(2), e0189335.

Reid, J. F. (1974). *Breakthrough in Action: An Independent Evaluation of Breakthrough to Literacy*. Longman for the Schools Council.

Rosenshine, B. (2012). Principles of instruction: Research-based strategies that all teachers should know. *American Educator*, 36(1), 12. https://www.teachertoolkit.co.uk/wp-content/uploads/2018/10/Principles-of-Insruction-Rosenshine.pdf

Rosenthal, R., & Babad, E. Y. (1985). Pygmalion in the Gymnasium. *Educational Leadership*, 43(1), 36–39.

Rosenthal, R., & Jacobson, L. (1968). Pygmalion in the classroom. *The Urban Review*, 3(1), 16–20.

Rubie-Davies, C. (2014). *Becoming a High Expectation Teacher: Raising the Bar*. Routledge.

Rubie-Davies, C. M., Peterson, E. R., Sibley, C. G., & Rosenthal, R. (2015). A teacher expectation intervention: Modelling the practices of high expectation teachers. *Contemporary Educational Psychology*, 40, 72–85.

Salisu, A., & Ransom, E. N. (2014). The role of modeling towards impacting quality education. *International Letters of Social and Humanistic Sciences*, 32, 54–61.

Schiefele, U., & Schaffner, E. (2015). Teacher interests, mastery goals, and self-efficacy as predictors of instructional practices and student motivation. *Contemporary Educational Psychology*, 42, 159–171.

Sharples, J., Webster, R., & Blatchford, P. (2018). *Making Best Use of Teaching Assistants, Guidance Report.* EEF. https://d2tic4wvo1iusb.cloudfront.net/production/eef-guidance-reports/teaching-assistants/TA_Guidance_Report_MakingBestUseOfTeachingAssistants-Printable_2021-11-02-16 2019_wsqd.pdf?v=1731158852

Silby, A. (2013). *From Composition to Transcription: A Study of the Conceptual Understanding and Levels of Awareness in Thinking Used by Children during Specific Genre Writing Tasks*. https://bura.brunel.ac.uk/bitstream/2438/8123/1/FulltextThesis.pdf

Simpson, E. J. (1972). *The Classification of Educational Objectives in the Psychomotor Domain*. Gryphon House.

Singer, J. (2017). *NeuroDiversity: The Birth of an Idea*. (2nd ed.). Singer.

Skyrme, S., & Hunt, T. (2022). *A Guide for Teachers with Maths Anxiety*. https://mathsanxietytrust.com/Maths%20Anxiety%20Trust%20Teachers'%20Guide.pdf

Sousa, D. (2015). *Brain-Friendly Assessments: What They Are and How to Use Them*. Learning Sciences International.

Speech and Language UK. (2023). *Written Evidence Submitted by Speech and Language UK*. https://committees.parliament.uk/writtenevidence/116638/pdf/

Standards and Testing Agency. (2016, October 19). *Rochford Review: Final Report*. GOV.UK. https://www.gov.uk/government/publications/rochford-review-final-report

Standards and Testing Agency. (2020). *The Engagement Model*. GOV.UK. https://www.gov.uk/government/publications/the-engagement-model

Stearns, S. A. (2013). Motivating students to offer their best: Evidence based effective course design. *College Teaching*, 61(4), 127–130.

Swartz, R. J., & Perkins, D. N. (1989). *Teaching Thinking: Issues and Approaches*. Midwest Publications.

Sweller, J. (1988). Cognitive load during problem solving: Effects on learning. *Cognitive Science*, 12(2), 257–285.

Sweller, J. (1994). Cognitive load theory, learning difficulty, and instructional design. *Learning and Instruction*, 4(4), 295–312.

Sweller, J. (2010). Element interactivity and intrinsic, extraneous, and germane cognitive load. *Educational Psychology Review*, 22(2), 123–138.

Theobald, M. A. (2006). *Increasing Student Motivation: Strategies for Middle and High School Teachers*. Corwin Press.

Van Merrienboer, J. J., & Sweller, J. (2005). Cognitive load theory and complex learning: Recent developments and future directions. *Educational Psychology Review*, 17, 147–177.

Vygotsky, L. (1978). *Mind in Society: The Development of Higher Psychological Processes*. Harvard University Press.

Warnes, E., Done, E. J., & Knowler, H. (2022). Mainstream teachers' concerns about inclusive education for children with special educational needs and disability in England under pre-pandemic conditions. *Journal of Research in Special Educational Needs*, 22(1), 31–43.

Warnock, M. (1978). *Special Educational Needs, Report of the Committee of Enquiry into the Education of Handicapped Children and Young People.* HMSO.

Wiliam, D. (2016). *Leadership for Teacher Learning: Creating a Culture Where All Teachers Improve So That All Learners Succeed.* Learning Sciences International.

Wiliam, D. (2018). *Embedded Formative Assessment* (2nd ed.). Solution Tree Press.

Willingham, D. T. (2002). Ask the cognitive scientist. Inflexible knowledge: The first step to expertise. *American Educator*, 26(4), 31–33.

Willingham, D. T. (2009). *Why Don't Students like School?* Jossey-Bass.

Woodcock, S., & Woolfson, L. M. (2019). Are leaders leading the way with inclusion? Teachers' perceptions of systemic support and barriers towards inclusion. *International Journal of Educational Research*, 93, 232–242.

Zimmerman, B. J. (1995). Self-efficacy and educational development. In A. Bandura (Ed.), *Self-Efficacy in Changing Societies* (pp. 202–203). Cambridge University Press.

Index

Zeitfracht Medien GmbH
Ferdinand-Jühlke-Straße 7
99095 Erfurt, Deutschland
produktsicherheit@kolibri360.de